Nothing to Admire

NOTHING TO ADMIRE

THE POLITICS OF POETIC SATIRE FROM DRYDEN TO MERRILL

Christopher Yu

2003

OXFORD
UNIVERSITY PRESS

Oxford   New York
Auckland   Bangkok   Buenos Aires   Cape Town   Chennai
Dar es Salaam   Delhi   Hong Kong   Istanbul   Karachi   Kolkata
Kuala Lumpur   Madrid   Melbourne   Mexico City   Mumbai   Nairobi
São Paulo   Shanghai   Taipei   Tokyo   Toronto

Copyright © 2003 by Oxford University Press, Inc.

Published by Oxford University Press, Inc.
198 Madison Avenue, New York, New York 10016

www.oup.com

Oxford is a registered trademark of Oxford University Press

All rights reserved. No part of this publication may be reproduced,
stored in a retrieval system, or transmitted, in any form or by any means,
electronic, mechanical, photocopying, recording, or otherwise,
without the prior permission of Oxford University Press.

Library of Congress Cataloging-in-Publication Data
Yu, Christopher, 1966–
Nothing to admire : the politics of poetic satire from Dryden to Merrill /
Christopher Yu.
p. cm.
Includes bibliographical references and index.
ISBN 0-19-515530-0
1. Verse satire, English—History and criticism. 2. Political poetry, English—
History and criticism. 3. Merrill, James Ingram—Criticism and interpretation. 4. Political
Poetry, American—History and criticism. 5. Verse satire, American—History
and criticism. I. Title.
PR508.S27 Y8 2003
821.009'358—dc21   2002015611

2 4 6 8 9 7 5 3 1

Printed in the United States of America
on acid-free paper

To

ALESSIA

ACKNOWLEDGMENTS

Thanks are due to a number of teachers, colleagues, family members, and friends who gave generously of their support during the conception and writing of this book. Of these, I should first acknowledge Thomas Hyde, who taught a Yale College seminar that was the beginning of my ongoing preoccupation with several of the poets whom I consider here. I am grateful to David Bromwich, Jill Campbell, Isaac Cates, Jeff Dolven, Kevis Goodman, Langdon Hammer, Arthur Kirsch, Edward Mendelson, Sara Suleri Goodyear, Rachel Wetzsteon, and Suzanne Wofford for their observations, encouragement, or assistance at one point or another along the way. The poetic examples of John Hollander, Richard Howard, Wayne Koestenbaum, and Charles Wright have persuaded me of the veracity of Pope's dictum regarding the origin of true ease in writing. At a critical juncture, Richard Feingold and Frederick Keener supplied invaluable counsel that helped to clarify my thinking regarding British Augustan satire and its relation to liberalism. To Claude Rawson, whose faith in this project and its author never wavered, I am most especially indebted. Through their friendship and good company, Ulrich Baer, Ian and Wendy Baucom, Stephen Metcalf, Mary Murrell, Charlotte and Nathan Scott, Armando Solis, Jared Stark, Niobe Way, and Koethi Zan all have helped to sustain the author of these scribblings. Special thanks to my parents, Anthony and Priscilla, for their abiding affection.

During the completion of my doctoral degree, a Mrs. Giles Whiting Dissertation Fellowship enabled me to write the bulk of my dissertation, and a Warnock Fellowship in Eighteenth Century Studies gave me a crucial summer at Yale for research and related work.

Elissa Morris, my editor at Oxford University Press, has been a model of professionalism and intelligence, as has Robert Milks, my production editor.

Finally, Alessia Ricciardi, to whom this book is dedicated, inspires me daily through her courage, brilliance, and integrity. I thank her for teaching me what Auden meant when he proposed that it is Love "to Whom necessity is play."

CONTENTS

Introduction, 3

1. *Satura Redux*: Dryden and the Augustan Ideal, 23

2. Arm'd for Virtue: Pope as Cultural Liberal, 49

3. Byron, Laughter, and Legitimation, 86

4. Auden in the Polis of the Absurd, 123

5. Imbued with Otherness: Merrill's Mock-Epics of Desire, 167

Notes, 195

Index, 213

Nothing to Admire

Introduction

Satire has now been for some time a blind spot for criticism. We have come to understand the term casually to mean any rhetorical procedure involving caricature, mockery, or irony, that is to say any act of comic distortion that encodes an ulterior agenda. Whether because of its covert manner or aggressive purposes or on account of textual uncertainty, satire is supposed to have arisen from a point of origin now hopelessly lost to historical scrutiny. Much of this confusion derives from the mistaken belief of early-Christian-era grammarians in a genealogical link between the Greek satyr play and Roman satire, a belief based on a false etymological derivation of Latin *satura* from Greek *satyros*.[1] This misreading is of more than merely philological interest inasmuch as it results, by the time of Renaissance critics such as George Puttenham, in the ascription of cult value to what he calls "verses of rebuke," a value that is predicated on the magical status of "the gods of the woods" who perform such speech acts.[2] Even after Isaac Casaubon in the early seventeenth century exposed the error behind this critical convention, the rules of the language-game of satire remained difficult to determine.[3] The very word *satura*, an inflection of the Latin adjective *satur*, meaning "full" or "replete" (and from which the English verb "saturate" descends), refers properly to the dish of mixed foods prepared for propitiatory ceremonies and more generally to a sense of miscellany or variety.[4] The noun publicizes its own all-inclusiveness and so ironizes its very taxonomic aim.

Recent attempts to determine the limits of the satiric mode have elaborated this ostensibly clarifying act of complication. In his survey of the critical literature, Dustin Griffin concludes: "satire is in my view rather an 'open' than a 'closed' form, both in its formal features (particularly in its reluctance to conclude) and in its more general rhetorical and moral features, in its frequent preference for inquiry, provocation, or playfulness rather than assertion and conclusiveness."[5] Griffin's insistence on the form's "reluctance to conclude" seems to harmonize with the poststructuralist supposition of an inherently paradoxical and self-contradictory quality in all signification. Fredric Bogel, in a recent investigation of the cultural role of the form,

3

equates satire with the effort "not to expose the satiric object in all its alien difference but to define it as different, as other: to make a difference by setting up a textual machine or mechanism for producing difference."[6] Bogel regards this mechanism as part of a broader "cultivation of structures of disequilibrium designed to resist, complicate, and disturb the stasis . . . that lurk[s] beneath the surface of what has been known as 'Augustan wit'" and thus as a counterargument to depictions of the late seventeenth and early eighteenth century as an "Age of Balance."[7]

As helpful as such studies may be, the project of rendering a definition of satire that is valid for all historical moments and cultural situations seems to me doomed to resort to partial truths and pointless generalizations. The graveyard of theoretical chimeras is crammed with attempts at such a definition. In what follows I will furnish not so much a definition as a historical account of the satiric practices of five representative English-language poets. The first two, John Dryden and Alexander Pope, are customarily perceived to be central to the British Augustan tradition; the third, Lord Byron, has a complex relationship to that tradition; the fourth and fifth, W. H. Auden and James Merrill, cannot be said to belong to the tradition in any meaningful sense. Yet, following Dryden's inaugural example, each successive figure looks back at his predecessors in order to learn not only an idea of how poetry works but of what it takes from life and adds to reality. I will argue in this book for the development of a shared language of ridicule and critique that is peculiar to these poets.

The language is neoclassical to the extent that it seeks self-knowledge in the present through the imitation of the past. A glimpse of the complex connotations the Augustans assigned the notion of imitation can be derived from Dryden's famous description of the process of translation—particularly translation of the works of antiquity—in terms of verbatim "metaphrase," reinterpretive "paraphrase," or "imitation, where the translator (if he has not now lost that name) assumes the liberty not only to vary from the words and sense, but to forsake them both as he sees occasion."[8] Clearly, Dryden assumes a high degree of exegetical engagement with the historical original as a precondition of any such "liberty" of imitation. Richard Kroll has summarized the neoclassical position vis à vis the past: "The chief architects of the social and literary scene after the Restoration . . . [visualized] their knowledge of the ancient world as a map of their present circumstances: unlike one earlier Renaissance habit that tended to treat the ancients as a unitary font of allusion and appropriation, the neoclassical habit sought rather to contextualize and discriminate consistently among its ancient sources."[9]

In response to the politically turbulent state of affairs inherited by Charles II after the Civil War and monarchical crisis of the mid–seventeenth century, Dryden gave new urgency to the myth of an Augustan restoration of republican values. As Howard Erskine-Hill reminds us, the modern expression of such an ideology dates back to the Elizabethan era, but the "eclectic practice of Dryden . . . imparts a new critical complexity to our concept of Augustan writing."[10] Philip Harth keenly observes that Dryden's great satires of the 1680s, composed as they were in the wake of the lapse of English censorship laws at the end of the previous decade, represent instances of his genius "in shaping a variety of literary genres into new and effective instruments of political propaganda."[11] Following Erskine-Hill, we might notice that the poet's use of the Augustan metaphor accommodated a broad range of perspectives. These could include outright praise of the royal patron, conscious ambivalence regarding an alternate, Antonian heroic standard, and, ultimately, Tacitean disapproval of the *princeps*. The language finally exemplifies an ideal of learned civility against the abuse of privilege by any public or popular luminary, whether Thomas Shadwell, the earl of Shaftesbury, or even, in an especially problematic sense, the king himself.[12] Dryden's satire thus interprets the relationship between poetic and political authority as implicitly antagonistic. Even his most celebrated defense of the throne, *Absalom and Achitophel*, at its conclusion affirms the legitimacy of Charles's reign through a reminder of Augustus's glorification by Virgil, a reminder that leaves the last word in the dialogue between benefactor and beneficiary to the scribe. This ending subtly refines the satire's pervasive impulse toward criticism of the king, thereby asserting the poet's freedom and independence of judgment. Dryden's masterpiece, as David B. Haley has put it, "is an allegory by means of which the public poet makes a radical criticism of the monarchy he seems to uphold."[13]

Absalom and Achitophel's remarkably equivocal portrayal of Charles II exhibits the Augustan impulse of commoner poets such as Dryden and, later, Pope to repudiate the bad words and deeds of their titled superiors by appeal to a principle of civility or wit that places a higher premium on learning, free-minded noncredulity, and eloquence than on birth or wealth. In Pope's writing especially, the appeal is articulated by means of a sustained invocation of Horace as the classical model of satiric perspicuity, hence of social merit. Horace's *Sermones* present themselves as the self-declarations of a moral and critical intelligence that has been painstakingly cultivated by a student of unmistakably humble station: the son of a *libertus* or freed slave. The Roman paradigm thus furnishes its modern imitators, Pope most of all, with the image of an imperial society that, while promoting itself as a return to the utopia of constitutional republicanism, unexpectedly found the measure of its claims to meritocratic inclusiveness being taken by a parvenu writer whom the state had subsidized in what might appear to be an attempt to purchase his service.

Although Horace is sometimes read as a mere propagandist for Augustus's administration, his political views are too iconoclastic in implication for the charge to stick. Indeed, any such accusation must ignore the urgency of the poet's habitual denunciations of Roman class prejudice, the worries attached to his pursuit of a scandalous and possibly unlawful literary vocation (as detailed in Satire 2.1), and his sympathy for some of the more marginalized constituents of the *principate* (as evinced in 1.4 by his likening of poets to Jews and his celebration in 2.2 of the equanimity of Ofellus, the dispossessed farmer). Accordingly, his encomiums to the *princeps* consistently arraign the social order over which Augustus presided as "first among equals," thus throwing into uncertainty the very logic of praise. Kirk Freudenburg captures the deviousness of Horace's rhetoric, particularly as it develops in the satires contained in the second book of *Sermones*:

> For while it is true that these poems do conform to the social and political pressures of the new post-Actian age . . . it is also true that they perform the activity of that compliance. . . . As that squeeze takes place, we hear the sounds of resistance in the unnerving hissings and pops of a forced, unnatural fit. And that noise is itself a searing commentary, a "real satire" on the way old freedoms get lost and power ultimately gets its way.[14]

In other words, Horace's poems on even the seemingly most innocuous domestic or literary topics (e.g., a dinner party in 2.8 or the appropriate curriculum of a young writer's training in 1.4) both dramatize and, in subtle ways, criticize the compromises with power necessitated by historical circumstance.

As Freudenburg has pointed out, Horace's analysis of such compromises reinterprets in an entirely original and more anxious light the Lucilian emphasis on the satirist's freedom or *libertas*.[15] Consequently, the *Sermones* propound an idea of the purpose of satire that is basically liberalizing. That is to say, they turn the exploration of the limits imposed by Roman society on intellectual and moral outspokenness into an indictment of the self-protective celebration of the status quo. The author of this indictment bequeathed to the British Augustans a language that allowed them to articulate the precariousness of their own positions as members of both a prestigious cultural elite and of a persecuted social community. The idiom moreover encouraged the poets to voice their anxieties regarding such a position in the mode of comic assault. Both Dryden, who converted to Roman Catholicism, and Pope, who was born into the faith, belonged to a religious minority that was disabled by law from many of the rights of property and the opportunities of education and office.[16] Indeed, Protestant chauvinism was so fierce in the post-Restoration era that Erskine-Hill has declared: "The opposition of Dryden and Pope to the powers-that-be might plausibly be attributed to religion and religious background alone," although he adds that the taking up of opposition rhetoric during the 1730s and 1740s by the decidedly Anglican

Dr. Johnson demonstrates the absence of a direct link between the discourse and Catholicism.[17]

I will argue that the Augustan satirists perceived themselves as victims not only of religious intolerance but also of the snobbery of those aristocrats who disparaged them as upstarts, as well as the increasingly virulent forces of commerce that threatened to eradicate the humanist ideal of learned association they inherited from the Renaissance. Their peculiar self-image drove them, in spite of their belief in monarchy, to the arguments of what I will call "cultural liberalism." Such arguments uphold a neo-Horatian attitude of worldliness that takes *nil admirari* as its proper motto and regards knowledge skeptically applied as the ultimate means of exposing the idols of the forum and the marketplace. My contention is that Dryden and Pope invented an admittedly jocose mode of poetic protest against the arrogance of a Whig hegemony that was consolidating throughout their lifetimes. Their style of thinking and writing would evolve in the works of their successors in ways they would never have foreseen and might not have applauded. The influence is nevertheless plain. Taken as a whole, this tradition advances a vision of liberal meritocracy that promotes openness in the form of poetic knowledge or judgment.

Cultural liberalism thus must be understood in terms of both its similarity and its opposition to the so-called classical liberalism that comes into being at the same moment and that has been identified with the very Whig ascendancy attacked by Dryden and Pope. Classical liberalism is usually regarded as originating with the political thought of John Locke, most notably as expressed in *The Second Treatise of Government* (written circa 1681 and published in 1689). Here Locke defines the understanding between a government and its governed population as a "compact," a consensual arrangement that endures on condition of the ruling body's fulfillment of its obligation to protect the natural rights of the citizenry, the chief of which, Locke contends, is the right to ownership of property. From this vantage point, Locke truly ought to be recognized as the most representative exponent of the "possessive individualism" that C. B. Macpherson saw as the source of liberal values.[18] By contrast, the Augustan poets and their successors embrace a liberal conception of education that in the end commits them to a critique of the self-rewarding impulses of power, including corporate or commercial power. By upholding a neo-Horatian emphasis on moral edification, the five satirists who constitute the subject of this book bring to light a fundamental contradiction at the heart of that constellation of ideas we now group together under the rubric of "the liberal tradition." Specifically, they raise the question whether an egalitarian principle of tolerance for cultural differences is ultimately compatible with an acquisitive self-interest that defines freedom in material terms and equates justice with the "rational" outcome of capital markets regulated only by the "Invisible Hand" Adam Smith thought deducible from the spontaneous order of competition.

Cultural liberalism may be said to represent an ethos of individualism that is nonpossessive to the extent that it warily views wealth as a form of political power, subject to criticism and to limitation for the sake of the common good. According to this ethos, individualism ought to be defined as a matter not of property rights but of intellectual and moral wisdom. Consequently, although alternative terms such as "skepticism" or "libertinism" may capture aspects of the outlook I have been describing, these designations do not adequately evoke the ethical awareness of the attitude. Skepticism, for example, refers somewhat more restrictively to issues of epistemology and probabilism (as in David Hume) and libertinism to issues of metaphysics and theology (as in Pierre Charron and Pierre Gassendi) than the disposition I am after. Although I do not dispute that such positions may come near and in some instances contribute to the urbane broadmindedness for which I admire the modern Augustans, neither posture captures the specific moral and political implications of their neo-Horatian insistence on knowledge as a means of social equalization. By mobilizing a rhetoric of classical allusion that seemed to represent a common birthright, while at the same time making sharp intellectual demands on its adherents, Dryden and Pope struck a note of caustic worldliness that effectively trumped all aristocratic claims to authority based on lineage or riches.[19] Through this effort, the Augustans supplied their successors with a satiric arsenal that the later poets would use to attack the institutions of a bourgeois culture.

So, an epoch after Pope, Byron revolts against the commercial ideology of the Regency years, partly through invocation of standards that, in a characteristically Augustan manner, expose by contrast the coarse satisfactions of the present. His grand satire, *Don Juan*, depicts an epoch of conservative despotism and imperial strife that refuses to consort with the available narratives of progress, whether articulated as the myth of a Pax Augustana that inaugurates a golden age in the arts and sciences or the fable of a supposedly civilizing "westering of empire," or the Whiggish fiction of commercial exchange as a means of controlling humanity's aggressive instincts.[20] His poetry instead conveys the melancholy scorn of a mind alienated from the history of human strife as written by its victors. This scorn leads him to reject the triumphal equation of Western modernity with what Hegel would have termed the world-historical destiny of Spirit. Consequently, Byron writes from the perspective of an exiled wanderer whose fascination with the foreign culture of the Levant or Orient often takes on a political edge, a pointedness that Saree Makdisi has evoked: "[Byron's] fascination with the otherness of the Orient is predicated . . . on its inviolate non-Westernness as much as on its own pure and essential Easternness—indeed, these are, for him, one and the same. . . . The East is for Byron not only a refuge from modernity—that is, a space from which to flee modernity—but also a space from which to critique modernity and the West itself."[21]

Rather than a theory of progress, Byron's satire, like Rousseau's *Second Discourse* on the "Origin and Foundation of Inequality among Men," presumes an idea of corruption, a sense of the inevitable decline of civilization from a natural state of sympathy, or *pitié*, between human beings. Byron argues from his own presumption of a natural law of sympathy for a revolutionary overthrow of the hierarchy of social categories: the privileging of civilized West over savage East, old over young, male over female. Whereas Rousseau defines inequality primarily in terms of class, as demonstrated in the *Second Discourse* by his identification of the introduction of property as the catastrophic moment of humanity's fall from the state of nature, Byron enlarges the concept to include all of the terminologies that supply the epistemological foundations of power in nineteenth-century British and European society: that is, the languages of religion, race, gender, and even sexual preference, in addition to those of class.[22] Cultural liberalism, as propounded by his satire, may be understood as beginning to entail a critique not only of class oppression but also of cultural intolerance.

Satire's ancient claim to represent a controversial *libertas* ranged in opposition to a censorious *lex*, which in Lucilius and Horace's cases had to do primarily with the legality of *ad personem* lampooning of the famous and well-to-do, is revised by Byron in keeping with a Romantic disdain for the repressive "law" of a generalized public opinion invoked to confirm the identity of the nation. He aspires not to the Shelleyan role of an unacknowledged legislator of the world but rather to the position of acknowledged historian of its wrongs. By insisting on the corrupt incapacity of modern "Civilization" to produce anything other than "War, Pestilence, the despot's desolation" (*Don Juan* 8.68), he bears witness to the catastrophic failure of the promise of bourgeois society. Insofar as he regards language as inadequate to such a state of affairs, he anticipates Jürgen Habermas's thesis that the emergence of "advanced" capitalism has instigated a crisis in the legitimation of the "world-maintaining interpretive systems" or norms that society invokes in order to establish political consensus.[23] Satire acquires the analytic function of dissolving false normative structures and thus of representing through laughter viewpoints beyond the sphere of legitimation.

Even more than Byron's, Auden's poetry gains its urgency from capturing the contradiction and mutual invalidation of competing historical narratives: classical versus modern, imperial Roman versus early Christian, psychoanalytic versus socialist, fascist versus democratic. His writing is neoclassical, among other ways, in its sense of being consciously historiographical. Satire, for Auden, gives expression to an iconoclastic impulse in order to recover an awareness of the plight of those whom the accepted record of events has overlooked. Perhaps the most obvious examples of such unfortunates are the children who "died in the streets" in "Epitaph on a Tyrant" and the horrified figure of Thetis in "The Shield of Achilles," but instances abound throughout the poet's oeuvre. That the communities with whom he sympathizes often belong to a larger, tacitly homosexual mythos of schoolboy obligations and insecurities gives his satire a hidden dimension of political awareness. It was precisely in order to denounce the fascist ideal of a purity achieved by eliminating racial, religious, and sexual deviance that Auden in "September 1, 1939" formulated his credo "We must love one another or die." The Pauline rhetoric of the injunction is radicalized through its juxtaposition to an alternative intimation, quasi-Hobbesian in its realism, of the human propensity for cruelty. Auden's emphasis in the poem falls on earthly love as a sign of fallibility and need, a sign that urges the reader to solidarity with all human beings and to action in the secular dimension of mortal existence. Accordingly, he identifies himself as part of a community of individuals whose defining characteristic is that they are composed "of Eros and of dust."

Similarly, for James Merrill, the desire of a gay man, particularly as avowed in his mock-epic of same-sex marriage, *The Changing Light at Sandover*, constitutes the horizon within which the poet is forced to confront the homophobic decorum espoused by his parents and by the sexually repressed establishment and to assert his ethical and libidinal autonomy in dissent. The poem's conceit of recounting the education of its author and his companion, David Jackson, by ghostly and divine presences conjured up through the Ouija board illustrates a fundamentally satiric understanding of human nature. For the device of the Ouija board symbolizes memory as a conduit for irrational and precivilized impulses that call into question the "naturalness" of the codes of legitimated or conventionalized social conduct. By representing consciousness as a symbolic game, Merrill implies a definition of the human that resists conscription into the service not only of heterosexism but of other varieties of conformism as well. The unruly interplay of desire and pleasure impels him to reexamine his assigned roles within the economies of group affiliation—from that of family to those of age, class, nation, race, gender, and sexual orientation—and gives structure to his emotional life. His playful questioning of straight manners and institutions culminates in the disclaiming of identification with the available exemplars of erotic propriety. Travestying the expected Oedipal narrative of subject-formation in poems such as "The Thousand and Second Night," "From the Cupola," and "Up and Down," Merrill repeatedly associates the recognition of his gay sexual inclination with moments of lapsed or failed object-identification, a condition of alienation or "otherness" (as he himself calls it) that may be said to resemble what lately has been called a position of "disidentification."[24] In the course of a comic exposure of entrenched prejudice and misperception, he cultivates a language of irreverence that enables him to give voice to a subject hitherto deemed unspeakable, unpresentable, inauthentic. His satire thus functions as a version of what Judith Butler has called "gender parody": it casts into radical doubt received ideas of male and female identity and makes possible the acceptance of new configurations of desire.²⁵ Merrill's writing may be said to advance the project of cultural liberalism by positing a hermeneutic consciousness of language as the first step toward an ironic nonadmiration of philistine complacency and parochialism.

Having aligned a particular genealogy of poetic satire in English with the skeptical, oppositional, individualistic civility I have dubbed "cultural liberalism," I wish to take a step back in order briefly to review the historical origins of the core tradition of classical liberalism in response to which modern discourses of pluralism inevitably have taken shape. Such an exercise, I hope, will suggest precisely how the satiric dialect of liberalism I have ascribed to Dryden, Pope, Byron, Auden, and Merrill diverges from the classical framework and, under certain circumstances, might be directed against it in criticism. By positioning cultural liberalism in contrast to the main current of contemporaneous political thought, I will seek to show how the ideas of freedom propounded by these poets can be ranged against the commercialism generally understood to be implicated in the classical liberal conception of a free society.

That "classical liberalism" is an anachronism, that those thinkers now regarded as its chief expositors would not so have identified themselves, is by now routinely acknowledged.²⁶ In general, however, theorists of classical liberalism agree on a notion of political freedom that presumes the guarantee by the state of negative liberties ("freedom from" as opposed to "freedom to") and a dispersal of material goods through private ownership.²⁷ F. A. Hayek, probably the most celebrated twentieth-century expositor of this idea, identifies it with a "tradition, much older than the name 'liberalism,' [that] traces back to classical antiquity and took its modern form during the late seventeenth and the eighteenth centuries as the political doctrines of the English Whigs."²⁸ Hayek locates the antique origins of this tradition in the Greek ideal of *isonomia*, or equality before the law, and the Roman achievement of "a highly individualist private law, centering on a very strict conception of private property."²⁹ The modern revival of the tenets of the rule of law and of limited political authority he perceives as having occurred with the formation of the Whig Party in the late seventeenth century; as he declares, "[t]he classical formulations were supplied by John Locke's *Second Treatise on Civil Government* [sic]."³⁰ Hayek plainly means by "classical" something like "pure" or "emblematic." Classical liberalism on this reckoning properly refers to the belief, original to post-Restoration England, that political freedom and vigorous economic competition are inextricably linked. On this score, Locke's crucial contribution is an account of property that conflates the term's larger meaning of "the mutual preservation of . . . lives, liberties, and estates" with its narrower signification of "the partage of things in an inequality of private possessions," an allocation made possible by the invention of money.³¹ For Hayek, such a conflation exemplifies the spirit of classical liberalism per se:

> For the British tradition the two [dimensions of political and economic liberalism] are inseparable because the basic principle of the limitation of the coercive powers of government to the enforcement of general rules of just conduct deprives government of directing or controlling the economic activities of the individuals, while the conferment of such powers gives government essentially arbitrary and discretionary power which cannot but restrict even the freedom in the choice of individual aims which all liberals want to secure. Freedom under the law implies economic freedom, while economic control, as the control of the means for all purposes, makes a restriction of all freedom possible.³²

In this last sentence, Hayek argues that legal freedom in fact more than merely implies economic freedom: the latter is the *conditio sine qua non* of the former and indeed of "all freedom."

Subsequent intellectual historians largely have accepted this interpretation even as they have proposed various different configurations of the canon of classical liberal theory. Consider David Conway's concise defense of classical liberalism as the best safeguard against the meddling of government in the private lives of the governed: "A liberal polity . . . must prohibit and seek to prevent anyone depriving any member, who is a proprietor of any material item, of the liberty to use or dispose of that item innocuously. . . . This, in effect, amounts to a liberal polity having to acknowledge and enforce property rights in all material things."³³ Conway recapitulates Hayek's basic stance but makes little mention of Locke when naming the foundational proponents of the ideology, citing instead Adam Smith and David Hume as the earliest champions and Ludwig von Mises and Hayek himself as the latest.³⁴ Again, Razeen Sally, who wishes to enlarge the province of classical liberalism beyond an Anglocentric context, expounds a synthesis "of the Scots (Smith and Hume), Americans (Knight and Viner), Germans (Eucken, Böhm and Röpke) and others (such as Tumlir) in a common intellectual tradition."³⁵ Whatever the perceived inaugural moment of such a synthesis may be, Sally's essential assessment of this tradition is indistinguishable from Hayek's: "The normative core of classical liberalism is the approbation of economic freedom or *laissez faire*—Adam Smith's 'obvious and simple system of natural liberty'—out of which spontaneously emerges a vast and intricate system of cooperation in exchanging goods and services and catering for a plenitude of wants."³⁶ Both Sally and Conway share with Hayek a belief that the "system of cooperation" that free markets appear to represent encourages the widest attainable diversity of human means and ends. They reason that such a system emancipates the almost infinite multiplicity of social interactions from the rational constructivist interventions of a paternalist state. For such exponents of classical liberalism, even freedom of thought ultimately depends on freedom of pricing. As Hayek puts it, "If it is the mind which chooses the ends of human action, their realization depends on the availability of the required means, and any economic control which gives power over the means also gives power over the ends."[37]

Those interested in a kind of liberalism concerned with liberty of thought rather than of capital might reply that Hayek allows too much by way of implication to ride tacitly on his deployment of the adjective "any" in the final clause of this sentence. (Does "any" control of means confer absolute power over ends? Are there no grounds on which to speak of the regulation of exchange beyond those forbidding individual parties to injure one another?) Moreover, such readers ought to notice how reductive is the classical liberal interpretation of Locke's notion of natural law. In the eyes of Hayek and his followers, the ambivalence between the extended and restricted connotations of the central Lockean concept of "property" is inevitably resolved in favor of the latter. At this point, it is helpful to compare the classical liberals' relentless insistence on the primacy of the material aspect of proprietorship to what Locke actually says on the topic in an important passage from "Of Paternal Power," the sixth chapter of the *Second Treatise*, where he indicates that he has good reason to keep alive the widest spectrum of the word's valences:

> The law that was to govern Adam was the same that was to govern all his posterity, the law of reason.... [T]he end of law is not to abolish or restrain, but to preserve and enlarge freedom.... But freedom is not, as we are told, "a liberty for every man to do what he lists," for who could be free when every other man's humour might domineer over him? But a liberty to dispose and order as he lists his person, actions, possessions, and his whole property, within the allowance of those laws under which he is; and therein not to be subject to the arbitrary will of another, but freely follow his own.[38]

Assigning "property" to the climactic position in the inventory of attributes developed by the individual through exercise of personal freedom under the rule of reason and highlighting such emphasis by adding the qualifier "whole," Locke appears to imply that the final category comprehends or at least supplements its antecedent terms, thus taking on something of their importance. This is what Peter Laslett means when he writes in a celebrated essay on the *Two Treatises* that "Property [as Locke presents it] ... seems to give the political quality to personality."[39] Laslett's point is that Locke elaborated a theory of property much more idiosyncratic than we, working with the benefit of historical hindsight, usually suppose, that he deliberately allowed the word to resonate in psychological and even quasi-metaphysical registers because he meant his project to be construed as moral description rather than economic prescription. On this reading, Locke remains neutral as to the optimal distribution of wealth within the popular society he envisions because he simply is not concerned with such a question. Communism, redistributive taxation, or nationalization might all be reconciled to his doctrine of property as long as the majority of the populace formally expresses its consent. Property, in connoting the full range of the individual's powers, chiefly comes to mean something very like "character" for the philosopher: "The property he defends is never confined to substantial possessions, or looked on as what we (not Locke) call capital."[40] We may speak of bringing "market choices" to bear on property, then, only insofar as we are aware that such choices at best mime the far more complicated moral decisions that personally burden our consciences. Lockean property cannot aptly be evaluated by recourse to a utilitarian language of costs and benefits.

If this is true, then neither can his ideas of liberty be so evaluated. Laslett's sensitivity to the moral, philosophical, and theological underpinnings of Locke's argument shares much of the interest of John Dunn's clarifying depiction of that philosopher's political thought as a version of Calvinist theodicy.[41] From this perspective, Locke's repeated denunciations in the *Second Treatise* of government intrusion on the individual's property rights (as when he declares that "the supreme power cannot take from any man any part of his own property without his consent") ought to be understood as aimed at denying to civil authority such license as would allow it to pose an obstacle to the individual's fulfillment of her or his religious duty, a spiritual task that Puritans referred to as "the calling."[42] Because God has placed every human being on the earth to fulfill a unique role, each one must be free to employ his or her gifts to the fullest, hence to respond to the deity's summons or calling. Dunn in short perceives Locke in his political writings as endeavoring to draw the boundary lines between the jurisdictions of earthly and divine power:

> The calling was an undertaking which under the best of terrestrial circumstances taxed the moral capacities of human beings to the limits. The political norms which Locke affirms are to be seen as insistences that conventional social morality has no right to make the assignment still more difficult. No human authority had a status which justified it in encroaching upon men's individual religious understanding. Similarly no human authority enjoyed a status which would justify it in treating a human being as a means to its own ends.[43]

Such a reading makes manifest the existential loneliness inherent in Locke's ideal of freedom and its realization in the unconstrained operations of the mind. To the degree that he disallows any moral judgment or choice reached by recourse to an external authority, irrespective of whether the authority is civil or sectarian in nature, he places the onus of responsibility on the individual for the achievement of rational ends. This point almost exclusively constitutes the logic of *The Letter Concerning Toleration* (1685), where he vigorously rejects any notion that the state may preside over the question of religious or denominational affiliation, declaring that "true and saving religion consists in the inward persuasion of the mind" and defining a church in pointedly ethical language as "a free and voluntary society of men."[44]

In the *Second Treatise*, Locke argues this point with particular force in the chapter on paternalism: "The freedom, then, of man, and liberty of acting according to his own will, is grounded on his having reason, which is able to instruct him in that law he is to govern himself by, and make him know how far he is left to the freedom of his own will."[45] It is revealing that in this formulation he describes reason as teaching or training the subject to understand the responsibilities that come with independence of thought and even more telling that the sentence occurs in a chapter concerning parental offices. For the family provides the philosopher with a synecdoche of the sort of ethically conscientious use of power on which civil society fundamentally relies. Children, born without the full strength and proficiency of their faculties, are subject temporarily to the governance and care of adults: "The bonds of this subjection are like the swaddling clothes they are wrapped up in, and supported by, in the weakness of their infancy."[46] Over the course of time, each child grows into adulthood and thereby into accountability for her or his own decisions, including the decision to assume in turn his or her own parental duties, should such circumstances arise. Locke, it seems to me, strongly implies in this chapter that such parental duties are a subset of the general moral debts that human beings owe to one another and must acknowledge in order to demonstrate their obedience to the calling: "Adam and Eve, and after them all parents, were by the law of nature under an obligation to preserve, nourish, and educate the children they had begotten, not as their own workmanship, but the workmanship of their own maker, the Almighty, to whom they were to be accountable for them."[47]

We are all, in other words, the "property" of God. The drift of Locke's thesis is that submission to the injunctions of the divine necessitates that we treat one another individually not with the indifference of an instrumentalist or indeed economic mentality but rather with the care and attention we would show to one of our own family members. Consequently, the parallel he repeatedly draws in the *Second Treatise* between the consent of children to parental authority and of people to civil government cannot be understood without recalling the sentence where he explicates the exact metaphysical conditions under which parents are authorized to make decisions for their dependents: "God hath made it their business to employ this care on their offspring, and hath placed in them suitable inclinations of tenderness and concern to temper this power, to apply it as his wisdom designed it, to the children's good, as long as they should need to be under it."[48] Such passages as these make evident that it is precisely the differential between parents and children in experience, means, and force that argues for the succor of the weak and needy by the more powerful. Moreover, the model of social relations enacted within the family has direct political applications to society at large, as Locke asserts when he speaks in a later chapter of monarchs as "nursing fathers, tender and careful of the public weal."[49] In the light of his analysis of the relationships of power within the family, this characterization stands the existing conventions of royalist paternalism on their head.

To recover the religious dimensions of Locke's political philosophy may undermine to a significant degree the conventional view of his writings as collectively constituting the inaugural manifesto of classical liberalism. Dunn has identified two clear reasons why, once such dimensions are restored, Locke's reasoning does not consort with a capitalist apologetics. The first is that Locke gives his readers every reason to believe that the market was a coercive evil of terrestrial existence that could be accepted because its harm fades into inconsequence beside the demands of the calling. The second is that such an acceptance of social and material inequities can be judged comprehensible only within a framing conception of rational action, a conception oriented toward the reward of salvation in the afterlife, not of earthly riches.[50] By dwelling on the relation between the natural law of reason and the social structure of the family, I have tried to refine and to amplify Dunn's second point in one respect. My contention is that, in the *Second Treatise*, Locke gives concrete examples of the effort of moral and spiritual commitment required to give reason a binding sense of urgency on individual agents and that these examples envision action in the worldly present of this life as the basis of our election in the otherworldly future of the next. Dunn's judgment that Locke's Calvinism inures him to the economic and social inequalities of his society thus holds only up to a point. If I am correct, Locke's theology cannot be lumped together with a stereotypical reading of the Puritan work ethic as a displaced and domesticated form of greed. Once we have recognized the ambiguity of the concept of property at work in the *Second Treatise*, or the quasi-Calvinist sense of vocation that for Locke motivates the work of reason, or the significance of his extended comparison of the family to civil society, we cannot paint him as a settled apologist for material consumption.

Here, then, are grounds on which to begin to question certain assumptions central to the classical economic interpretation of liberalism. Hayek's position that freedom of mind (or ends) is absolutely dependent on freedom of action (or means) cannot be sustained if we look on even the selection and employment of our means and resources as ethical choices. At any rate, it cannot be sustained if we view action principally in moral terms, as I believe Locke does. The liberty that Locke holds dear is not readily conformable to the basic posture of classical liberalism as Hayek delineates it when he writes: "As in the intellectual so in the material sphere, competition is the most effective discovery procedure which will lead to the finding of better ways for the pursuit of human aims."[51] Competition so conceived is not an activity for which Locke would have had any special praise. To present him as the progenitor of a basic faith in the beneficial contributions of free-market commerce to the achievement of the good life is to falsify his point of view. If we may doubt the line of descent that Hayek traces from Locke's ideas to the philosophers of the Scottish Enlightenment such as Hume and Smith, and from there to the grand summary of Whig historiography by Thomas Babington Macaulay in the nineteenth century, we may also begin to doubt the claims he advances for the integrity, logical consistency, and pivotal importance of this line of thinkers. Such claims are reductive, particularly as regards the alternative model of liberal society that he ascribes to the alleged rationalism and constructivism of Continental philosophy, which Hayek distrustfully views as aspiring to a sweeping revision of social foundations according to abstract tenets of reason.[52]

In a cogent recent study of the tension between liberalism's two aspects as a universalist philosophy on the one hand and a pluralist on the other, John Gray is at pains to dismiss Hayek's core propositions: "The dangers of seeking to define an essential liberal tradition are well illustrated by Hayek's attempt to identify 'true' or 'classical' liberalism as a whiggish, 'English' tradition running from Locke to Adam Smith, which was swamped by a 'new' or 'French' liberalism towards the end of the eighteenth century."[53] Gray plainly discerns that the success of Hayek's overall historical picture far too frequently rests on a one-sided or selective consideration of his sources, as in his treatment of Adam Smith:

> Hayek's attempt to define a tradition of "true" or "classical" liberalism deforms the thought of Adam Smith. True, if anyone was a liberal in the late eighteenth century, it was Adam Smith; but he was just as much a critic of liberalism. Smith was an early critic of the moral hazards of capitalist societies.... In fact, so far is Smith from being an exemplar of "true" or "classical" liberal thought that one could just as well say of him that he is one of the chief sources of later critiques of liberalism.[54]

A certain irony attends Gray's just objections to this slanting of the history of ideas. His own assessment of liberalism, as a political philosophy torn between peaceful toleration and rational consensus, may be construed in some respects as a revision of Hayek's distinction between the pragmatist focus on executive limitation by the rule of law and the constructivist focus on administrative leeway under the courts. Still, Gray's revision is bracingly realistic. For he drops both Hayek's partitioning of liberalism into separate schools whose divergence reflects purportedly incommensurable differences of national character and his unquestioning adherence to the myth of Whiggish commercial triumph. What separates Gray from his predecessor is an interest in the philosophical consequences of a split between ethical attitudes. As he sees it, the question that needs to be addressed now by liberal thought is not "Which ordering of institutions best enables us as rational agents to achieve our agreed-on purposes?" but rather "What sets of purposes may serve as conventions for peaceful agreement between groups whose claims no longer can be adjudicated by appeal to a transcendent standard of reason?" The current conflict that threatens human freedom in other words lies between a realist *modus vivendi* that embraces value-pluralism in the name of tolerance and a blinkered rationalism that pursues cohesion in the name of universality.[55]

Gray ends his book with a declaration of his skeptical intent to dispel the illusion that well-formulated theoretical foundations would obviate the agonistic necessity of politics in liberal society. Then he finely adds:

> It would be idle to deny that *modus vivendi* is a sceptical view. But what it gives up is not the belief that we can know the difference between right and wrong. It is the traditional faith, which contemporary liberal orthodoxy has inherited, that questions of value can have only one right answer. To relinquish this is no loss, since it means that the diversity of ways of life and regimes is a mark of human freedom, not of error.[56]

Skepticism on this reckoning comes to the aid of the fragile ideal of cultural open-mindedness or lenity. This orientation, which for Gray is the starting point of the effort to salvage what is left of a viable liberal project, is not far different from the repertory of ideas espoused by the satirists I have called cultural liberals. Gray, who wishes to establish an origin for liberal toleration in political philosophy, nominates Hobbes as its initial author: "A Hobbesian state extends to private belief the radical tolerance of indifference. Hobbes is thereby the progenitor of a tradition of liberal thought in which *modus vivendi* is central."[57] However, if we contemplate the wider epistemological and ethical contours of the mentality, we can discover much of its substance already set forth in the observations of the great satiric moralist of the Roman *principate*:

> Nil admirari prope res est una, Numici,
> solaque quae posit facere et servare beatum. . . .
> insani sapiens nomens ferat, aequus iniqui,
> ultra quam satis est virtutem si petat ipsem.
>
> Never to marvel is the one good, Numicius,
> that can grant and preserve our happiness. . . .
> Let the sage be called mad, the just unfair,
> should he pursue virtue beyond what's right.[58]

Horace's articulation in Epistle 1.6 of the Epicurean precept of *ataraxia*, or equanimity, captures a texture of thought and feeling that presupposes detachment from dogmatic conviction or enthusiasm of any kind. As he points out, to push even virtue to an extreme is to indulge in a form of zealotry.

As I indicated earlier in passing, these lines may be said to constitute a motto for the English Augustans and thus to enunciate a perspective that remained influential on their successors. Dryden and Pope both subscribed to a theory of knowledge that regarded an acceptance of a significant amount of uncertainty as the unavoidable price of an inferential or probabilistic understanding in matters of language, history, and ethics.[59] They therefore viewed with suspicion all claims to immanent authority in the human realm and found in Horace a model of how poetic judgment might work as a corrective to such claims. Moreover, they regarded such claims, which they associated with the intolerance of the Protestant majority in England, as the manic excesses of a historically corrupt modernity—as "nothing to admire" in the parodic sense of a self-gratifying impulse entirely at odds with the moderating principle of *nil admirari*. (Accordingly, I mean the title of this book to suggest not a translation of the Horatian formula but rather its bathetic or ironic paraphrase.) Adopting such a view, Dryden and Pope confirm that for their classical predecessor "the issue is . . . one of status, and what one is born with."[60] On this reckoning, the Roman satirist's very advocacy of the traditional ideal of *libertas* only serves in his poems as a reminder of, for example, "the great gulf that separates [the lowborn] Horace from [his aristocratic forerunner] Lucilius not just in terms of connections, money, and power, but especially in terms of being able to say what he wants to say."[61]

Commenting on Pope's "imitation" of Epistle 1.6, James Noggle exactly apprehends the satire's peculiar critical cast, its modernization of the Horatian effect of "both renouncing the sources of apparent happiness—wealth, popularity, power, sensory indulgence—and pointedly declining to represent good living otherwise than negatively as the lack of admiration for such things."[62] Noggle situates his perceptive reading of the doctrine of *nil admirari* and its importance for Pope in the course of an overarching proposition that "writers [such as Dryden and Pope] share a skeptical tendency to refuse the individual subject any access to absolute authority . . . [an] epistemological posture that must be seen as a staple of political conservatism even if it does not always translate into a doctrine of the political subject's subservience to royal, church, or state authority."[63] He goes on to say flatly that "skeptical philosophy always advises extreme conservatism, finding the status quo to be the safest bet in a radically dubious world."[64] Noggle bases his reasoning on the insight that the drastic skepticism of the Tory satirists casts into doubt the Whig faith in a providential, universal order that harmonizes "the competing economic and political interests of individual citizens, general necessity with personal liberty, and absolute justification with probabilistic skepticism."[65] Much of the plausibility in his use of political tags thus hangs on the customary equation of liberalism with the Whig Party itself, hence on the conviction that any discussion of our personal, individual dignities and freedoms inevitably presupposes as its enabling condition the entire complex of social institutions and practices advocated by the Whigs during the period of their political ascendancy. I have tried in this introductory essay to voice appropriate reservations with respect to the alleged necessity of the connections drawn to support the thesis that liberalism is by definition a Whig creation. My assertion through the rest of this book is that Dryden, and Pope, and their successors mount in their satires a sustained critique of power and of commerce that gives to their inheritors the linguistic resources with which to expose the illiberal, regressive, and mystifying forces of their own political and social communities. As an effect of this argument, I hope to undermine the habit of applying "liberal" and "conservative" labels to protagonists in the ideological skirmishes of the post-Restoration or Augustan period simply based on nominal party affiliations. To look at the reciprocal favoritism of political and commercial privilege during the Whig Robinocracy as an incumbent regime's mechanism of self-perpetuation allows us to look at a writer like Pope who shares that perception as an enemy of the status quo precisely on account of his "skeptical philosophy."

To readers familiar with J. G. A. Pocock's work in the history of political thought, my analysis will look like a corollary of his thesis. Pocock has advanced a view of the period roughly from Charles II's reign through the American Revolution that rejects the idea of Locke as the framer of political debate during the period and thus as responsible for policies that, after the Glorious Revolution, kept the peace and nurtured prosperity. His interpretation rather accentuates a sustained conflict between two discourses that competed for the ideological upper hand in the formation of society and culture. The older of the two idioms, associated with a civic humanism inherited from Francesco Guicciardini and Niccolo Machiavelli, crystallizes around the self-fulfillment of the individual "as a conscious and autonomous participant in an autonomous decision-taking political community, the polis or republic."⁶⁶ It expresses approval for such a personality via the codeword "patriot" and celebrates an ethic of independence "entailing a conception of property that had more to do with Harrington than with Locke," whereby freedom or "virtue" is assured by the stable expedient of land ownership.⁶⁷ This language is renewed with particular subtlety and sophistication by a group to which Pope and his political mentor Henry St. John, the Viscount Bolingbroke, were central, namely the Country Party of opposition to the Walpole administration. The younger of the two idioms revolves around the conversion of the feminized, unpredictable phenomenon of "credit" into "opinion" or confidence and, because it interprets this process as a sign of historical advancement, invokes "those schemes of natural law and *jus gentium* propounded by Grotius, Pufendorf, Locke and the German jurists, which stressed the emergence of civil jurisprudence out of a state of nature."⁶⁸ It defends commerce on the grounds that exchange tames the passions and teaches "politeness," and its chief self-conscious proponents are Daniel Defoe and Joseph Addison.

Pocock's riveting and, in many ways, indisputable reading of the period casts into doubt the narrative of the linear development of a uniform political tradition called "liberalism" that centers around the private interests of the individual and that supposedly "had held the field—or had expanded control of the field without effective opposition—from the days of Hobbes and Locke even to the days of Marx."⁶⁹ This is a liberalism that grants a generous measure of self-determination to the individual on the view that the proper relation between personality and government occurs "only through a series of social relationships of which commerce was the paradigm if not the efficient cause."⁷⁰ The target of Pocock's criticism, in other words, is the triumphal Whig historiography that, as I already have shown in some detail, takes as its intellectual centerpiece the complex of ideas that Hayek identified as "classical liberalism." What is not entirely clear from the explicit terms of this criticism is precisely how far Pocock wishes to go in pressing the attack from the interpretation of history to the social doctrine at its core. It is still less clear as a matter of overt exposition whether he believes or takes interest in a language of individual self-rule that does not chiefly resort to the metaphors of the free market. When pressed, he declares: "I am not calling into question the historical reality of 'liberalism' or 'possessive individualism,' so much as those 'liberal,' or rather antiliberal, interpretations of history, in which everything leads up to and away from a monolithic domination of 'liberal' ideas somewhere in the nineteenth century."⁷¹ His accomplishment of recovering for intellectual history the importance of the clash between the discourses of virtue and commerce, however, necessarily implies a shift in our understanding of historical reality. For the insight suggests that by repressing the tension between these ideals we risk mistaking our own limiting and liberating circumstances: "There is no greater and no commoner mistake . . . than to suppose that the tension ever disappeared, that the ideals of virtue and unity of personality were driven from the field, or that a commercial, 'liberal' or 'bourgeois' ideology reigned undisturbed until challenged by the harbingers of Marx."[72]

The polemical success of Pocock's inquiry consists in its open-endedness. By refusing to close off entirely the ideological debate he perceives at the heart of modernity, he leaves the reader to ponder a set of specific, corollary questions. What indeed is the historical reality or referentiality of liberalism? If the "undisturbed" rise of the bourgeoisie is a fiction, where are we to locate the sources of discomfort and how are we to judge the politics of such resistance? Is there a way of defining liberalism that does not amount in the end to a romanticizing of possessive individualism? Might a reexamination of the antithetical tradition of republican virtue constitute a first step toward such an alternate definition? Although the scope of this study does not permit lingering consideration of such questions, I hope that the critical account I will give here of the legacy of the Augustan satirists may be seen as one episode in the vicissitudes of literary culture that has implications for the dispute between the depiction of humans as either essentially economic or essentially political beings. Ultimately, I wish to affirm a liberalism that places greatest faith in intellectual, as distinct from material, exchange and that therefore perceives the domain of culture as having a distinct importance.

It may be that many contemporary readers are arriving at a similar point of departure. In a recent study of "early modern liberalism," Annabel Patterson has named Milton as a source of our modern ideas of free, yet sociable, communities when he advocates what she calls "massive decentralization of the law and the fiscal apparatus" in order to achieve a condition in which, to use his own words, "all distinction of lords and commoners, that may any way divide or sever the publick interest [is] remov'd." Patterson goes on to note that this vision is wedded in Milton's mind to an emphasis on "education," to the exposure of all members of society to "all liberal arts and exercises."[73] Her emphasis on liberalism as a mode of socially and culturally critical freedom of mind is timely; and I believe the five poets I have brought together here articulate a similar understanding. For by giving it a satiric voice, they call attention to the absurdity or triviality of such a proposition from the perspective of established power. The very acknowledgment of the ludicrousness of their own devices as satirists, however, exposes to interrogation in turn the claims to authority of the entrenched, conventional views against which the poets protest. In the process, Dryden, Pope, Byron, Auden, and Merrill teach us to interpret laughter as the sign of a freedom that has yet to be realized. In a mood of Horatian skepticism, they expose the disenchanting privileges of commercial society and its culture of the marketplace as objects of the satirist's derision and therefore as nothing to admire.

1

Satura Redux

Dryden and the Augustan Ideal

> Forgive th' allusion; 'twas not meant to bite,
> But Satire will have room, where e're I write.

Strictly speaking, the myth of a British Augustan age did not originate with Dryden. As early as the posthumous publication in 1595 of Sir Philip Sidney's *Defence of Poesy*, an overtly Horatian notion of literary value had advanced to the forefront of critical discussion in England with the claim that poetry ought to "teach and delight." Ben Jonson, in his 1601 stage satire *Poetaster*, depicted Augustus as an ideal arbiter of cultural disputes who could be trusted to defend Horace and the virtue of scholarly wit against the criticism of pretentious and opportunistic courtly rivals. On the occasion of King James's triumphal entry into the City of London in 1604, Jonson heralded the arrival of "the greatest, perfectest, and last" historical round of "change and sway" in a commissioned verse of welcome that echoed the passage from Virgil's Fourth Eclogue inaugurating a new golden age under Augustus ("Ultima Cumaei venit iam carminis aetas," etc.).[1] Subsequently, to measure English society against the Augustan standard became something of a *topos*. Robert Herrick bestowed the title of "great Augustus" on Charles I for bringing "dearest peace after destructive war" in his lyric of 1647, "To the King, Upon his Welcome to Hampton Court." Howard Erskine-Hill has pointed out that Marvell's poem *An Horatian Ode Upon Cromwell's Return* would have provoked instant thoughts, in the classically trained readers of its day, of Horace's Actium Ode, 1.37, which "uniquely among Horace's Odes ... describes the fall of an hereditary monarch, Cleopatra, with the victory of a Caesar, Octavian, not yet but soon to be Augustus."[2]

After the end of the Protectorate and the subsequent restoration of Charles II to the throne, however, the myth of a programmatic reunification of empire by a strong ruler acquired a new urgency. Much of the reason for the renewal of this narrative may be ascribed to the formation of a Tory propaganda machine during the last years of Charles's reign. The establishment of a coterie of apologists for the throne came in response to the torrent of Whig tracts unleashed by the expiration in 1679 of the Licensing Act that had been in effect since 1662. Although Dryden's involvement in the Tory counteroffensive may have been "slow in coming," according to Phillip Harth's characterization, the laureate on entering the fray "would lead the way in shaping a variety of literary genres into new and effective instruments of political propaganda appealing to a reading public whose own interests had been increasingly concentrated and politicized by a long succession of public crises and partisan debates."[3] The growing stridency of public debate that followed the collapse of censorship in England appears to have supplied the right environment for the development of a new kind of poetic authority. Dryden's feat of "uniting politicks with poetry" during the 1680s, to borrow Samuel Johnson's phrase, permanently changes our understanding of the poet's office or proper role in society.[4] It is this sense of the new possibilities for imaginative expression that become available after the Restoration on which the notion of an Augustan epoch of unparalleled cultural vitality in England ultimately rests.

Attentive throughout his learned study to his project of delineating the connection between the emergent Tory propaganda effort and Dryden's satires of the 1680s, Harth does not observe the consequences of this linkage for the larger picture of English cultural and political history. My feeling is that the consequences are noteworthy. To view the poet as exercising a new mode of cultural influence by courting the judgment of an autonomous general readership is to confirm, at least partially, Jürgen Habermas's sense of Augustan England's pivotal importance to the establishment of the public interest "as an organizing principle of our [modern] political order."[5] Habermas argues that a number of historical circumstances, including the lapse of censorship laws and the burgeoning of "the coffee houses in their golden age between 1680 and 1730," combined during the period to transform culture, particularly in its literary manifestations, into "a forum in which the private people, come together to form a public, readied themselves to compel public authority to legitimate itself before public opinion."[6] A crucial contributor to this process, on the philosopher's reckoning, was "Dryden, [who,] surrounded by the new generation of writers, joined the battle of the 'ancients and moderns' at Will's" and thus participated in the formation of "centers of criticism—literary at first, then also political—in which began to emerge, between aristocratic society and bourgeois intellectuals, a certain parity of the educated."[7]

Habermas has had detractors, it should be acknowledged. The most eminent of these was Jean-François Lyotard, who famously raised certain complicating questions in *The Postmodern Condition* regarding the German philosopher's project: whether it is possible to reach universal agreement on the rules of social legitimation, whether the aim of dialogue is in fact such agreement or whether it is the proliferation of alternative propositions, and consequently whether the validity of particular statements depends on the degree to which they facilitate a supposedly emancipating rational consensus.[8] Lyotard's complaints, however, revolve around Habermas's proposed theoretical corrective to the domination of the public sphere by corporate private enterprise since the middle of the nineteenth century.[9] Such objections leave untouched his account of the historical origin and function of the public sphere. In general, Habermas's reading of the relation between popular debate and the liberalization of British society during the eighteenth and nineteenth centuries demonstrates an imposing command of the record. Particularly with respect to the operation of literary culture as a catalyst for the emergence of a populist opposition politics, his argument has been indirectly borne out by scholars who subsequently have called for greater recognition of Tory and Country participation in the affairs of the day.[10]

Concentrating on the celebrated poems of the 1680s, I shall argue in what follows that in order to acquire a sense of satiric prerogative adequate to defend the throne, Dryden paradoxically had to develop figurative strategies that enforced the stance of a cultural liberal. Despite the poet's explicit and unwavering adherence to a conservative, royalist political agenda in his satires, the poems implicitly argue for an idea of human nature grounded in a use of language, an exercise of wit or poetic invention, that undermines a strict social conservatism. His particular use of the Augustan metaphor, that is to say, commits him to a meritocratic rather than aristocratic ideal. The metaphor permits Dryden the liberty of rebuking in more or less covert ways his social superiors and even Charles for failing the ideal, thus placing imperial order and plebeian satire in an inherently problematic relation to one another. Dustin Griffin has captured an aspect of this attitude when he says we meet in Dryden's dedicatory epistles with the poet's belief that "literature . . . is too serious a matter to be left wholly in the hands of the class of leisured aristocrats who traditionally bore responsibility for creating and overseeing it."[11] David B. Haley has identified another aspect when he ascribes to the satirist "a strain of Puritan radicalism . . . [that] can still be detected beneath the Tory propaganda of *Absalom and Achitophel*."[12] Haley traces Dryden's radicalism on matters of belief back to a tradition of Erasmian humanism that embraced "free will in theory, tolerance in practice, and the amenability of religious problems and texts to reason."[13] In England, such principles were associated with Arminian doctrines that issued "from the pens of liberal theologians like William Chillingworth and Archbishop William Laud, who were thought to be soft toward papists."[14] According to the critic, it is from this intellectual inheritance that Dryden learned in *Absalom and Achi-*

tophel to propound "an allegory by means of which the public poet makes a radical criticism of the monarchy he seems to uphold."[15]

Dr. Johnson's famous comment on Dryden, I think, best describes the sense of change that the poet precipitated in our very conception of culture: "What was said of Rome, adorned by Augustus, may be applied by an easy metaphor to English poetry embellished by Dryden, 'lateritiam invenit, marmoream reliquit,' he found it brick, and he left it marble."[16] As an encomium to Dryden, Johnson's reappropriation of the approving comment by Suetonius concerning the legacy of monuments that Augustus left to Rome suggests a nearly oxymoronic contradiction. On the one hand, the Latin quotation pays tribute to the poet's success in reviving an overtly classical, rhetorical style of expression. On the other, the formula argues that Dryden has contributed something new and original to "English poetry," that he has raised the state of the literary culture to an unprecedented level of sophistication. By an allusive trick of the voice, Johnson makes the innovation for which Dryden is responsible in our very consciousness of writing look like a self-effacing homage. However, the radical nature of the innovation is given away by the metaphoric substitution at the heart of the figure. For in the transition from the classical to the modern reality, the poet has inserted himself into a position as central to his culture as Caesar's was to Rome. Having turned poetry into a means of shaping public opinion, Dryden has found the authority to usurp Augustus's place as the spokesman for the civilization.

At the beginning of *MacFlecknoe*, Dryden draws a comparison between writer and ruler that might seem to anticipate Johnson's "easy metaphor," if the overall effect were not one of ludicrous inappropriateness.

> All humane things are subject to decay,
> And, when Fate summons, Monarchs must obey:
> This *Fleckno* found, who, like *Augustus*, young
> Was call'd to Empire, and had govern'd long:
> In Prose and Verse, was own'd, without dispute
> Through all the Realms of *Nonsense*, absolute.
> (1–6)

The opening line's emphasis on "decay" subtly moralizes the imperial simile, so that even the long duration of Flecknoe's reign over "the Realms of *Nonsense*," ordinarily an index of the monarch's judgment and statesmanship, here comes to look like an attribute of nerveless quietism. The Virgilian rhetoric of prophecy, which in *MacFlecknoe*'s putative ur-text, the *Aeneid*, celebrates the desired historical triumph of "all Julius's descendants" ("omnis Iuli / progenies," 6.789–790), modulates at once into a delicately cynical register, a sort of understated doomsaying. As a consequence of this shift, all the usual clichés of praise for the sovereign's magnificence are inverted. In the line immediately following the citation, for example, Dryden's description of the hack Flecknoe as an "aged Prince now flourishing in Peace" surreptitiously rescinds the very compliment it pretends to pay. Since it is an "Empire" of (corrupted) arts over which Flecknoe presides, "Peace" in this context cannot mean the political and economic stability achieved by efficient government but rather connotes unresponsiveness of wit or imagination.

The guile of the poem's language, the eagerness with which it courts this kind of semantic confusion, is emblematic of both Flecknoe's and Shadwell's role in the cultural economy here being detailed. While the versifying fraud sets himself up as an Augustus of the intellect, hence as *primus inter pares* when it comes to questions of taste, he in fact makes no direct contribution to the lasting, public edifice of the civilization. Rather, in his capacity as "absolute" literary dictator, he exerts a deleterious power of persuasion over weak-minded contemporary readers. He embodies the kind of "peace" in which a healthy, critical mind would rather not be "flourishing." And not only does the bungling Flecknoe threaten injury to the general sensibility, he adds the insult of having guaranteed the perpetuation of his influence through his inheritor, Shadwell. *MacFlecknoe* sarcastically affirms the traditional equation of the nation's interest and well-being with its ruler's and in so doing perhaps follows the lead of Hobbes's *Leviathan*. The special relation between the "Artificiall Man" of the civil state and the "Artificall *Soul*" of "Soveraignty," which Hobbes envisions "as giving life and motion to the whole body," is reflected parodically in Flecknoe's portrayal of Shadwell incarnating an anarchic and uncultivatable "Nature" and thereby laying claim to a certain emblematic status.[17]

> Besides his goodly Fabrick fills the eye,
> And seems design'd for thoughtless Majesty:
> Thoughtless as Monarch Oakes, that shade the plain,
> And, spread in solemn state, supinely reign.
> (25–28)

Hobbes declares in chapter 35 of *Leviathan* that "the Kingdome of God is a Civill Kingdome" and goes on to add: "The King of any Countrey is the *Publique* Person or Representative of all his own Subjects. And God the King of Israel was the *Holy one* of Israel."[18] What these sentences imply is that the Christian kingdom derives "life and motion" from its king insofar as it recognizes him as God's lieutenant on earth. His position is exemplary because he is a reminder of the original covenant of the Jews through Moses with the deity.[19]

Shadwell, by contrast, personifies an order thoroughly detached from divine providence or reason. Unluckily, he has managed nevertheless by sheer, artless force of imposition to catch and hold the attention of the larger society: "his goodly Fabrick fills the eye." The result promises to be disastrous. Whereas a Hobbesian sovereign would inspire the polity to dynamic action, Shadwell, once enthroned, will transform his readers into a nation of inert wooden trunks like himself. The very texture of the verse in this passage exacerbates the air of comic peril; the persistent repetition on the adjective "thoughtless," the replication of the diphthong [ej] through the last two lines ("shade...plain / ...state...reign"), and the promiscuous alliteration in the final line all conspire to suggest a linguistic environment menaced with the possibility of infection by an all-too-catching insipidity of manner. Not only does the jibe at Shadwell's weight recall to his discredit the image of his hero, Ben Jonson, as if to say the only resemblance between idol and imitator consists in their bulk, but it warns the reader against a laziness of mind that has left Shadwell no other claim to fame than existence as a "goodly Fabrick."[20]

Fear that the body politic may lapse into gross Shadwellian dilapidation is well founded, we see, as the poem proposes through the repetition of the key word, "fabrick," a deepening affinity between England's capital and its would-be emperor.

> Close to the Walls which fair *Augusta* bind,
> (The fair *Augusta* much to fears inclin'd,)
> An ancient fabrick rais'd t'inform the sight,
> There stood of yore, and *Barbican* it hight:
> A watch Tower once, but now, so Fate ordains,
> Of all the Pile an empty name remains.
> From its old Ruins Brothel-houses rise,
> Scenes of lewd loves, and of polluted joys;
> Where their vast Courts the Mother-Strumpets keep,
> And, undisturbed by Watch, in silence sleep....
> Great *Fletcher* never treads in Buskins here,
> Nor greater *Johnson* dares in Socks appear.
> But gentle *Simkin* just reception finds
> Amidst this Monument of vanisht minds:
> Pure Clinches, the suburbian Muse affords;
> And *Panton* waging harmless War with words.
> Here *Fleckno*, as a place to Fame well known,
> Ambitiously design'd his Sh — 's throne.
>   (64–73; 79–86)

Having declined visibly into an "empty name," the once functional watchtower "called Burgh-kenning, i.e. Barbican" provides a revealing synecdoche for the fallen condition of "fair Augusta" and thus for a cityscape of "Ruins" and "Brothel-houses" which under other circumstances might have been the site of ancient Rome's historical resurrection (hence the use of London's archaic, latinate name "Augusta").[21] Flecknoe's choice of the spot for the coronation of his adopted son is appropriate because the neighborhood literally unites in one locale the businesses of prostitute and playwright that, Dryden with no special delicacy intimates, combine figuratively in Shadwell's career. The poet's repudiation of the "polluted joys" offered by the "Mother-Strumpets" clearly implies a larger indictment of a decadent, hence feminized, reading public and the emasculated scribblers who pander to such an audience (their sexual incapacity is highlighted by Flecknoe's later command to Shadwell, "learn thou from me / Pangs without birth, and fruitless Industry," 147–148).

The moral of these lines thus might seem to look ahead to the end of *Absalom and Achitophel*, where David in effect blames the Exclusion Crisis on undomesticated female sexuality (the Errour-like "Mother Plot" of l. 1013) and the threat it poses to the sanctity of patriarchal succession. Susan C. Greenfield has explained that the poem entertains a maternal theory of conception in order to excuse Charles II from responsibility for the crisis. As she points out, Dryden's argument runs directly counter to Locke's emphasis on the maternal in order to question the institution of monarchy in his *First Treatise of Government*, which itself responds to Sir Robert Filmer's *Patriarcha*. She observes that *Absalom and Achitophel* articulates a politically conservative distrust of the subject masses (and, it might be added, in this light resembles *MacFlecknoe*): "If the populace believes that Kings are made, not designated—if it assumes the right to create a ruler—then like the mother viper, it too will become the breeder of chaos."[22]

If the lines I have been examining from *MacFlecknoe* betray signs of their author's somewhat nervous concern for the security of Charles's reign, however, they also startlingly give indications of a kind of exhilaration, perhaps unwittingly or unwillingly felt, toward the incongruities of contemporary life. The description of the whorehouse district, "Where their vast Courts the Mother-Strumpets keep, / And undisturb'd by Watch, in silence sleep," is a good case in point. Although scholars often remark that the lines revise Abraham Cowley's description of Hell from book 1 of his *Davideis* (1668), they seldom clarify how the revision works. On this score, it is worth recalling in full the original:

> Beneath the dens where unfletcht Tempests lye,
> And infant Winds their tender Voyces try,
> Beneath the mighty Oceans wealthy Caves,
> Beneath th'eternal Fountain of all Waves,
> Where their vast Court the Mother-waters keep,
> And undisturb'd by Moons in silence sleep,
> There is a place deep, wondrous deep below.[23]

What is noticeably absent from Cowley's landscape is any impression of the cosmopolitan traffic that gives the vista painted by Dryden its smirched glamour. Whereas Cowley's tableau is all of a piece, Dryden's is all in pieces, and the pieces all converge in an exuberant whirl of contrasts: great piles collapse to empty names, "old Ruins" give rise to new bordellos, the "Watch" marches by as the strumpets luxuriate in oblivious dreams.

The one poet whose example might have helped to show the way for Dryden is Milton in *Paradise Lost*, not so much in his actual depiction of the infernal city, Pandemonium, which radiates a supernatural opulence that does not really enter into the scene from *MacFlecknoe*, but in his characterization in book 9 of Satan's memory of Hell on visiting Eden in the guise of the serpent. Milton pictures Satan

> As one who long in populous City pent,
> Where Houses thick and Sewers annoy the Air,
> Forth issuing on a Summer's Morn to breathe . . .
>
> from each thing met conceives delight.
>
> (9.445–447; 449)

These few lines do no more than give a hint, however; here the poet glances at the overcrowding and dirtiness of the city and briskly turns away. Dryden's lines bring London to life in all its teeming variegation and linger over the spectacle. When he envisions scenes of "polluted joys," he forces us to recognize the pull these sensations exert on us in both directions: they are *both* "polluted" experiences *and* "joys." Accordingly, even the theaters that provide the despised Shadwell with an outlet for his wares are allowed their flicker of excitement. Of course, on those stages "great Fletcher" and "greater Johnson" would never be caught dead in any footwear, whether tragic "Buskins" or comic slippers, "But gentle *Simkin* just reception finds / Amidst this Monument of vanisht minds."

The last line is of particular interest. At first glance, "vanisht minds" might seem to refer, in a conventional show of critical piety, to the pantheon of dead geniuses such as Fletcher and Jonson who preceded the present generation of dramatists. We have just been told, however, that Fletcher and Jonson in reality never make any appearance in these shabby establishments. At second glance, then, we realize that "vanisht minds" must refer to the current theatergoers and performers who are mutually responsible for the fashions of the moment and thus for the popularity of such inane characters as the burlesque clown Simkin. The "minds" are "vanisht" not because they belong to the past but because they belong too wholly to the present. Expectations of grandeur raised by "this Monument" undergo a sharp revision downward when the formula is read with careful attention to its position in its local context. Yet some ghostly residue of the expectations clings even to the revised perception.

This effect of revision, interpreted as a disappointment of cultural hopes that the poem nevertheless refuses to let the reader abandon, occurs at a number of points throughout *MacFlecknoe*. Consider the moment at which Flecknoe claims responsibility for the literary fathering of Shadwell, thereby denying the younger man any opportunity of membership in the Tribe of Ben.

> Thou art my blood, where *Johnson* has no part; . . .
>
> Where sold he Bargains, Whip-stitch, kiss my Arse,
> Promis'd a Play and dwindled to a Farce?
> When did his Muse from *Fletcher* scenes purloin,
> As thou whole *Eth'ridg* dost transfuse to thine?
> But so transfus'd, as Oyl on Waters flow,
> His always floats above, thine sinks below.
> (175, 181–186)

Dryden not only hands Shadwell an exquisite and withering put-down here, by anointing him king with an oil that by nature cannot touch him, but also delivers a quietly displaced encomium to Jonson, whose death in 1637, some forty odd years before the composition of *MacFlecknoe*, would have made him a distant but perhaps not totally vanished (to use Dryden's adjective) figure on the theatrical landscape.[24] As readers we are prompted by the insistent rhetorical questions to regard the modern poseur's falling off from the standard of the past as an oblique vindication of the measure. Shadwell's clumsy inability to "transfuse" Etherege only serves to point up Jonson's authorial self-sufficiency, his freedom from the need to "purloin" the designs of his immediate peers.

Unable to disguise its own derivation from Flecknoe's "blood," Shadwell's watery fancy "sinks below" Etherege's subtler "Oyl," leaving Jonson at his high level still more removed from the muddy depths. The subliminal echo of the ponderous Shadwellian "flow" in the instant at which Etherege "floats above" mockingly accentuates the separation. Dryden's editors in the twentieth century have discerned a likeness between his ingenious metaphor and the description by Cowley in *Davideis* 4 of Samuel's anointing of Saul ("Drops of that Royal Moisture which does know / No Mixture, and disdains the place below").[25] On the topic of literary standards, however, Dryden perhaps might have been thinking as well of Jonson's rendering into English of Horace's *Ars Poetica*.[26]

> As jarring music doth, at jolly feasts,
> Or thick gross ointment, but offend the guests:
> As poppy, and Sardane honey; 'cause without
> These, the free meal might have been well drawn out:
> So, any poem, fancied, or forth-brought
> To bettering of the mind of man, in aught,
> If ne'er so little it depart the first,
> And highest; sinketh to the lowest, and worst.
> (557–564)

As in *MacFlecknoe*, the point here is the rapidity of the drop-off; any straying from the "first and highest" place, be it "ne'er so little," will elicit the disenchantment and ill will of the reader. Whereas Horace enumerates uniformly damning analogies for poetic miscalculation, that is, "jarring music," gummy "ointment," and bitter Sardinian honey, Dryden presents us with a picture not only of the imagination's disreputable retreat (into coarse attempts at humor, for example, with expressions such as "kiss my Arse") but of the shimmering play of wit that represents the ideal it has forsaken. The ridicule of Shadwell, which by means of the liquid figure literally puts him in his place, also brings to the reader's attention a counterexample to the process of historical decline with which the delinquent playwright is complicit. Etherege, at least, does no discredit to the modern English stage. Although the other writers (Jonson, Fletcher) whom Dryden praises are dead, Etherege among the living sustains the possibility of a true Augustan flowering of the arts. Naming him with approval, the poem aligns itself with the struggle to recover the writer's vocation for the forces of cultural progress.

This struggle may be said to be motivated in part by a peculiar political agenda of its own. As Richard Kroll has remarked in the case of *Absalom and Achitophel*: "The poet implicitly inhabits the world that the king has tainted, and he must therefore discover a source of linguistic authority that permits him to admonish David and buttress his poem, without becoming, like the plotters, an idolater, a 'God-smith' or '*Adam*-wit.'"[27] In *MacFlecknoe* Dryden clearly picks his quarrel with Shadwell rather than Charles (as in the later satire he picks his quarrel with Achitophel rather than David), but the pervasive stress on Flecknoe and Shadwell as failed imperial figures may be meant to imply that the royal patron is not quite living up to all of his duties.[28]

Whether or not the side on which *MacFlecknoe* enlists has any chance of success is another matter. When "Empress Fame" spreads the news that Shadwell is to be crowned Flecknoe's heir, enticing the true-blue Protestant poet's supporters to appear from "Bun-Hill" and "Watling-Street" (the former an area associated with the Dissenters and thus with the Whigs), the poem manages to insinuate into its description of the ensuing celebration what may be a faint signal of its own opposition to all the festivity: "No *Persian* Carpets spread th'Imperial way, / But scatter'd Limbs of mangled Poets lay" (98–99). The "scatter'd Limbs of mangled Poets" translates the famous phrase from Horace's Satire 1.4, where he claims that in the work of a new poet endowed with divine judgment ("mens divinior," 43), however he may strain the limits of artistic license, "You would find the limbs of a poet, albeit dismembered" ("invenias etiam disiecti membra poetae," 62). Those readers who catch the allusion might wonder if Dryden means us to consider the "mangled Poets" whom he lists a few verses later ("*Heywood, Shirly, Ogleby,*" 102) as deserving of their punishment in no uncertain terms. The memory of the Latin original in fact may argue that some of the writers who line the streets have been victimized by the professional grind and the desperation it inspires and are awaiting the leadership of Horace's notional paragon, identified with "whoever has genius" ("ingenium cui sit," 43).

At the conclusion of the poem, however, it becomes evident that rescue is a long way off. There Shadwell's accession to the throne is sealed with a wickedly droll description of Flecknoe's removal, while he obliviously goes on "declaiming" about the merits of his successor, through a trap-door sprung beneath him by a pair of pranksters.

> Sinking he left his Drugget robe behind,
> Born upwards by a subterranean wind.
> The Mantle fell to the young Prophet's part,
> With double portion of his Father's Art.
> (214–217)

Flecknoe's descent is a familiar comic stage device, of the sort that, since the invention of the motion picture, has achieved something of a formal perfection in cinematic animated cartoons, where the contrast between the solidity of the falling body and the airy weightlessness of the afterimage it leaves behind reaches hyperbolic levels of exaggeration. Unlike the fluid sinking of Shadwell relative to Etherege, which effects the distillation of their two types of genius into separate essences, Flecknoe's fall through the floor emphasizes his corporeality and thus his resemblance to the Shadwell, who is a "goodly Fabrick" and of whom Flecknoe says: "A Tun of Man in thy Large bulk is writ, / But sure thou 'rt but a Kilderkin of wit" (195–196). To assume the mantle of this precursor, in other words, is to accept a "double portion" of a nonexistent virtue. The continuance of the House of Flecknoe means the victory of shoddy or meaningless "Art" and thus of a politics (with historical origins in Puritanism) that has little or no vision of civic culture. Shadwell's successful installation of himself in the public "eye," promised at the very beginning of the poem, thus is an affront of the most egregious kind to good taste. His crowning as Flecknoe's heir not only represents the elevation of an unworthy writer to a central position of social authority but the demotion or pushing aside of more deserving writers in the overall scheme of things.

The discomfort with which *MacFlecknoe* contemplates the demands of popular opinion, even while surreptitiously placing all hope of cultural reform on the shoulders of a literate (rather than propertied) class, evinces the poem's anxiety specifically with respect to its status as an economic commodity. The Whig commemoration in early 1682 of the *ignoramus* verdict rendered on the government's charge of treason against Anthony Ashley Cooper, first earl of Shaftesbury, provided Dryden with an occasion to rephrase this anxiety in hotter and more pointed terms. His response to the celebration of Shaftesbury's acquittal, *The Medall*, moralizes its own rhetorical function by means of a quotation from Ovid that is appended to the end of the satire as a kind of postscript: "Pudet haec opprobria, vobis / Et dici potuisse, et non potuisse refelli" ("It is a disgrace that these reproaches could be made against you and could not be refuted," *Metamorphoses* 1.758–759). To utter these "opprobria," or obloquies, is to expose the truth by default, to mount attacks so harsh that the silence of the accused can only be taken as assent. This silence, this inability of the derided to formulate an answer, logically ought to be construed to ratify the derision itself, to certify the validity of the satire. The muteness of the medal struck by the Whigs in tribute to their leader thus appears to cede to the loquacity of *The Medall* the status of the last (and only) word on recent history. On this evidence, the two works would seem to belong to two categorically separate and unrelated aesthetic economies. Whereas the false coinage of the Whig medal is consigned to the order of the nonlinguistic or insignificant, the legal tender of Dryden's work *The Medall* is added to the fund of language or significance.

In his commentary on the poem, however, Phillip Harth reminds readers not to take *The Medall* too hastily at its word. Replying to those who portray Dryden as adopting a new and more sincere manner in the satire and therefore as complying with an unprecedented feeling of crisis, Harth writes: "His tone of anger and exasperation in *The Medall* . . . is an effective rhetorical tactic to which his real feelings, whatever they may have been, are irrelevant. Along with other Tory propagandists in the winter of 1681–82, Dryden has raised the pitch of his discourse and adopted . . . the rhetoric of outrage."[29] Harth's foregrounding of the pragmatic nature of the satire, of its function as public speech and participation in a coordinated program of polemic, undermines not only the theory that the poem's furor is motivated by some singular, novel fear on Dryden's part but also that this violence of expression demarcates once and for all the boundary between the dumb and the speaking, the counterfeit and the genuine, the base and the precious. Viewed in its proper historical context, *The Medall* looks less like a deciding, interpretive act of demystification than like one more of a series of transactions between Whig and Tory within a single, continuous circuit of exchange. The useful posture maintained by the poem of spontaneous and aesthetically pure indignation appears even more dubious if we recall Joseph Spence's allegation that the king gave Dryden the idea to undertake the writing and rewarded him with "a present of a hundred broadpieces" on its completion.[30] Given the satirist's arraignment of Shaftesbury for "Bart'ring his venal wit" (32), the apocryphal image drawn by Spence skeptically reinterprets the poem's evocation of the Augustan mythos (associated with Ovid, for example) and advertisement of its privileged connection to the center of a revived age of gold.

Already in the "Epistle to the Whigs" that opens the satire, Dryden acknowledges the changeable value of his currency, the volatility of the standard to which his coin is pegged. Castigating his enemies for their plan of armed "Association" to resist a Catholic succession, he depicts the clash between parties as a kind of competition for popular investment: "So now, when your Affairs are in a low condition, you dare not pretend that to be a legal Combination, but whensoever you are afloat, I doubt not but it will be maintain'd and justify'd to purpose."[31] Elaborated in a mood of warning, the fiscal trope makes clear whose capital, relative to that of Shaftesbury's followers, is "afloat" at the moment, presently enjoying a high estimation. Yet the metaphor encourages a problematic confusion here between talk of intrinsic worth and of market value. What stands in danger of being lost in the course of this confusion is the ultimate referent (call it Nature, or the word of the monarch) of the larger chain of signification that permits commerce and its regulation, the rational order that Foucault has described as "the whole of that great *taxinomia* that makes it possible to know things by means of their identities... that area where being and the Same reside."[32] In the actions and sentiments of the Whigs, use threatens to overtake and to exhaust real wealth. "If God has not bless'd you with the Talent of Rhiming," writes Dryden, alluding to his opponents' efforts to compete with the recently published *Absalom and Achitophel*, "make use of my poor Stock and wellcome: let your Verses run upon my feet: and for the utmost refuge of notorious Blockheads, reduc'd to the last extremity of sense, turn my own lines upon me, and in utter despaire of your own Satyre, make me Satyrize myself."[33]

Despite his evident sarcasm, Dryden's tone wavers between boastful defiance and something less confident; it is hard to tell whose "despaire" will run deeper if the Whigs indeed must resort to appropriating and managing his "poor Stock." The "extremity of sense" that he reviles here denotes an intellectual avidity or mania that is the opposite of wit and must distort hopelessly the "great *taxinomia*." According to Michel Foucault, the development of monetarist policy in the "Classical" period, of an attempt to ensure prosperity through the regulation of currency, presupposes "analyses [which] are important because... they provide the interplay of signs and representations with a temporal index that gives progress a definition of its condition of possibility."³⁴ The *episteme* that draws on these analyses does not glimpse the limits of the "definition" until late in the eighteenth century, when it first encounters "the enormous thrust of a freedom, a desire, or a will, posited as the metaphysical converse of consciousness," a thrust that Foucault claims "is contemporaneous with Sade."³⁵ Such a generalization may be plausible from a French perspective. We perhaps may wonder if the language and mentality of English neoclassicism does not actually originate as a kind of reaction-formation against the thought of this "will," associated with the Civil War of the 1640s and the execution of Charles I.

Certainly, *The Medall*'s satirizing of popular caprice depicts the appetite of the plebeian masses as a hostile encroachment on the dominion of reason that, carried to an extreme, will culminate in a negation of the *lex naturalis* and its logical underpinnings. This logic of self-preservation, to adopt a Hobbesian interpretation once more, is precisely what argues for the transference of rights from the individual to society as it is symbolized by the throne.

> That Kings can doe no wrong we must believe:
> None can they doe, and must they all receive?
> Help Heaven! or sadly we see an hour,
> When neither wrong nor right are in their pow'r!
> Already they have lost their best defence,
> The benefit of Laws, which they dispence:
> No justice to their righteous Cause allow'd;
> But baffled by an Arbitrary Crowd:
> And Medalls grav'd, their Conquest to record,
> The Stamp and Coyn of their adopted Lord.
> (135–144)

To deny the king's authority to dispense justice is to subjugate everyone alike to the whims of the "Arbitrary Crowd" and thus to render language per se ineffectual as a means of deciding questions of moral accountability. Note that the ambiguity of the possessive adjective in the line "When neither wrong nor right are in their pow'r" indicates that when the hour we "sadly" foresee arrives, both the sovereign will have lost his proper office and the names "wrong" and "right" will have lost their real meaning. The appeal to "Heaven" in the third line evokes in a technical sense the idea of the ruler's special centrality to a Christian monarchy. More important, the appeal helps to reinforce the message of the last two lines that the issuing of a medal that bears Shaftesbury's image in the place ordinarily reserved for the king does not simply amount to a criminal act of counterfeiting but rather to the blasphemous act of idolatry. Whiggish efforts to substitute "their adopted Lord" for the rightful lieutenant of God betoken a more profoundly corrupt understanding than operated behind even the worst excesses of the past. Although formerly the people of England may have been guilty of committing regicide, at least by facing the practical consequences of their extravagance they came, however self-righteously, to an amendatory realization: "Crowds err not, though to both extremes they run; / To kill the Father, and recall the Son" (99–100). The crime was grave, but it taught a serious lesson: "to destroy the seeds of Civil War" (113).

Now, however, the lesson will be forgotten if the mob succeeds in setting up Shaftesbury as its chief object of veneration. Pushing beyond any previous "extremes" of self-involvement, the "Arbitrary Crowd" attains the final limit of presumption, what Dryden already has identified contemptuously in the "Epistle" as an incompetence with words, "the last extremity of sense." To illustrate the readerly ineptitude that he maintains is the precondition of Shaftesbury's popular support, Dryden draws a scathing portrait of the Whig jury members and witnesses responsible for the earl's undeserved acquittal.

> Then, Justice and Religion they forswore:
> Their Mayden Oaths debauch'd into a Whore.
> Thus Men are rais'd by Factions, and decry'd;
> And Rogue and Saint distinguish'd by their Side.
> They rack ev'n Scripture to confess their Cause;
> And plead a Call to preach, in spite of Laws.
> But that's no news to the poor injur'd Page;
> It has been us'd as ill in every Age . . .
>
> But, since our Sects in prophecy grow higher,
> The Text inspires not them; but they the Text inspire.
> (152–159, 165–166)

Dryden makes witty use of the prosodically overdetermined last line as a figure for the egotistical self-inflation of the Protestant sects in their insistence on the right to individual interpretation of scripture. Despite the modest joke of the alexandrine, however, the overall impression here is one of bitter acrimony. The "ill" usage or usury of the "poor injur'd Page" by the Whig partisans constitutes a work of misreading that appears motivated by avarice on the one hand, inasmuch as the jurors and witnesses stand to profit from Shaftesbury's patronage, and by lechery on the other, insofar as they have compelled the entity of language, their "Mayden Oaths," to serve their pleasure rather than the common good. As a consequence, the entire symbolic structure by which personal desire is sublimated into socially productive expression or exchange is twisted out of shape. The breakdown of this system will clear the way for the natural state of war under which condition human life becomes inevitably nasty, brutish, and short: "Lords envy Lords, and Friend with every Friend / About their impious Merit shall contend" (308–309).

Shaftesbury makes the perfect chief for such a morally and mentally impoverished crew of "Lords" and "Friends" (all "hot Zealots," as the poet calls them elsewhere in the satire, 238), because throughout his career he has played "the Pander of the Peoples hearts . . . / Whose blandishments a Loyal Land have whor'd" (256, 258). Dryden drops several references in *The Medall* to the fact of the earl's having begun his ministerial career in the service of the king ("The Wretch turn'd loyal in his own defence / And Malice reconcil'd him to his Prince," 51–52, and again: "When his Sovereign, by no impious way, / Cou'd be seduc'd to Arbitrary sway; / Forsaken of that hope, he shifts the sayle," 77–79) and blends these allusions with sexual innuendoes based on contemporary gossip ("His open lewdness he cou'd ne'er disguise," 37) in order to turn Shaftesbury into an emblem of ruthless self-interest. The Whig aristocrat is a semiotic debauchee, bodying forth Foucault's "metaphysical converse of consciousness" with a proto-Sadean abandon. Throughout the poem, and particularly toward the end, Dryden plays on the notion of Shaftesbury as a libertine, elevating what would be matter for mere mudslinging in a lesser writer's hands into a mythic denunciation of opportunism: "Religion thou hast none: thy *Mercury* / Has pass'd through every Sect, or theirs through Thee" (263–264). The use of mercury as a desperate treatment for syphilis clearly provides the primary meaning of the figure here. However, the alchemical importance of the element also connects the word peripherally both to the Egyptian ruler Hermes Trismegistus, the supposed inventor of alchemy, and to the Greek Hermes, patron god of science, commerce, and language (hence, of course, "hermeneutics"). Dryden's ringing assertion "Religion thou hast none" and talk of sects thus implies a denial of Shaftesbury's fitness to supply the figure of a deified, magical, mercurian king.[36]

Even if we wish to minimize these resonances, it is apparent from the lines following that Shaftesbury's "mercury" assaults the body like a kind of perverted poetic invention or afflatus; it "inspires the Tongues, and swells the Breasts / Of all thy bellowing Renegado Priests" (268–269). A crucial, early passage in the satire proposes through its adoption of a familiar rhetoric that his restless political ambition builds on the urgings of a defective and frustrated poetic talent: "His nimble Wit outran the heavy Pack. / Yet still he found his Fortune at a stay; / Whole droves of Blockheads choaking up his way" (45–47). The last line of this little character sketch evokes the parade that heralds Shadwell's coronation in *MacFlecknoe*, where "loads of Sh— almost choakt the way" (103). Shaftesbury's grasping imagination in other words is a (perhaps more virulent) strain of the artistic pretension of the hack writer. So as ultimately to gain public office, he first must usurp the poetic. The initial line is most interesting in this regard, picturing as it does Shaftesbury's "Wit" agilely outdistancing the "heavy Pack" on the scent of advancement. With this line Dryden reaches even further back in memory to revive a trope from one of his earliest published performances, *Annus Mirabilis*, where he writes in the prefatory "Account" addressed to Robert Howard: "The composition of all Poems is or ought to be of wit, and wit in the Poet ... is no other than the faculty of imagination in a writer, which, like a nimble Spaniel, beats over and ranges through the field of Memory, till it springs the Quarry it hunted after."[37]

This simile itself recollects a passage from *Leviathan* in which Hobbes articulates the distinction between "Man and Beast," which he locates in the human capacity for reasoned speculation, or "the Discourse of the Mind, when it is governed by designe."[38] The mind's soliloquizing or self-address is "governed by designe" to the degree that it involves the patterning and repatterning of memory into a legible narrative. "Sometimes a man knows a place determinate, within the compasse whereof he is to seek; and then his thoughts run over all the parts thereof, as one would sweep a room, to find a jewell; or as a Spaniel ranges the field, to find a sent."[39] Hobbes devises the analogy between "a man" and "a Spaniel" precisely to drive home the difference between the search conducted by design and by instinct; the similarity consists in the mounting excitement of the searcher as the end of the chase draws near, but not in the manner of the pursuit. The analogy is imperfect and, by means of differentiating the terms, points up how the human trait is universal among human beings but only among human beings. Dryden takes this a step further when he revises the metaphor in the letter to Howard. Whereas Hobbes strives to define in an exact sense what makes a common human feature identifiably human, Dryden seeks to describe a talent that all humans may share in some measure but only a select number are able to nurture. The argument of increasing exclusivity from Hobbes to Dryden will climax in *The Medall* with the image of Shaftesbury's neurotic wit compelling him to run ahead of the pack until at last he is running in isolation. This is Dryden's way of saying that Shaftesbury and the Whigs who follow him never can be trusted to do anything of an uncalculating or altruistic nature; that is not the way their reasoning or skill moves them.

Dryden imagines no cure for the infection of the nation at the end of *The Medall* other than England's felt need to manage its energies and resources as efficiently as possible. That is to say that the economy of the society, in the largest sense, eventually will force the populace to return to its senses (or else cease to exist).

> Thus inborn Broyles the Factions wou'd ingage,
> Or Wars of Exil'd Heirs, or Foreign Rage,
> Till halting Vengeance overtook our Age:

> And our wild Labors, wearied into Rest,
> Reclin'd us on a rightfull Monarch's Breast.
>
> (318–322)

The "rightfull Monarch," naturally, is Augustus. The image of the exhausted English people seeking refuge on the breast of their true king from "Factions" and "Foreign Rage" slyly rehabilitates the terms applied to Cromwell by Edmund Waller in the "Panegyrick to my Lord Protector" (1655), where Waller declaimed that just as "the vex'd World" at one time in "Augustus' arms" had sought refuge, "So England now does with like toyle opprest, / Her weary Head upon your Bosome rest" (171–172). The irony of Dryden's appropriating the laurels that Waller laid on Cromwell's brow for stepping into the breach after the collapse of the "Nominated Assembly" or "Barebone's Parliament," and of his reworking the crown of praise to fit Charles II, is wickedly pointed. Indeed, the sarcasm is all the sharper because Dryden has been charging the Whigs throughout *The Medall* of attempting to extend the Dissenters' religious agenda.

At the same time, the ease with which Dryden redirects the encomium from Cromwell to Charles perhaps encodes a deeper and more problematic moral that the satirist would have admitted only with great reluctance, if at all. For the ruler that Dryden praises in these last lines is evidently an allegorical ideal rather than a historical reality. He is the product of a recurrent English dream of a cultivated and judicious monarch, as much the archetype of statecraft as the Horatian *mens divinior* is the epitome of poetic skill. Like all complicated principles, the aspiration behind the dream is easily travestied. Avowing a position that subsequently has become common opinion, George Lord wrote a number of years ago that Dryden's "ubiquitous Virgilian theme of the establishment of the peace of Augustus after the Roman Civil Wars" was well tailored for "a conservative age bent on imitating the classics."[40]

All cultural and social commitments, in other words, ultimately are determined by the individual's conception of history. To opposition writers such as Andrew Marvell, Lord ascribes a linear, eschatological view of time that derives mostly from the apocalyptic books of the Old and New Testament and supports a revolutionary politics. To Dryden and the loyalist cause, the critic ascribes a cyclical, retrospective view of time that derives mostly from the Augustan and Davidic myths of restoration and supports a regressive politics. "In contrast to the excitements of apocalyptic myth with the prospect of imminent divine intervention," he asserts, "the conservative myth as Dryden used it was deliberately quiescent and cool. Apocalypse riveted its vision on the immediate future and emphasized the need to act; the conservative myth saw the present in the past and emphasized passive acceptance."[41] According to Lord, Dryden's attachment to the status quo results in an "aversion to innovation" so great that it encourages "antiintellectualism" (161). In support of this thesis, the critic cites the poet's famous indictment of Shaftesbury in *Absalom and Achitophel*: "Great Wits are sure to Madness near ally'd; / And thin Partitions do their Bounds divide" (163–164).

Such a reading underestimates the artistic and political seriousness of Dryden's satire. "Passive acceptance" in particular strikes me as the wrong moral to extract from *Absalom and Achitophel*, since complacency is the very mood of thinking against which the poem aims to warn Charles and, implicitly, the reader. Dryden's "cool" demeanor, that is to say, represents not the smugness of social privilege but the self-discipline of critical intelligence reasoning in the teeth of an emergency. Moreover, "antiintellectualism" is not at all in keeping with the demands his works make on readers, nor does he recommend approaching with an attitude of mental laziness the final consequences of the Exclusion Crisis. In fact, a crucial theme sounded by the poem is the heroic difficulty of maintaining an autonomous sense of judgment at a moment when the tenor of civil colloquy is growing ever more partisan and shrill.

Hence Dryden praises John Sheffield, third earl of Mulgrave (or "sharp judging *Adriel*"), for remaining always "In Sanhedrins debate / True to his Prince; but not a Slave of State" (878–879). A hostile reader could argue, of course, that the poet delivers this compliment in bad faith, that he is paying mere lip service to Mulgrave's independence of perception. Yet in an atmosphere of deepening hysteria, it should be added, even a commonplace appeal to principle may have a sobering and corrective force.

> The Prophets Sons by such example led,
> To Learning and to Loyalty were bred:
> For *Colleges* on bounteous Kings depend,
> And never Rebell was to Arts a friend.
> (870–873)

Occurring late in the poem, these lines allude to the close association between the Stuart court and the Westminster School during the tenure of its erudite, Arminian headmaster, Richard Busby, from 1638 until 1695. (Dryden could write of the connection with authority, because he himself earned his secondary education at the London school and continued to correspond with his former teacher in later years.)[42] Although the poet acknowledges that the king's generous benefaction is a necessary prerequisite of this arrangement, Dryden's account of the relation between the royal donor and the institutions of learning he sponsors is by no means cynical.

Rather, the description implicitly argues that patronage of the contemporary culture redounds to the mutual honor of giver and recipient. Because the arts belong to no faction, their sustenance bespeaks some disinterested expansiveness of imagination on the part of the monarch, and such magnanimity merits in return a degree of recognition, if not by the public then at least by that sector that profits from his largesse. This belief is what lends force to Dryden's claim that Westminster students "to Learning and to Loyalty were bred." The priority that the line assigns the nouns makes clear it is the devotion to knowledge that ratifies political affiliation, rather than the other way around. (By way of contrast, consider the effect of reversing the formula: "To Loyalty and Learning they were bred.")

On the whole, this supposition may be understood to exert a subtle pressure on Charles to attend to his civic obligations, and it does so not only through the shrewd deployment of the adjective "bounteous." Dryden's application of the epithet "Prophets Sons" to the scholars of Westminster provides a case in point. At the most obvious level, the epithet associates the students with John Dolben, then dean of Westminster and bishop of Rochester, to whom the couplet immediately preceding refers in all but name: "Him of the Western dome, whose weighty sense / Flows in fit words and heavenly eloquence" (868–869). At a more removed level, however, the designation also hints at a genealogical link between the students and the king.

If we reflect that in Christian and postbiblical Judaic writings David himself was identified as a prophet by virtue of his imputed authorship of the Psalms, we might conclude that the appellation is meant to remind Charles who his true inheritors are. The label makes manifest who stands to lose if he permits the parliamentary opposition free reign and if, as a consequence, political tensions escalate to the point of civil war. "Prophets Sons" on this view allows itself to be read almost as a synonym for "King's Scholars," the select group of Westminster prize-winners sponsored by the throne and privileged with admission to Commons and the law courts to listen to speeches. At any rate, the formula contributes to the satire's disapproval of Charles's past indulgence of his natural son, the duke of Monmouth, and Monmouth's subsequent disobedience. The epithet clearly resonates with the biblical image of David as a ruler whose partiality for his son Absalom, even after the younger man dies in rebellion, threatens to alienate the kingdom until Joab reproaches the king: "Thou hast shamed this day the faces of all thy servants, which this day have saved thy life, and the lives of thy sons and daughters" (2 Samuel 19:5). In effect, Dryden's satire admonishes Charles to worry about the fate of the nation's future Solomons rather than its present Absalom.

To read a cautionary note into these lines of acclaim for the munificence of the Crown is to read the poem's ultimate idealization of David in accordance with its famously ambiguous opening, which offers the "vigorous warmth" of a monarch who "scatter'd his Maker's Image through the Land" as a case study in an at once charming and problematic unconstraint. "Warmth," it should be noted, is a term of approval that the prefatory epistle to the reader already has prepared us to regard in a halfway negative light. It is a word that belongs to the domain of the epistle's last paragraph, where Dryden in a sustained metaphor alleges the necessity of treating the "inveterate Disease" of religious and political faction with "harsh Remedies" in order to avoid the more desperate measure of "an *Ense rescidendum*": "To conclude all, If the Body Politique have any Analogy to the Natural, in my weak judgment, an Act of *Oblivion* were as necessary in a Hot, Distemper'd State, as an *Opiate* would be in a Raging Fever."[43] Playing out the "analogy" between the bodies "politique" and "natural," Dryden stops just short of reminding us in what instance the two aspects exactly coincide. That his proposition derives its vocabulary from the Elizabethan legal doctrine of the king's Two Bodies is hard to miss, however, and sharply indicates when the analogy is most pertinent:

> For the King has in him two Bodies, *viz.*, a Body natural, and a Body politic. His Body natural . . . is a Body mortal, subject to all Infirmities that come by Nature or Accident. . . . But his Body politic is a Body that cannot be seen or handled, consisting of Policy and Government, and constituted for the Direction of the People, and the Management of the public weal, and this Body is utterly void of Infancy, and old Age.[44]

The idea of the sovereign's metaphysical person "that cannot be seen or handled," as Ernst Kantorowicz once noted, is "related to theological thought, or, to be more specific, to the medieval concept of the king's *character angelicus*."[45]

Although he employs a language associated with the divine-right theory of monarchy, Dryden at the same time describes David unflatteringly as a ruler who makes "promiscuous use of Concubine and Bride" (6) and who is denounced in public by the very son to whom he is most "indulgent" (31) for having "grown in Bathsheba's Embraces old" (710). This last comment is a thinly veiled reference to Charles's unpopular French Catholic mistress, Louise de Kéroualle, whom he had made duchess of Portsmouth. Although James Winn has claimed that the "phrase hardly constitutes criticism," a reader might wonder who knows the disapproving biblical account of David's and Bathsheba's adulterous affair and its culmination in his murder of her husband, Uriah (1 Samuel 2:4 and 27).[46] At least in potential, Dryden's swipe at the duchess must have been a tricky joke to deliver before the king, and the touchiness of the business would explain why the charge is placed in the mouth of Absalom at a point in the narrative after he has fallen under Achitophel's corrupting sway. The jibe is part of a larger strategy to portray David as a ruler who, throughout most of the poem, runs the risk of allowing himself, and thus the nation of Israel, to be victimized by his natural, all-too-human impulses.

As a result, the heated sexual vitality by which he is identified at the outset comes to look like a strain of the humoristic disorder that jeopardizes the workings of popular reason in the world depicted by the satire and threatens to plunge Israel into irremediable divisiveness. Signs of this ailment, a sort of infectious, egoistic mania, are evident in numerous characters and recur throughout the narrative. The symptoms may be glimpsed in the "warm excesses" of Absalom that precipitate "*Amnon*'s murder" (37–39), in the avarice of Shimei whose "Brains were hot" (621), in the "Zealous Cry" of the "Hot *Levites*" or nonconforming clergy who were forced by the 1662 Act of Uniformity to resign their positions (519–521), and perhaps most revealingly in the capriciousness of Achitophel, whom Dryden in a famous triplet describes as "A fiery Soul, which working out its way, / Fretted the Pigmy Body to decay: / And o'r inform'd the Tenement of Clay" (156–158).

To depict the parliamentarian forces as pathologically reckless, it should be observed, Dryden falls back on a rhetoric of disparagement that was a standard instrument of royalist propaganda. The metaphor of the nation as a body wracked by the fever of sectarian fanaticism may have been taken from no less a source than Charles I, the presumed author of the apologetic *Eikon Basilike* (1649). Early in this treatise, the "tumults" of the Civil War are described as no "short fit or two of shaking, as an ague, but a quotidian fever, always increasing to higher inflammations, impatient of any mitigation, restraint, or remission."[47] Similarly, the king's declaration in the first paragraph that, when he called for the Long Parliament in November 1640, "I was not forgetful of those sparks which some men's distempers formerly studied to kindle in Parliaments" bears a strong resemblance to Dryden's portrayal of the maddening effect on Absalom of Achitophel's counsel.[48]

> What cannot Praise effect in Mighty Minds,
> When Flattery Sooths, and when Ambition Blinds!
> Desire of Power, on Earth a Vitious Weed,
> Yet, sprung from High, is of Caelestial Seed:
> In God 'tis Glory: And when men Aspire,
> 'Tis but a Spark too much of Heavenly Fire.
>   (303–308)

Whereas Charles I in *Eikon Basilike* represents himself as the ultimate restraining principle on popular unrest, Dryden suggests in *Absalom and Achitophel* that David, that is, Charles II, has contributed to the turmoil of his day in no insignificant measure.[49]

Behind the satirist's criticism of the throne (which, of course, is altogether more respectful and approving than his vilification of opposition figures such as Shaftesbury) stands a carefully balanced analysis of the king's role in recent history. On the one hand, in dealing with his enemies David has erred on the side of leniency; as he himself admits, "Thus long have I, by native mercy sway'd, / My wrongs dissembl'd, my revenge delay'd" (939–940). To underscore this point, readers have noticed, Dryden makes particularly ironic use of the trope of king-as-father. According to Phillip Harth, the "poem has begun with the English David's complaisance toward Absalom . . . because it epitomizes Charles's behavior toward those he governs. His indulgence of his coddled son is an exact reflection of the father-king's forbearance toward . . . his subjects."[50] With regard to this "forbearance," Dryden probably had in mind the concessions Charles had to make, especially on matters pertaining to foreign policy and the Popish Plot, before the dissolution of the Oxford Parliament in early 1681.

On the other hand, David's own lapses of self-restraint as ruler have played to the advantage of his adversaries and readied the public to look with greater indifference on the conspirators' agitations. Indeed, the poem firmly hints that, if we are to condemn the narcissism of Absalom to which Achitophel appeals when he urges the younger man to seize the crown, we ought to acknowledge that Absalom's displays of vain self-regard take their cue from David's example: "With secret Joy, indulgent *David* view'd / His Youthfull Image in his Son renew'd: / To all his wishes Nothing he deny'd" (31–33). Absalom's misguidedness of ambition thus reflects back ominously (albeit indirectly) on his father, especially given the poem's supposition that "inspir'd by some diviner Lust, / His Father got him with a greater Gust" (19–20). David appears in this light very much the author of his own woes as king.

Consequently, Dryden's *sotto voce* reproach to Charles with respect to his personal affairs, his attachments to figures such as Monmouth or the duchess of Portsmouth, implies more broadly a reminder to the monarch to be pragmatic in his choice of associates and thus in his management of the popular will. The critical view that the satire takes of David's lenity toward Absalom, in other words, has distinct applications to the wider historical and political picture. It is interesting to remark on this score that *Absalom and Achitophel* takes pains to demonstrate a correspondence between the prelapsarian libidinal freedom enjoyed by David in an epoch before taboo law, "when Nature prompted" (5), and the social anarchy that Dryden fears will ensue if Shaftesbury and his followers are permitted to meddle in the succession and to encroach on the royal prerogatives with impunity.

> Nor only Crowds, but Sanhedrins may be
> Infected with this publick Lunacy:
> And Share the madness of Rebellious times,
> To Murther Monarchs for Imagin'd crimes.
> If they may Give and Take when e'r they please,
> Not Kings alone, (the Godheads Images,)

> But Government it self at length must fall
> To Natures state; where all have Right to all.
>
> (787–794)

At its foundation, the dispute over Exclusion crystallizes around a test of wills between Parliament and the court that promises to unhinge the ideal of mixed government. In this event, all legal curbs on the aggressive self-interest of the mob will dissolve. Of course, Dryden's idealization here of "Kings" as the "Godheads Images" reveals on which side of the conflict his allegiances lie. But the poem's linkage of "Natures" competitive amorality, "where all have Right to all," with the false sexual Eden of polygamy, "e'r one to one was, cursedly, confind" (4), belies, if only by inference, any attempt to present David within the allegory as a morally idealized or blameless archetype.

Although it seems true to say, therefore, as Anne K. Krook does, that Dryden endeavors in *Absalom and Achitophel* "to construct a world in which David remains both satirized and finally powerful," I think it is quite wrong to conclude as a result that Dryden allows David "to remain uninterpretable."[51] To the contrary, as the satire advances it may be said to render an increasingly well-nuanced interpretation of the sovereign's character. The overall assessment is, in the end, positive but measured; it is offered with all the qualifications of a candor that enhances rather than abates the force of the judgment. Indeed, David begins his climactic speech in the poem by chastising himself for having been an ineffectual leader prior to the current exigency. He was, as he puts it, "So willing to forgive th'Offending Age, / So much the Father did the King asswage" (941–942).

Further along in the speech, however, his imperious judgment against himself will turn against his rebellious subjects and wayward son, deepening in anger as David contemplates the enormity of the upheaval that Absalom is fomenting.

> Kings are the publick Pillars of the State,
> Born to sustain and prop the Nations weight:
> If my young *Samson* will pretend a Call
> To shake the Column, let him share the Fall.
>
> (953–956)

The sarcastic transformation of Absalom into a pseudo-Samson is a particularly cunning bit of poetic reinterpretation in its own right, not only of the biblical paradigm in Judges but of the satire's own earlier, comic depiction of Absalom's patron.

> *Achitophel*, grown weary to possess
> A lawfull Fame, and lazy Happiness;

>   Disdain'd the Golden fruit to gather free,
>   And lent the Croud his Arm to shake the Tree.
>   (200–203)

In spite of the evident resonance, the overall effect of the two passages is quite different. The last line of Dryden's sketch of Achitophel, with its terse stringing-together of monosyllables (not quite as arch as Pope's "ten low words"), wittily conveys an impression of blunt frustration, especially coming on the heels of the stately, alliterative parallelism of "A lawfull Fame, and lazy Happiness." When the grandee consorts with the "Croud" for the sheer pleasure of making trouble, he establishes the bottom line, so to speak, of his own moral imagination. While here the tone is playful, the note struck by David as he envisions the labors of his "young Samson" sounds in contrast altogether sterner. The king's description of Absalom's revolt places a heavy stress on the theme of crime and punishment, a stress made manifest by the strong dialectical and syntactic closure of the "if . . . then" couplet with David's verdict "Let him share the Fall." The rhyming of "Call," which has its meaning here of a duty or right (*Oxford English Dictionary [OED]*, sense 8), with the grave finality of "Fall" neatly dramatizes the corrective logic of the king's judgment. It is as if the phonological likeness of the words frames for us all the more clearly their semantic antagonism. Holding the terminal position in the rhyme scheme, the threat of punishment has, in every sense, the hermeneutic upper hand here.

Throughout his last speech, David reasserts his power as the ultimate arbitrator of legal conflicts within the state and, by virtue of his revelatory exegesis of the plotters and the quandary they present the nation, redeems the satire's appraisal of his own mettle. "True, they Petition me t'approve their Choice," declares the king with regard to the opposition's outcry in favor of Exclusion, "But *Esau*'s Hands suite ill with *Jacob*'s Voice" (981–982). The allusion to the story in Genesis of Jacob's usurpation of the rights of his firstborn brother by masquerading as Esau in their father's presence signals Charles's perceptive dismissal of the phony good wishes mouthed by his adversaries regarding his "Safety" (983). Some three months before his arrest on charges of treason, Shaftesbury in a face-to-face meeting directly submitted to the king a plan to settle the crown on Monmouth (an idea Charles had rejected on its previous circulation), capping his presentation with an assurance to the monarch of "how earnest the whole Nation was for His Preservation."[52] David's parabolic alignment of the opposition's pretended solicitousness for his well-being with Jacob's dissimulation before Isaac evinces the king's refusal to be hoodwinked by the Whigs' pietistic avowals of concern or to be cowed by the threat they imply. And it is due to the incisiveness of his reading of recent events that *Absalom and Achitophel* finally can declare "Once more the Godlike David was Restor'd" (1030).

The epithet "Godlike," conferred on David at the poem's start ("for several Mothers bore / To Godlike *David*, several Sons before," 13–14), returns here with peculiar and unexpected sharpness. For the godlike justness of David's opinion at the end represents no less than a negation of the embarrassment created by his "Godlike" sexual capacity highlighted earlier. At the same time, the restoration of David to his proper status as sole judge in the court of final appeal is clinched by another allusion that sublimes the whole analogical structure of the satire into an elaboration of an original, Roman paradigm of reparation: "Henceforth a Series of new time began, / The mighty Years in long Procession ran" (1028–1029). The last line unmistakably recalls the fervent exclamation with which Virgil's Parcae greet the reign of Augustus in the *Eclogues*: "Such ages run on" ("talia saecla . . . currite," 4.46). It is of no small interest that at the moment at which David reaffirms his ability and resolve to live up to his divine destiny, he becomes another Augustus.

Of course, the view that the poem takes of this event is entirely approving and celebratory. Yet the sudden imposition of the Augustan framework on a narrative that, to this point, has made the Old Testament its chief source of historical metaphor is somewhat disconcerting. The allusion seems to encode a subtle reminder of the independence of the poet's perspective from the ruler's. By assigning the rhetorical roles of Virgil to Dryden and Augustus to Charles, the poem presents itself as the site of a dialogue between the forces of history, synonymous with the *princeps*, and of culture, synonymous with the poet-scribe, in which the last word inevitably falls to poetry. Thus at the end of *Absalom and Achitophel* the Davidic myth of the king-as-poet is displaced, or at least complicated, by the Augustan myth of Caesar-as-patron. We need not share, consequently, Howard Weinbrot's strong sympathy for the damning, Tacitean tradition of depicting Augustus to see that the language of neoclassicism enabled Dryden to craft a supple and often disarming critique of the center of power of his day.[53] Each of his three satires taught readers, and continues to teach readers, what sort of liberties great poetry is capable of taking.

2

Arm'd for Virtue

Pope as Cultural Liberal

To broach the topic of Pope's political commitments is to venture onto slippery ground. Much of the difficulty of defining his allegiances by means of the standard party labels stems from the poet's air of skeptical ambivalence toward ideology per se, as his famous self-description from his imitation of Horace's Satire 2.1 makes clear: "In Moderation placing all my Glory, / While Tories call me Whig, and Whigs a Tory" (*The First Satire of the Second Book of Horace Imitated*, 67–68). Dustin Griffin recently has noted that it has become something of a critical convention to describe Pope broadly as a "Tory satirist," or else as a Stuart supporter and anti-Hanoverian, or yet otherwise as a member of the Patriot cause supporting Frederick, prince of Wales, against the Whig oligarchy headed by Robert Walpole.[1] Griffin quickly adds, however, that "it might be more accurate to regard Pope as a writer who, throughout his career, aspired to serve the state as 'My Country's Poet,' but who—even from the beginning—looked with some ambivalence at the prospect of joining the patriot with the poet."[2] With an eye to the example of *Windsor-Forest*, he concludes that "even at a time when Pope delights in the state of the British nation, there is something that holds him back from embracing the role of national poet, something that makes him fear that a poet must ultimately choose between serving the muse and serving the state."[3] His examination of the poet's equivocal, and in some cases harshly critical, treatment of Patriot mythology shows how quickly the clichés of demagoguery unravel under the pressure of Pope's attention to historical ironies. Yet such a lesson also tantalizes readers with intimations of the care the poet devoted to political thought and language.

In an earlier essay that anticipates some of the revisionist implications of Griffin's argument, J. A. Downie deplored the habit of explaining all of Pope's views in terms of his so-called emotional Jacobitism, or identification with the Jacobite camp.[4] Although he perhaps underestimates the force of certain royalist sentiments in Pope's poems, Downie surely is right to remind us that the poet described himself as a Whig on several occasions in his correspondence and to insist on the crucial importance of the key word "liberty" to the poetry, a term the critic notes "was more likely to have appealed to Whigs with revolution principles than to Jacobites."[5] In spite of such observations, however, he argues that the poet elaborated a nonpartisan appeal to authority and tradition, advancing particularly in *Windsor-Forest*, the *Epistle to Burlington*, and the *Epistle to Augustus* an ideology that "is conservative, sure enough, but not specifically Tory" and thus resorting to "a rhetoric not so much of Jacobitism but of order, hierarchy, and stability."[6] Not only does such a characterization overlook the very evidence that Downie himself marshals against a Jacobite reading of Pope's writings but it falsely suggests a sense of historical optimism on the poet's part. Moreover, the interpretation trivializes Pope's problematic character in his role of satirist. When he declares that "when I aim at praise they say I bite" (*To Augustus*, 409) or depicts his culture as "a Land of Hectors, / Thieves, Supercargoes, Sharpers, and Directors" (*Satire* 2.1.71–72) or proclaims the triumph of the "great Anarch" at the end of the *Dunciad*, he does not sound like a poet of "stability."

The most incisive recent account of Pope's attitude of doubt toward claims of cultural authority is James Noggle's exploration of what he dubs the "skeptical sublime" in the work of the so-called Tory satirists. This reading of British Augustan literary rhetoric, it should be noted, splendidly elucidates the sense of radical philosophical uncertainty that informs Pope's critique of eighteenth-century culture. Yet Noggle's alignment of such a critique with the stereotypical view of the poet as an admirer of established political institutions and traditional social hierarchy seems oddly self-contrary, particularly in the scholar's insistence on the catchall adjective "conservative" to define Pope's ethical and political disposition. I have glanced at Noggle's argument already in the introduction but wish to review briefly his thinking here. I believe the discrepancy between his accounts of Pope's intellectual positions and political beliefs clarifies the difficulty of positioning the poet within the customary ideological spectrum.

Noggle grounds his observations on the work of the last two decades by intellectual historians such as Douglas Lane Patey, Barbara J. Shapiro, Richard Kroll, and Steven Shapin, which "establish[es] beyond doubt the remarkable dominance of the probable order" in Restoratian and Augustan theories of knowledge.[7] With a glance at Patey, however, Noggle keenly remarks that "by emphasizing the stability of procedures of inference and the 'hierarchy of probable signs' . . . in the period's institutions, intellectual historians tend to neglect the ironies evolving from probabilism's roots in more radical skepticism."[8] In order to correct this tendency, he wishes to redirect our attention to these roots and thereby to demonstrate "not that . . . probabilism [is] unworkable or our picture of its dominance in the period wrong but that a constitutional instability is crucial to the period's epistemological functioning."[9] Noggle moreover intends to highlight the radicalism of Dryden, Swift, and Pope within this picture. He thus distinguishes between a "mitigated skepticism" that, by affirming a providential view of history, supplies a theoretical "justification of what has been called the ideology of eighteenth-century liberalism" and the poets' more problematic sense of alienation from epistemological foundations.[10] At the very least, the alienation of the Augustan satirists differs from mitigated skepticism in emphasizing the unknowability of experience "only to guard against the appropriation of transcendent authority by any putatively knowing subject or group."[11] At its most extreme, this satiric doubt leads to a paradoxical assertion of "a power to remain ironic . . . in the very insistence that the ironic distance between . . . [the satirist] and the satirized butt has collapsed."[12] The paradigm of such insistence is Pope's "incorporation" of himself into the bathetic domain of Dulness in the *Dunciad*.

To my mind, Noggle's exposition of Augustan satiric irony is persuasive but for one detail. His acceptance of the standard profile of the Tory satirist compels him to argue that the Augustans' attitude toward received structures of thought "must be seen as a staple of political conservatism even if it does not always translate into a doctrine of the political subject's subservience to royal, church, or state authority."[13] He seems to think the questioning of such institutions or of social hierarchy in general must be understood to reinforce a conservative point of view whenever such questioning complicates the progressivist history generally held to be the centerpiece of the Whig liberal tradition. Such a definition of conservatism is so conditional and restrictive as to beg the question. In order to retain the political terminology that is habitually applied to the discussion of Pope's writings, Noggle is forced to make statements such as "[*An Essay on Man*'s] insistence on our limited perspective also tends to expose . . . the emptiness of our invocations of providence. Pope's refusal to resolve this contradiction with an account of sublime experience expresses a conservative skepticism but one that emerges only through his best efforts to be liberal."[14] Here Noggle stretches the conventions of political description to the breaking point.

If not a "conservative," what are we to call Pope? A clue, I think, may be had from Pat Rogers's portrayal of the poet as a "parvenu and an outsider" whose satires represent the imaginary revenges of a victim of anti-Catholic persecution on the privileged and hostile Anglican establishment of his day.[15] Rogers reminds us of the legal restrictions against the education, property ownership, holding of public office, and even medical treatment of Catholics during the poet's lifetime. He concludes: "The style of a civilization which made . . . [Pope] a 'convict' and a pariah is turned with exquisite artistry into a satiric vehicle: its language of polite acceptance is converted into an idiom of oblique criticism and ironic qualification."[16] To this bold assertion a reader might respond that Rogers is relying too heavily on Pope's life for the meaning of his poetry. In an analysis of the poet's representations of slavery in his Homeric translations and in *Windsor-Forest*, however, Howard Erskine-Hill has corroborated the general outlines of Rogers's thesis. Scrutinizing in particular the conclusion of this last poem, which anticipates the abolition of the slave trade and the moment when "the freed Indians in their native Groves / Reap their own Fruits, and woo their Sable Loves" (409–410), against the background of contemporaneous celebrations of the European colonization of the New World, Erskine-Hill restores a carefully historicized sense of Pope's resistance to the current of social opinion and political practice in his day. Erskine-Hill's essay brings to consciousness the delicate imaginative solidarity between various degrees and forms of servitude that Pope's denunciation of slavery advocates: "Pope's repudiation of 'slavery' is the affirmation of one whose community and values had been drastically marginalised by the events of 1699, and again by those of 1714. Like Dryden in the 1690s, Pope probably hoped for a restoration, but as the years rolled by and the House of Brunswick hung on, it became a point of honour to say: 'So proud I am no Slave.'"[17]

Without denying the complexity of Pope's political views or minimizing his failings, I hope to build on Rogers and Erskine-Hill's foundations in order to show that the poet's satire of paper-credit society entails a critique of modernity that ultimately serves the ideal of political freedom. When he assumes the role of advocate for disenfranchised interests and calls for the inauguration of a new social order determined neither by birth nor wealth but by something like artistic or poetic judgment, Pope takes up an outlook that anticipates the position of later writers whom we usually characterize as liberals and even as radicals. The reasons for his posture of mixed iconoclasm and historicism are rooted in his political circumstances. At the same time that Pope held membership in a prestigious cultural elite, he felt himself to belong to a persecuted social minority. His ways of thinking and writing came to reflect this precariously exemplary standing, hence his perpetual recourse to the poetic resources of "wit" or irony. The central strategy of his poems is the deliberate subversion of linguistic convention in order to achieve effects of surprise, effects that encourage a feeling of skeptical disbelief toward the truisms of the prevailing consensus.

Of course, it might be argued that such a tactic does not in itself bespeak a specific ideological perspective. I will begin this chapter by examining how Pope's explication of strictly aesthetic rules in *An Essay on Criticism* turns at key moments to explicitly political metaphors in order to uphold an open-minded idea of culture. The basic tension in his poetry between shared standards of reason and radical individuality moreover enables him in works such as the *Epistle to Augustus* and the *Dunciad* to retool the devices of civil rhetoric for the purposes of controversy, criticism, and opposition. Griffin's emphasis on the poet's ambivalent patriotism, which I remarked on earlier, is pertinent here. Above all, it is in his cunning reinterpretation of Horatian *libertas* in the *Imitations of Horace* that Pope deploys wit in support of what must be regarded as a liberal politics in a precise sense. For by affirming a Horatian faith in the mind's independence from the tyranny of social privilege, he calls into question the institutions of early eighteenth-century England's incumbent political powers, including, crucially, the commercial marketplace. I label his position a politics of cultural liberalism in order to distinguish it from the classical liberalism that comes into being at roughly the same moment and has been identified with the very Whig bureaucracy he attacks in his satires.

In a broad sense, then, the poet's mode of irony gives latent ethical force to Dr. Johnson's observation in the *Lives* that Pope's writing balances "the two most engaging powers of an author: new things are made familiar, and familiar things are made new."[18] "Engaging," I think, is the right word in all its nuances, for the pleasures of reading Pope never feel like disinterested pleasures (and that is part of their appeal). The playful manipulation of the fictive resources of language in his writings works, in other words, to enlist the reader in a shared hermeneutic task. We may ponder what curious twist of history made John Locke the foremost censor of such language-games, which he belittled as "perfect cheat" in the pursuit of "Things as they are," in the period a generation or so before Pope:

> Since Wit and Fancy finds easier entertainment in the World, than dry Truth and real Knowledge, figurative Speeches, and allusion in Language, will hardly be admitted, as an imperfection or abuse of it. . . . But yet, if we would speak of Things as they are, we must allow, that all the Art of Rhetorick, besides Order and Clearness, all the artificial and figurative application of Words Eloquence hath invented, are for nothing else but to insinuate wrong Ideas, move the Passions, and thereby mislead the Judgment; and so indeed are perfect cheat. . . . Eloquence, like the fair Sex, has too prevailing Beauties in it, to suffer it self ever to be spoken against.[19]

Poems "cheat" in the sense that they pretend to the offices of criticism while circumventing criticism's official rules and protocols. This is to say that the fundamental procedure of poetic writing is parodic—it aims to "abuse" confirmed truths into new and startling figures that do not present to consciousness the real knowledge of what is but rather represent to the imagination the possibility of what might be. Such figures are "wrong Ideas" insofar as they appeal to the emotions rather than to reason. Locke's peevish imputation in the final sentence that the feminine beauties of eloquence corrupt the objective, dispassionate, and implicitly masculine standards of judgment in civil society demonstrates a rationalist suspicion of the nonutilitarian that, as

Linda Zionkowski observes, hostile readers directed against Pope persistently during his career: "The open questioning of Pope's masculinity occurred frequently throughout his life. . . . Barred by his religion and political sympathies from positions of influence in the church and state, Pope had a difficult time placing himself within the traditional boundaries of elite masculine activity."[20] Although Zionkowski shows that in many instances the poet reacted to such questioning by defending the masculinity of the bourgeois literary professional, I will argue that he also responded by mounting a sustained satiric attack on an increasingly commercial culture that sought to reformulate "the traditional boundaries of elite masculine activity" in such a way as to promote the ideal of *homo economicus*.

What animates poetry for Pope, in other words, is a playfulness or impertinence that eludes codification and therefore stands outside the established order of social institutions.

> Some Beauties yet, no Precepts can declare,
> For there's a *Happiness* as well as *Care*.
> *Musick* resembles *Poetry*, in each
> Are *nameless Graces* which no Methods teach.
> (141–144)

These lines from *An Essay on Criticism* have been thought to rehearse the doctrine of the *je ne sais quoi*, the notion that all true art incorporates an element of the unexplainable.[21] A savvy reader might take the lines to assert that the procedures involved in an artistic performance, such as the composition of a poem, mimic the procedures of what we call "knowing" or "understanding" without working to provide a scientific depiction of the world and so without inviting the customary doubts about the verifiability of knowledge.

Music and poetry bring into existence "graces" that cannot be understood by an appeal to "methods" in the same sense that for Kant objects that fall within our experience either of the beautiful or the sublime stand in "an indeterminate reference to concepts" or universal rules, as he attests in his third critique (sec. 23).[22] Because aesthetic opinions are based on purely subjective feelings of pleasure or displeasure, they cannot be considered "determinant" judgments that proceed from universal to empirical principles but rather are "reflective" judgments that proceed from empirical to universal. Given that such responses ultimately are determined by subjective criteria, they achieve what the philosopher calls "objective universal validity" only by analogy; it is "by taking the singular representation of the Object of the judgment of taste, and by comparison converting it into a concept according to the conditions determining the judgment, [that] we can arrive at a logically universal judgment" (sec. 8).[23] Kant's discussion of the critical pronouncements of taste and the type of authority such assessments exert addresses epistemological questions that have their roots in the theory of probability. In his learned study of Augustan probabilism, Douglas Lane Patey has argued persuasively that Pope conceives of artistic "rules as descriptive generalizations arrived at by probable inference."[24] The poet accepts, then, a certain necessary indeterminacy to aesthetic rulings (and in this light, we might add, anticipates the Kantian break from the realm of objective universality). A reader cannot arrive at the rules through a priori reasoning, because nameless graces "bypass the judgment of writers in the sense of not being the product of any yet formulated rule," although Patey will add that this is only in a "limited and temporary sense."[25]

Kant's highly complicated notion of taste links the domains of the beautiful and the sublime in the subject's indifference to the object's ontological presence. His idea of the beautiful emphasizes a subjective disinterest that arises from the harmony of understanding and imagination, whereas his notion of the sublime stresses the subjective freedom that arises from the dissonance between the two. If we take Pope's lines to rehearse the *je ne sais quoi* as the doctrine customarily is understood (as descriptive of lower order harmonies), then the lines describe the beautiful rather than the sublime. But Nicolas Boileau, with whose writings Pope was well acquainted, uses the phrase in chapter 7 of his *Traité du Sublime* to describe sublimity of thoughts or ideas, when he declares "le silence d'Ajax aux Enfers dans l'Odyssée . . . a je ne sçai quoy de plus grand que tout ce qu'il auroit pû dire."[26] And indeed for Pope, too, minor "graces" can swing toward grander uncertainties. It is worth noting how he gets from the one to the other:

> Thus *Pegasus*, a nearer way to take,
> May boldly deviate from the common Track.
> Great Wits sometimes may *gloriously offend*,
> And *rise* to *Faults* true Criticks *dare not mend*;
> From *vulgar Bounds* with *brave Disorder* part,
> And *snatch* a *Grace* beyond the Reach of Art,
> Which, without passing thro' the *Judgment*, gains
> The *Heart*, and all its End *at once* attains.
> In *Prospects*, thus, some *Objects* please our Eyes,
> Which *out of* Nature's *common Order* rise,
> The shapeless *Rock*, or hanging *Precipice*.
>   (150–160)

Scholars have long observed the indebtedness of this passage to René Rapin's *Reflexions sur la Poétique de ce Temps* (1674), where what is being described are clearly small-scale merits (though Rapin does not refer to the *je ne sais quoi* overtly): "Il n'y a point de préceptes pour enseigner ces grâces secrètes, ces charmes imperceptibles de la poésie: et tous ces agrémens cachez qui vont au coeur."[27] Notice, however, what happens to Pope's "Grace beyond the Reach of Art." The supercrowding of the verse with the grammatical pattern adjective-noun or adverb-verb (a strategy that commences at line 151 with "boldly deviate") calls to our attention the increasingly paradoxical relation, from a lexical standpoint, between the qualifiers and principal parts of speech thrown together as the lines advance. When the adverb "gloriously" deflects the verb "offend" from its ordinary meaning in line 152, for instance, the effect adds to a general sense that the customary terms of praise and blame are subtly being reversed, an impression that coalesces most vividly at line 154 with the juxtaposition of "vulgar Bounds with brave Disorder." By the time we reach the last line, we are meant to feel that "the shapeless Rock, or hanging Precipice" exemplifies the sublime inasmuch as each disorientingly represents a freak of nature, that Pope's use of "shapeless" and "hanging" to express admiration forestalls the linguistic "common Order" from settling into an expected regularity.

We might say that Pope's *Essay* composes an intricate argument about the relation between wit and rules that affirms nature's rationality while denying our ability to grasp its rationale with certitude and thereby propounds an early notion of the sublime. When he adopts such a position, Pope may be said to anticipate Kant by siding with Boileau against Rapin. Yet though such a reading is in one sense true, it is clearly not the whole, or even the basic, truth. To say that in *An Essay on Criticism* Pope sends up or travesties the demeanor of scholarly argumentation would be nearer the point. His virtuosic yoking together of mismatched orders of meaning repeatedly points up the divide between convention and aberration by violating it. Whereas the canonical association of the *je ne sais quoi* brought to mind by "nameless Graces" operates within the precincts of convention, the impromptu sensation of the sublime conjured by "The shapeless Rock, or hanging Precipice" operates beyond them.

The *Essay*'s effort simultaneously to define and to perform the mode of great wit that "may gloriously offend" ultimately precludes a Kantian reading of the poem in terms of the disinterested apprehension of form. For the ideal of independent reason that the poem espouses and that undergirds its treatment of the sublime ultimately sponsors an attitude of irreverence toward all doctrinaire or ideological certainties and thus prepares the way for a larger argument on behalf of political freedom. Patey remarks that Pope's depiction of the innate genius who achieves beauty without method hinges on an idea of the relation between human beings and nature as central to Augustan England's moral and political thought as to its poetics: "Such 'graces' are as yet 'nameless' precisely because they have not yet been formulated into precept (reduced to rule); we find their effects in the works of 'genius,' those artists who (like saints in theology) have the deepest and surest implicit grasp of natural law, and hence of the sometimes extraordinary means necessary to achieve their ends."[28] The capacity for probabilistic supposition that enables human beings to intuit the laws of nature thus is equally capable of judgment in the ethical pursuit of the good life as in the making of art or the advancement of knowledge: "Because the rules of art are formally the same as the laws of nature, Pope can extend his analogy of a well-lived life not only to a well-constructed work of art, but to good criticism."[29]

In the lines immediately following, Pope proposes that such a talent for probable inference carries with it immediate political responsibilities:

> But tho' the *Ancients* thus their *Rules* invade,
> (As *Kings* dispense with *Laws* Themselves have made)
> *Moderns*, beware! Or if you must offend
> Against the *Precept*, ne'er transgress its *End*,
> Let it be *seldom*, and *compell'd by Need*,
> And have, at least, *Their Precedent* to plead.
> The Critick else proceeds without Remorse,
> Seizes your Fame, and puts his Laws in force.
> (161–168)

Laura Brown has observed that these lines advance the *Essay*'s argument regarding the rule of natural law but maintains that the mere introduction of the political metaphor "seems to suggest instead the prerogative of the monarch in an absolutist state, where the notion of royal license signifies the unrestricted powers of the king."[30] Although Brown is correct that the passage evokes the language of arbitrary rule, she seems to think that the very presence of such terms indicates the poet's uncritical support of the monarchy. Yet his warning to errant "Moderns" not to indulge an overly casual attitude with respect to the law clearly equates such an attitude, in a negative light, with the dangers of tyranny. If it is true that expressions of approval for the ideal of an enlightened (not absolute) ruler may be found in Pope's poetry, these lines, however, articulate no such sentiment, and at any rate careful attention must be paid to the peculiar manner in which he interprets and qualifies the ideal.

His caveat against the willfulness of historical ignorance prepares the reader for the extended satire on "*Pride, the never-failing Vice of Fools*" (204) that constitutes the heart of *An Essay on Criticism* (201–473). Pride, according to his description, deceives the intellect by encouraging an unself-questioning trust of superficial details at the expense of a thorough and sobering knowledge of the facts in all their complexity. Dogmatic "Moderns" thus flout the laws of creation in a dangerous way, because an egotistical love of their own achievements drives them like petty dictators to choices predicated on the denial and distortion of history. In their shortsightedness, they exemplify the imaginative inadequacy that Pope generally ascribes to readers who are academic in a pejorative sense or unworldly:

> Thus *Criticks*, of less *Judgment* than *Caprice*,
> *Curious*, not *Knowing*, not *exact*, but *nice*,
> Form *short Ideas*; and offend in *Arts*
> (As most in *Manners*) by a *Love to Parts*.
> (285–288)

Bad critics fasten on isolated aspects of a text to the neglect of the whole and thereby falsify the truth; as Patey succinctly puts it, "in the *Essay on Criticism*, pride is said to cause fragmenting readings of literary works, readings that attend solely to parts."[31] The fragmentation of meaning due to a reader's prejudice, or, to use the Popean term, "caprice," culminates in factionalism within the public sphere, which is to say in overtly political conflict: "Parties in *Wit* attend on those of *State*, / And publick Faction doubles private Hate" (456–457).

Indeed, it is precisely this intuition that the cultural domain of literature has become the fundamental battleground of politics that for Jürgen Habermas marks the emergence of the modern phenomenon of the public sphere in what he calls "the model case of British development."[32] In his eyes, the formation of a bourgeois liberal public in England commences with the establishment of the opposition newspaper the *Craftsman* under Bolingbroke and continues with the appeal to independent reason in the name of political dissent by the coterie that included Bolingbroke, Pope, John Gay, Jonathan Swift, and John Arbuthnot:

> From 1727 on, under the impact of the *Craftsman*, a systematic opposition arose which (for a while even equipped with something like a shadow cabinet) until 1742, via literature and the press, informed the public at large about the political controversies in Parliament....
> Until then political opposition at the national level had been possible only as the attempt to push one's interests by resorting to violence in the forms of the Fronde and the Civil War; now, through the critical debate of the public, it took the form of a permanent controversy between the governing party and the opposition.[33]

The very articulation of an opposition critique at the level of what Pope calls "publick Faction" thus signifies for Habermas the dawning of a modern conception of consensus achieved through rational debate as a precondition of political legitimacy, hence as a political brake or check on entrenched social authority. While he warns that such a limitation of power is not the same as the rule of popular opinion, he nonetheless declares that "the ongoing commentary on and criticism of the Crown's actions and Parliament's decisions transformed a public authority now being called before the forum of the public."[34] On its inception in the early eighteenth century, then, the public sphere reflected the emerging importance of the bourgeois merchant classes before their reorganization under the pressures of mass production and consumption. It thus supplied a new horizon for the criticism of material and class privilege.

Although the publication of *An Essay on Criticism* in 1711 precedes by several years the establishment of the Whig oligarchy, the formation of the opposition, and the creation of the *Craftsman*, the poet's invocation of critical judgment against the mystifying influence of pride affirms Habermas's general intuition of the pivotal role of literary culture in the liberalization and democratization of Western society. For in his denunciation of pride, Pope saves his greatest contempt for the pride of association that upholds the ideology of class:

> Some ne'er advance a Judgment of their own,
> But *catch* the *spreading Notion* of the Town. . . .
>
> Of all this *Servile Herd* the worst is He
> That in *proud Dulness* joins with *Quality*,
> A constant Critick at the Great-man's Board,
> To *fetch and carry* Nonsense for my Lord.
> What *wofull stuff* this Madrigal would be,
> In some starv'd Hackny Sonneteer, or me?
> But let a *Lord* once own the *happy Lines*,
> How the *Wit brightens*! How the *Style refines*!
> Before *his* sacred Name flies ev'ry Fault,
> And each *exalted* Stanza *teems* with *Thought*!
> (408–409, 414–423)

The sarcastic paraphrase of the sycophant's dismissiveness toward "some starv'd Hackny Sonneteer, or me" emphasizes the purchasable character of the "constant Critick at the Great-man's Board" and aligns the poet with the cultural underclass in a pointed manner that differs markedly from the attitude of later writings composed after the initial success of his translation of the *Iliad*. Nevertheless, such later claims to independence as the celebrated boast "Scribblers or Peers, alike are *Mob* to me" (140), from his imitation of Horace's Satire 2.1 (1733), share with these lines from *An Essay on Criticism* a pronounced suspicion of both lordly patronage and plebeian deferentiality. Pope's condemnation of the "Servile Herd" consorts with the poem's basic ideology of political and intellectual self-determination, an ideology that crucially and idiosyncratically affirms the ideal of liberty.

At its climax, the *Essay* propounds a curious image of this ideal as it rehearses the story of the spread of neoclassical learning from Italy during the Renaissance:

> But soon by Impious Arms from *Latium* chas'd,
> Their *ancient Bounds* the banish'd Muses past;
> Thence Arts o'er all the *Northern World* advance;
> But *Critick Learning* flourish'd most in *France*.
> The *Rules*, a Nation born to serve, obeys,
> And *Boileau* still in Right of *Horace* sways.
> But *we*, brave *Britons, Foreign Laws* despis'd,
> And kept *unconquer'd*, and *unciviliz'd*,
> Fierce for the *Liberties of Wit, and* bold,
> We still defy'd the *Romans*, as of *old*.
> (709–718)

The "Liberties of Wit" that Pope ascribes to the "brave Britons" of the past suggest an ambiguous variation of the mythical state of nature of the political philosophers, neither as brutal as the Hobbesian paradigm nor as idyllic as the Lockean notion of a cooperative law of nature that ensures that "our moral obligations are not in conflict with each other."[35] Clearly, such liberties as Pope has in mind belong to a condition of precivilized instinct rather than of learned reason. British writers in this sense exactly resemble the early Greek tragedians in the times before Aristotle's composition of the *Poetics*, dramatic artists whom the poet describes as "Poets, a *Race* long unconfin'd and free, / Still fond and proud of *Savage Liberty*" (649–650). By the same token, Britain's "unconquer'd" culture exemplifies a vigorous freedom of wit or imagination that has saved it from decadence, particularly in comparison to the "*Critick Learning*" of France, "a Nation born to serve."

In his illuminating study of the friendship between Pope and Bolingbroke, Brean Hammond has explained how a tension between negative and positive conceptions of the state of nature informs the poet's handling of the topic in *An Essay on Man*. According to the scholarly commentator, Pope associated the positive conception, at least in his verse treatise on human nature, with the Arcadian mythos of classical pastoral poetry. Although in correspondence Bolingbroke scolded his friend for allegedly confounding the philosophical doctrine of what Hobbes called the "condition of Warre of every one against every one" with the pastoral Golden Age, he predicated his own theory of mixed government on much the same idealization of primitive society for which he chided Pope. For, as Hammond notes, what the political theorist and the poetic satirist shared was a pessimistic view of history as a process of degeneration:

The nature of Bolingbroke's political platform that he developed to fight the parliamentary and extraparliamentary battles against Walpole in the 1730s was such that it united both the philosophic and the poetic notions of a purer state of society. Crucial to Bolingbroke's ideology is the conception that there has existed in British political life a free and ancient constitution, functioning as an index of the health of that life and constituting the primary condition of political liberty. When the balance between the king, nobles, and commons that the proper functioning of the constitution requires is overturned, as Bolingbroke argued it had been by the Walpole clique, the result is a moral and political decline that can be described as a state of "corruption."[36]

The fall from communal harmony into corruption occurs as a result of the demagogue's egomaniacal lust for power, but the process may be combated through the critical efforts of individuals exercising their autonomy of thought and thus sustaining the civic ideal of virtue. As I have shown, a rhetoric that pits the virtue of moral independence against the corruption of monied influence and mercenary interests is already present in *An Essay on Criticism*, even if it awaits the occasion to be honed into an instrument of topical satire.

The political language to which Pope has most consistent recourse in his poetry, then, is the idiom in which, J. G. A. Pocock has pointed out, the early eighteenth century debated the consequences of the establishment of the Bank of England, public credit, and an increasingly speculative system of exchange relations: "If we pay attention to the actual records of debate . . . we find that the origins of commercial ideology lay largely in the controversy between 'virtue' and 'corruption' and in the associated debate between 'landed interests' and 'monied interests' which was revitalised by the Financial Revolution."[37] Pocock has argued over the course of several important books about intellectual history that the enemies of commercial ideology in Augustan England used the term "virtue" to evoke the familiar classical image of the individual as an altruistic political agent.[38] They thus sought to reprimand the new society of creditors and speculators with reminders of the ancient conviction that "the highest form of active life was that of the citizen who, having entered the political process in pursuit of his particular good, now found himself joining with others to direct the actions of all in pursuit of the good of all."[39] Adopting what the historian has defined as a neo-Harringtonian position, proponents of this conviction furthermore viewed the autonomy of the citizen as best secured by the stabilizing means of land ownership. In a precise sense, therefore, "the concept of the citizen or patriot was antithetical to that of economic man."[40]

By restoring the debate between virtue and commerce to a central place in British Augustan culture, Pocock calls into question the fundamental narrative of Whig historiography, which for most of the twentieth century dominated scholarly views of England's political development. This narrative depicts the restraint of government and the vindication of the individual's political rights during the period from the Glorious Revolution of 1688 to the latter nineteenth century as the result of a gradual but thorough acceptance of Locke's political ideas, most especially as regards property. The general assent to his perception of civil society as the guarantor of the individual's property rights, so the reasoning goes, led to the early success of the Whig Party in financial administration and to the establishment of England as a commercial power. On this view, the protection of personal liberties is a function of the economic imperative to rationalize exchange relations by maintaining free markets. Some of the basic elements of this interpretation may be traced back to Macaulay's *History of England* (published in successive volumes from 1848 to 1862). The view that our freedoms of conscience depend entirely on our freedom of ownership, however, does not come into full focus until the twentieth century, when such authors as Ludwig von Mises and F. A. Hayek promote this perspective as the foundation of so-called classical liberalism.[41]

Pocock advances his objections to the classical liberal thesis on two distinct fronts. To start with, he casts doubt on the universal acceptance of an allegedly Lockean identification of freedom with the private ownership of material goods. This is what he means when he declares that "there is no greater and no commoner mistake in the history of social thought than to suppose that the tension [between virtue and commerce] ever disappeared, that the ideals of virtue and unity of personality were driven from the field, or that a commercial, 'liberal' or 'bourgeois' ideology reigned undisturbed until challenged by the harbingers of Marx."[42] Such a recognition of the division in the Augustan mind between competing varieties of political rhetoric and their attendant historical outlooks implies in turn a second, subtler point. For once we acknowledge that whatever democratization of English society took place during the period was not the necessary result of a consensus about the material basis of freedom, we may perceive that the appeal to liberty and to personal rights meant different things to different groups. Far from the founding of a classical liberalism, then, the eighteenth and nineteenth centuries saw an efflorescence of several more or less loosely related and at times rival liberalisms. The historian locates the origin of one such alternative (though he does not acknowledge it by the name "liberalism") in the Polybian theory of mixed government that envisioned the ideal polis as a democratic republic in which no one individual or faction could coerce the others:

To lose one's due share of authority, or to have more than one's due, amounted to a loss of virtue, and since virtue consisted in a relation between equals its loss was not private but mutual. It might be thought of as coming about either when some became so strong that they could use others as their instruments, or when some became so weak that they could be so used. The republic could persist only if all its citizens were so far autonomous that they could be equally and immediately participant in the pursuit of the universal good.[43]

Freedom in this case is synonymous with equality, although of a sort that to the modern mind may appear to demand intolerable sacrifices of the individual. According to Pocock, the republican or civic humanist tradition grants autonomy to the citizen in exchange for the voluntary suppression of private or personal needs, because "only a Spartan rigidity of institutions could enable men to master the politics of time."[44]

The historian has declared that his recovery of civic humanism hinges on "a context too rich and complex to be unmade all at once by any great cultural revolution, or made to yield to any one set of revolutionary demands."[45] In this sense, Pocock's project entails what he calls "a conservative theory of freedom."[46] In spite of this self-characterization, however, he gives emphasis to an irony that further complicates the historical picture. Because the Bolingbrokean language of opposition invoked a "rhetoric of outsiders" that in an earlier era had been employed by the Old Whigs to articulate the disaffection of urban populations marginalized by the Septennial Act, "we encounter . . . the problem that Tory language, which ought to have been and often was High Church and Jacobite, ought not to have been but often was radical and republican, Commonwealth as well as country."[47] On this point, Pocock arrives at an insight that to a greater or lesser degree has struck other students of the period as well; Isaac Kramnick notices that "nearly eighty years before John Cam Hobhouse coined the phrase 'His Majesty's Opposition,' Bolingbroke described Parliament as divided into two parties: a government party and an opposition party."[48] Yet it is Pocock who has brought to light most sharply the importance of the clash between the neoclassical ideal of virtue and the modern ideal of commerce in Augustan England for the later history of political thought. Summing up the critique of economic man mounted by thinkers of the Scottish Enlightenment such as Adam Ferguson and John Millar, for example, he concludes: "It is clear . . . that it was the civic humanist ideal which provided the point of departure for the concept of alienation. The undistracted, unspecialised man—hunter in the morning and critic in the afternoon—whom Marx and Lenin hoped to restore to his universality is in the long view an Aristotelian citizen, participant in all the value-oriented activities of society, and his history is in large part the history of civic humanism."⁴⁹ The "conservative theory of freedom" that authorized the Country attack on what we have since come to think of as classical liberalism thus supplies the basis of those later populist and anti-commercial strands of liberal and radical thought that connect figures as diverse as William Godwin, Hobhouse, John Stuart Mill, and even, if we are to take Pocock's analysis at face value, Marx and Lenin.

By now it ought to be plain that Pope, who depicts himself in Satire 2.1 as "arm'd for Virtue, when I point the pen" (105), in an exact sense propounds the civic humanist ethos elucidated by Pocock. Yet we should be careful not to blindly equate Pope's political ideas either with those of Bolingbroke or with Pocock's exposition of the ideology to which both poet and statesman contributed. Of course, Pope made complicated allegorical use of the vocabulary of virtue and corruption to repudiate the Whig monopoly on place and pension and so in a real sense took up the opposition banner.⁵⁰ However, his views on property and social class are so ambivalent as to make the Harringtonian position ascribed by the historian to the Country side of the debate seem naively simplistic. I do not mean by any stretch of the imagination that Pope saw himself as an enemy of the landed gentry. What I rather wish to notice is that his distrust of the corrupting influence of wealth is so strong that his satires typically conclude in a state of cynical incredulity at the prospect of ever determining a material basis of freedom.

This disbelief is sharply at work even in a poem as ostensibly complimentary to the figure of the British country squire as the imitation of Horace's Satire 2.2, whose dedicatee, Hugh Bethel, according to Pat Rogers represented in the poet's eyes "an exemplar of oldfashioned 'virtue.'"⁵¹ Although Pope certainly put the satire's moral of moderation in his friend Bethel's mouth ("He knows to live, who keeps the middle state, / And neither leans on this side, nor on that," 61–62), he switches to his own voice at the end in order not to promote the value of landownership but rather to explode the concept of ownership altogether.

> Fortune not much of humbling me can boast;
> Tho' double-tax'd, how little have I lost? . . .
>
> My lands are sold, my Father's house is gone;
> I'll hire another's, is not that my own? . . .
>
> What's *Property*, dear Swift! you see it alter
> From you to me, from me to Peter Walter,
> Or, in a mortgage, prove a Lawyer's share,
> Or, in a jointure, vanish from the Heir,
> Or in pure Equity (the Case not clear)
> The Chanc'ry takes your rents for twenty year:

> At best, it falls to some ungracious Son
> Who cries, my father's damn'd, and all's my own.
> Shades, that to Bacon could retreat afford,
> Become the portion of a booby Lord;
> And Hemsley once proud Buckingham's delight,
> Slides to a Scriv'ner or a City Knight.
> Let Lands and Houses have what Lords they will,
> Let Us be fix'd, and our own Masters still.
> (151–152, 155–156, 167–180)

Rogers paints Bethel as a type of the prosperous steward of the land whose "suitability . . . for his role as the modern Ofellus in *Satire* 2.2" derives from the fact that his "deepest involvement lay in the country life."[52] Pope's displacement of Bethel from the role of poetic speaker at the conclusion of the satire, however, complicates the approving identification of the modern peer with the Roman *rusticus* (2.2.3). It should be noted as well that Horace's and Pope's poems advance somewhat different moral arguments. Ofellus declares at the climax of the Latin original that nature itself disallows any human authority from sole proprietorship of the earth ("nam propriae telluris erum natura neque illum / nec me nec quemquam statuit," 2.2.129–130). Pope pointedly omits any equivalent of these lines in his imitation and, by adhering to a contractual language of "mortgage," "jointure," and "equity," interprets the instability of property as a function of the adversarial or agonistic impulses unique to human society. A characteristically supple use of anaphora and syntactical parallelism highlights the remarkable argumentative turn of the final lines. The formulaic repetitiveness of Pope's description in lines 169–171 of the circuitous movements of property suggests the self-perpetuating shocks of a modernity that bestows social agency on the individual at the price of a thoroughgoing alienation and commodification of personality.

Against such traumatic changes, the final couplet sets the image of a mental equilibrium that disdains the acquisitiveness of commercial society. The return of anaphoric repetition, which in the preceding lines allegorically signifies the mutability of material circumstances, throws into high relief the constancy of a moral intelligence that distinguishes between being a lord of lands and titles and a master of one's own mind and that therefore is well equipped to overcome the vicissitudes of fortune. Making specific reference to a line in which the poet praises Bethel's "equal mind" (131), Erskine-Hill points out that "Pope introduces into his imitation the idea of a balance or equality of mind. There is no such reference in *Sat.* 2.2. Yet it is an immediately recognizable Horatian *motif*."[53] Clearly, the motif supplies the last word of the poem's argument. Yet, as Erskine-Hill also has noted, Pope gives the theme an added drama when he "allows himself to allude, for the first time in any of his poems, to the disabilities suffered by Roman Catholics during his lifetime."[54] Without revising the earlier, flattering portrayal of Bethel, then, the satirist subtly differentiates between his own standing as someone whose "lands are sold" thanks to religious persecution and that of his friend, whose office of MP reflected the firm value of his own estate. The more decisive repudiation of corruption, so the satire seems to imply, is achieved by persevering against greater odds. The disparity between the satirist and his more comfortably situated friend thus facilitates the poem's sharpening of its Horatian skepticism toward immoderation or prejudice into a critique of what can only be called the illiberal traits of modern bourgeois society: its intolerance, its inequity, its deference to means and influence.

James Noggle astutely maintains that "one of the most thorough cases in the *Imitations* for the virtues of an 'equal mind' is made in . . . the *Nil admirari, Epistle* I.vi published in 1738."[55] He is, furthermore, right to say that the skepticism of the poem operates by "both renouncing the sources of apparent happiness—wealth, popularity, power, sensory indulgence—and pointedly declining to represent good living otherwise than negatively as the lack of admiration for such things."[56] From this observation, however, he appears to reason that Pope's reticence regarding the philosophical *summum bonum* represents a form of political accommodation, a way of surreptitiously "participating in civil society's providential order through a critique of it."[57] Such an affirmation of social foundations by implication consorts with a general impulse to "conservatism," which the critic defines as "a longing for old authorities and unquestioned modes of action."[58] Noggle's reading, however, downplays the critical point that Pope makes by applying skepticism to the accepted forms of trade and moneymaking in Augustan England. Once we have perceived the author's sustained contempt in the poem for "all the mad trade of Fools and Slaves for Gold" (13), it becomes harder to construe his articulation of the principle of *nil admirari* as some kind of backhanded approval of "civil society's providential order." Indeed, Epistle 1.6 might better be understood as a damning and surprisingly modern anatomization of the pathology of commodity fetishism:

> Is Wealth thy passion? Hence! from Pole to Pole,
> Where winds can carry, or where waves can roll,
> For Indian spices, or Peruvian gold,
> Prevent the greedy, and out-bid the bold:
> Advance thy golden Mountain to the skies;
> On the broad base of fifty thousand rise,
> Add one round hundred, and (if that's not fair)
> Add fifty more, and bring it to a square.
> For, mark th'advantage; just so many score,
> Will gain a Wife with half as many more,

> Procure her beauty, make that beauty chaste,
> And then such Friends—as cannot fail to last.
> A Man of wealth is dubb'd a Man of worth,
> Venus shall give him Form, and Anstis Birth.
>
> (69–82)

The verb "prevent" is used in line 70 in its etymological root sense of "precede" or "come before" and highlights the importance of the "Man of wealth" as an archetype or paradigm of greed. The perverseness of a fantasy life that sustains itself through relentless capital accumulation casts a negative light on the sociology behind the national project of commercial empire building, a project equated in line 71 with the pursuit of "Indian spices" and "Peruvian gold." That the Epistle's philosophically sophisticated reinterpretation of the ideal of *nil admirari* serves the aims of political critique is confirmed if we note the poem's sarcastic juxtaposition of the portrait of the "Man of wealth" to that of the exiled Prince Frederick in the lines immediately following ("Believe me, many a German Prince is worse, / Who proud of Pedigree, is poor of Purse," 83–84). Taking this reference to the opposition figurehead together with the Epistle's praise in an earlier passage of Henry Hyde, Viscount Cornbury ("Disdain whatever CORNBURY disdains," 61), who, Brean Hammond reminds us, was a central figure in plans for a Stuart restoration, we may begin to view the politics of Pope's critique of bourgeois ideology as being, more than conservative in the usual sense, revolutionary in implication.[59]

Another famous dictum from *An Essay on Criticism* helps to illustrate the almost dialectical sense of antagonism in Pope's writing between consumer culture and freedom of mind:

> Poets like Painters, thus, unskill'd to trace
> The *naked Nature* and the *living Grace*,
> With *Gold* and *Jewels* cover ev'ry Part,
> And hide with *Ornaments* their *Want of Art*.
> *True Wit* is *Nature* to Advantage drest
> What oft was *Thought*, but ne'er so well *Exprest*,
> *Something*, whose Truth convinc'd at Sight we find,
> That gives us back the Image of our Mind.
>
> (293–300)

Many readers seem to have preferred for simplicity's sake to interpret the famous definition of "true Wit" as a pledge of faith in orthodox canons of opinion. Interpretations of this type ignore the *Essay*'s clear suggestion that familiarity of thought derives not from obedience to authority but rather from a wide and deep course of critical engagement with cultural and intellectual history. Such interpretations further overlook the sharp opposition that the poem draws between true wit and the crass productions of an art that buys prestige through its calculated reification of the commodifying procedures of the market.

William Empson long ago advised against underestimating the force of Pope's ironies, but the tendency persists despite the warning.

> Critics may naturally object that the Augustans did not deal in profound complexities, and tried to make their words as clear-cut as possible. This is so, but it did not stop them from using double meanings intended as clear-cut jokes. The performance inside the word *wit*, I should maintain, was intended to be quite obvious and in the sunlight, and was so for the contemporary reader; that was why he thought the poem so brilliant; but most modern readers (unless I wrong them) do not notice it at all, and that is why they think the poem so dull.[60]

It is by way of outlining the personality behind "the performance inside the word *wit*" that Empson reveals the real weight of the term, which is political in the largest sense. Near the end of his essay he writes: "That word [wit] treats genius with a certain playfulness out of deference to the democracy of the drawing-room; but such a view could only be made plausible if the drawing-room were assumed to have a high standard. The whole strategy of Pope therefore makes large demands on the 'common sense' which is to become adequate to the task of criticism."[61] Empson's simultaneous stress on the "playfulness" and "high standard" of democratic parlor chat exactly registers the degree of ambivalence that Pope achieves in his exposition of the creative imagination. Empson intuits that, as Pope turns the phrase, "true wit" is not a repudiation of novelty so much as a celebration of the demystifying of intellectual, social, and political convention by experience. We are meant to feel as an honest paradox the protest lodged by the conjunction in the line "What oft was Thought, but ne'er so well Exprest," to feel that whatever "true wit" may lose by being identified with the historically known it regains from another perspective by being tested in the arena of critical debate. The critic's characterization of this formulation as "a deference to the democracy of the drawing-room" is largely correct, if facetious in tone. Empson understood that the Augustan ideal of intellectual privilege gained by true wit at some point works to contradict the ideal of social privilege gained by high birth, even while usurping its aristocratic hauteur.

Pope's poems prescribe a historically comprehensive education, pursued in a spirit of urbane curiosity, as a remedy against the sort of naivete that Hume would attack in his essay "Of the Standard of Taste" (1757) as "self-conceit."[62] To the readiness of ignorance "to call *barbarous* whatever departs widely from our own taste and apprehension," Hume opposed the "practice" that gives rise to "delicacy of taste."[63] Such practice, in other words, builds up the individual's comprehension of a range of experience that is ultimately incommensurate with the bigotry in which a mind too "full of the manners of [its] own age and country" confirms itself.[64] Experience in this sense readies us to overcome personal bias, clearing our pathway to a type of objective truth.

A critical tradition that teaches us to construe the past with respect for its strangeness, with a willingness to encounter the unexpected, teaches us mental independence. We acquire from the exploration of other times an enlarged perspective that steadies us against the conformist influences of fashion, superstition, and propaganda. The habit of following our enthusiasms beyond the bounds of what we already know, a habit that John Stuart Mill called "learning the grounds of one's own opinions," accustoms us to freedom of thought and thus makes possible the full exercise of our individuality.[65] The tradition that encourages such a practice, in other words, is a tradition of personal innovation. It will not evolve in a society that fails to guarantee the free circulation of ideas. And it is ranged against the "collective mediocrity" of the mass.[66]

To some of its detractors the very idea of a liberal tradition looks like an oxymoron. Because they cannot imagine a fixed course of education that would not program our reactions in advance of every task (whether for good or for ill), such critics do not believe the differences in our ways of thinking and feeling may be cultivated and made pertinent to one another. As David Bromwich points out, however, the course of education proposed in conjunction with the liberal tradition has never been so rigidly formulated.

> A liberal education tries to assure the persistence of a culture of responsive individuals—people who, in the course of a long experiment in learning, will have discovered ... the value of coming to know a tradition that is not the property of any party. A tradition on this view, far from being fixed forever, may be shaped by the voluntary choices of readers and thinkers. Indeed, it exists not only as something to know but as something to interpret and reform. But a difficult paradox holds together the idea of a nonrestrictive tradition. Before it can be reformed intelligently, it must be known adequately; and yet, unless one recognizes first that it *can* be reformed, one will come to know it only as a matter of rote.[67]

Our idea of human originality assumes, as its *conditio sine qua non*, an autonomy of reason that we achieve through a sustained effort of perception. The "habits of attention" that best resist secondhand sentiment are invigorated by an active career of reading and discussion. At any given moment, the subject of the reading and the terms of the discussion are open to revision. What ensures the heft and fit of every successive revision is the historical pressure exerted by the sequence of past revisions that constitutes the body of the tradition itself. As much as the tradition trains us to look on our idiosyncratic selves as participants in a larger narrative, however, the idiosyncrasy of each participant shifts and renews the drive of the tradition. In the encounter between the liberal tradition and the creative mind neither remains unchanged. I have been arguing that the concern with education and its proper application that leads to the liberal position has its source in the conception of the arts, and especially of literature, prevalent in England during the eighteenth century. On this theory, the work of the arts is always didactic, at least insofar as they supply the proving grounds of critical judgment and moral imagination.

Of all the classical authors to whom the period looked for inspiration, it was Horace who, according to Ian Watt, left the deepest impression, who "more than anyone else provided a common standard of thought and feeling and diction for almost the whole of literate society."[68] A freedman's son, a tribune who at one time commanded a legion of the Roman army, a satirist who fraternized with the likes of Virgil and Maecenas and who, recalling an especially memorable holiday in their company, wrote "Nothing, while in my right mind, would I compare to a pleasant friend" ("nil ego contulerim iucundo sanus amico," Satire 1.5.44), Horace suggested to the English the image of the poet as the center of a social order determined neither by birth nor wealth but by ability and conduct. At a relatively late moment in the period, for instance, Dr. Johnson appeals to the precedent of Horace as a means of justifying his own complicated vacillation between snobbery and progressivism in a celebrated remark in the *Rambler* of March 31, 1750, on the relation between readership and literary production.

> The task of our present writers is very different: it requires, together with that learning which is to be gained from books, that experience which can never be attained by solitary diligence, but must arise from general converse and accurate observation of the living world. Their performances have, as Horace expresses it, *plus oneris quantum veniae minus*, little indulgence, and therefore more difficulty. They are engaged in portraits of which everyone knows the original, and can detect any deviation from exactness of resemblance. Other writings are safe except from the malice of learning, but these are in danger from every common reader; as the slipper ill executed was censured by a shoemaker who happened to stop in his way at the Venus of Apelles.[69]

A more polemical essayist might have been tempted to decide the conflict staged in this paragraph between the "solitary diligence" of the bookworm and the philistinism of the "common reader" in favor of one or the other camp. Johnson's argument lies somewhere in the middle. The point here is that "learning" and "converse [with] . . . the living world" are not only desirable attainments in themselves but also necessary to each other's good growth and employment. The complaint that the public receives new compositions with "little indulgence" depends on a reader's prior awareness that at the time of the complaint the ranks of the literate public in England are growing, particularly among the middle classes. Of course, this increase in literacy will ultimately benefit writers who do not flinch in the face of the moment. Johnson may make light of the "shoemaker" who cavils at the "slipper" of Apelles, but he knows the society is better off that allows its cobblers to take an interest in paintings, and that the text equally able to overcome without condescension the narrow-mindedness of the common and the learned reader is a sounder piece of writing.

The lesson of the tale about the shoemaker who paused to criticize the Venus of Apelles is not that tradesmen should keep quiet before artistic monuments. The lesson is rather that in 1750 the serious writer or painter ought to be prepared for the attention of critics from every social class and walk of life. Johnson's passing jest at the specialized nature of the shoemaker's critique elaborates in bathetic terms one of the principal tenets that the British Augustans felt they had inherited from their Roman forebears: namely, the abiding belief in the exemplary status of the artist. To the English reader, the poet by reason of the occupation seemed to embody a higher standard of thinking, feeling, and doing that the entire society should have observed but for the most part ignored. Claude Rawson reminds us that in Pope's time the disparity between privilege and conscience was especially "disillusioning to authors whose model of the good life was an aristocratic one in a way that derived not from social rank . . . but from an ideal extending to all areas of mind, morality and manners: an ideal which bestowed on the word 'noble' its moral sense and ultimately aspired to a perfect order in which those who were noble in one sense were noble in the other."[70] Such an ideal paradoxically anticipates the disgust toward class barriers of a later brand of liberalism at the same time that it emulates an aristocratic scorn for the conformism of the popular masses. As Rawson adds, "Swift and Pope despised the pride of social rank, but they were not altogether without hankerings or affectations that way."[71]

There is at least one poem in which Pope commits what must be judged from the viewpoint of rank the most audacious impertinence of which a British Augustan poet was capable. The impertinence he offers the king in his imitation of Horace's Epistle 2.1, *To Augustus*, is audacious not merely because the poem masquerades as an encomium to George II while delivering a tart indictment of his reign but because delivery is achieved by means of allusions that continually revise and deepen the judgment behind the dispraise.

> In Days of Ease, when now the weary Sword
> Was sheath'd, and *Luxury* with *Charles* restor'd;
> In every Taste of foreign Courts improv'd,
> "All, by the King's Example, liv'd and lov'd."
> Then Peers grew proud in Horsemanship t'excell,
> New-market's Glory rose, as Britain's fell;
> The Soldier breath'd the Gallantries of France,
> And ev'ry flow'ry Courtier writ Romance.
> Then Marble soften'd into life grew warm,
> And yielding Metal flow'd to human form:
> Lely on animated Canvas stole
> The sleepy Eye, that spoke the melting soul.
> No wonder then, when all was Love and Sport,
> The willing Muses were debauch'd at Court;
> On each enervate string they taught the Note
> To pant, or tremble thro' an Eunuch's throat.
> But Britain, changeful as a Child at play,
> Now calls in princes, and now turns away.
> Now Whig, now Tory, what we lov'd we hate;
> Now all for Pleasure, now for Church and State;
> Now for Prerogative, and now for Laws;
> Effects unhappy! from a Noble Cause.
>
> (139–160)

This account of Charles II's court and the imbroglio over succession that erupted in its wake is often understood as the sounding of an alarm against the bad example of the past, especially as regards the potentially lasting, harmful influence of a dissolute monarch on the taste of the nation. Pope, however, is working on something tougher and more complicated here than a castigation of former sins. Indeed, the effect he achieves in these lines is more like nostalgia than self-righteousness, a nostalgia symptomized by the apothegmatic quotation at line 142, among other signs. The author of this verse was George Granville, Baron Lansdowne and the secretary for war during the brief Tory ascendancy prior to Queen Anne's death; he was also, of course, the friend to whom Pope dedicated *Windsor-Forest*, the poem published in 1713 to welcome the Peace of Utrecht. As the motto for his retrospective study of Stuart extravagance, in other words, Pope affixes a tag penned by a minister who contributed in no small part to the political victories that momentarily enlivened the last gasp of the House of Stuart on the throne. The remembered line signposts Pope's allegiance to a political and cultural agenda that may have been travestied at certain moments during Charles's and James's day (and may have evolved in significant ways since then) but that has been rejected without a second thought by the present powers.

Underlying the emblematic flourish of the quotation, then, is a careful admiration for an intemperance or excess that, in the final reckoning, Pope cannot quite bring himself to endorse. There is at least one less guarded moment, however, when the admiration rises to genuine enthusiasm: "Then Marble soften'd into life grew warm / And yielding Metal flow'd to human form." Here the sound structure of the verse briliantly seems an echo to its quasi-Ovidian sense.[72] The phonetic array [m], [l], [f] that organizes the initial half of the first line in "Marble soften'd" returns out of sequence ([l], [f], [m]) in the second half with "life grew warm," only to be restored to its original order early in the course of the next line: "Metal flow'd." It is as if the phonological atoms of the poem are being made to dance through a series of alchemical recombinations in order to demonstrate the molecular similarity of all aesthetically converted matter: marble as it softens, metal as it flows. Pope's superbly ambiguous use of the adjective "yielding" in the second line amplifies the message. On the one hand, the substance of the verse is surrendering passively to the poet's manipulations; on the other, the substance also actively furnishes or produces the meaning of the couplet. A fine balance is struck between connotations of an obliging pliancy and an abundant fertility.

Only after the exuberance of these lines does the language of the passage turn irrevocably toward disapproval with the introduction of words like "debauch'd" and "enervate" (although the sarcasm of the line "New-market's Glory rose, as Britain's fell" alerts the reader early on to the superfluity of the Restoration in one area). The infantile English whimsicality responsible for the vicissitudes endured by both monarchy and body politic since 1660 is thus made to seem the consequence most directly of an undisciplined and degrading voluptuousness, but more remotely of an enriching vivacity of feeling, too. The decline into political contortionism in the last few lines frustrates all the more keenly because of the subjectivity attributed by simile to the sufferer of the decline. If Britain has retreated into fickle childishness, it has just missed fulfilling the possibility of a vibrant maturity. The slap directed at George Augustus in the final line gains impetus from the historical movement of Pope's thesis. At least the unhappy effects of Charles's reign sprang from a "Noble Cause." He left behind a cultural legacy part of which will be an enduring source of pride for England. What can a boor like George, living in a mercenary age, hope to bequeath posterity?

The damning comparison Pope draws between Stuart and Hanoverian rulers is backed up in the poem by an even more damning (and more pervasive) comparison between Augustus Caesar and King George. The steady mimicry of the Horatian epistle by the Popean satire thoroughly colors the later poem's apostrophe of its royal nonpatron, as Erskine-Hill's reading of it has shown, and the coloration works to the diminishment of the addressee: "as many points in the poem recognize, George was not interested in poetry, while Pope is in the midst of a most detailed literary discourse, involving

Shakespeare, Jonson, *Gammer Gurton's Needle*, Sidney, 'Sprat, Carew, Sedley, and a hundred more.' Formally speaking the Epistle may be addressed to the reigning 'Augustus' but in the fiction of the poem a greater Augustus stands behind the Hanoverian monarch."[73] Pope is trading on a delicious irony in his imitation: the more faithful to Horace's eulogistic rhetoric he tries to be, the more unworthy appears the object of praise.

> Not with such Majesty, such bold relief,
> The Forms august of King, or conqu'ring Chief,
> E'er swell'd on Marble; as in Verse have shin'd
> (In polish'd Verse) the Manners and the Mind.
> Oh! could I mount on the Maeonian wing,
> Your Arms, your Actions, your Repose to sing!
> What seas you travers'd! and what fields you fought!
> Your Country's Peace, how oft, how dearly bought!
> How barb'rous rage subsided at your word,
> And Nations wonder'd while they dropp'd the sword!
> How, when you nodded, o'er the land and deep,
> Peace stole her wing, and wrapt the world in sleep.
>
> (390–401)

The superficially heroic strains that begin this speech swing decisively into the mock-heroic register with the line, "Your Country's Peace, how oft, how dearly bought!" That the nation's peace policy was unpopular when the poem was published in 1737 is not, I think, knowledge the reader must have in order to appreciate the put-down of holding George liable for a *Pax Brittanica* repeatedly purchased at high price. With the advent of the final couplet, the poem slips smoothly into a bathetically grandiose idiom that calls to mind the early editions of the *Dunciad* (and of course anticipates the 1743 masterwork). Pope further intensifies the bathos by overloading the final line with monosyllables, as if to mime the galling triviality of the theme by shortening the vocables. The paradigmatic instance of such shrinkage occurs in *An Essay on Criticism*: "And ten low Words oft creep in one dull Line" (347). John Hollander has established that the success of this poetic pratfall depends on "ten low words" and "one dull line" having the exact same stress contour in speech.[74] The distribution of stresses in "Peace stole her wing, and wrapt the world in sleep" is more even, but the impression given is equally of a quick, comic lapse in poetic inspiration.

After a closer glance, however, we might come to conclude that the passage is artfully insincere from its very inception. The first four lines follow Horace closely enough to sound to any reader schooled in the original like a verbatim translation, if only at one point: namely, "the Manners and the Mind," which pretty neatly renders "mores animique." Through the overt-ness of the echo, Pope's epistolary monologue refers the reader back to its classical model precisely for the purpose of drawing the attention to the dissimilarity of the circumstances imagined by the two texts. For when Horace announces that the minds and manners of great men are made visible in the work of the poet ("per vatis opus"), he substantiates the boast by pointing to the examples of certain specific poets ("Vergilius Variusque poetae") whom the *princeps* has had the good taste to patronize. The implicit thank-you to Augustus on behalf of Virgil and Varius reminds us that Horace was also on the imperial bankroll. Pope was not lucky enough to enjoy a similar favor, but then his own hard-won self-sufficiency was something he was proud of, as his famous claim of being "un-plac'd, un-pension'd, no Man's Heir, or Slave" in Satire 2.1.116 testifies. At any rate, the comparison to the cultural golden age of the Roman Empire whets our sense of how "dearly bought" is the British peace under George, since it is a peace, Pope reminds us three lines after the end of the quoted segment, that offers little reward to literary excellence: "But Verse alas! your Majesty disdains" (404).

The comparison flatters by bringing into proximity England's poetic achievement of the day with the grand flourishing of the arts in Rome, but the flattery comes at the price of any greater conviction regarding the historical kinship of the two civilizations. There is an expectation in Pope that history is about to repeat itself, but in a manner that for the reader only brings into sharper focus the sense of distance between past and present. Two sentiments in particular seem to contribute to this expectation: first, the idea that satire in Pope's age is more deserved than even during the classical period because the civic reality is more degraded and, second, the feeling that in order to live up to the example of their Roman predecessors the English writers must be original. The British Augustans indeed believed that they were following in the footsteps of the Romans, but to do so in good faith meant not to be slavish copyists.

What results are odd moments when what begins as a superficially straightforward feeling of resemblance, voiced as an allusion or commonplace, turns into a deeper and more ironic awareness of historical singularity. Rawson notes, for example, "Pope's famous line, 'Scribblers or Peers, alike are *Mob* to me,' occurs in a direct imitation of a famous Horatian satire, but it is not in the original, and its absence is conspicuous in the parallel text on the facing page."[75] Not only does the line occur in Pope's modernizing of Satire 2.1 (1733) but in a passage in which Pope is supposedly relaying Horace's own rationale for considering satire a necessary feature of the discourse of the *principate*.

> Envy must own, I live among the Great,
> No Pimp of Pleasure, and no Spy of State,
> With Eyes that pry not, Tongue that ne'er repeats,

> Fond to spread Friendships, but to cover Heats,
> To help who want, to forward who excel;
> This, all who know me, know; who love me, tell;
> And who unknown defame me, let them be
> Scriblers or Peers, alike are *Mob* to me.
>
> (133–140)

By now it is a familiar observation that, in the original lines after which this version is patterned, Horace names the satirist Lucilius as the object of his praise in order to diffuse, or at least complicate, the self-adulation involved in his defense of the mode, whereas Pope more boldly substitutes himself as the heroic paragon.[76]

> Quicquid sum ego, quamvis
> infra Lucili censum ingeniumque, tamen me
> cum magnis vixisse invita fatebitur usque
> invidia.
>
> Whatever I may be, although below Lucilius,
> in genius and in wealth, the envious nonetheless
> will have to recognize despite themselves
> that I have lived among the great.[77]
>
> (2.1.74–77)

The English poem in its first line sounds a note that manifestly harkens back to its Latin predecessor, "Envy must own, I live among the Great" succinctly picking up "tamen me cum magnis," and so on. Yet Pope, caught up in the momentum of self-assertion, hurries to conclude in the peculiarly ambivalent combativeness that simultaneously denounces "Scriblers and Peers." The Horatian original and the Popean imitation, in other words, give voice to two markedly different attitudes toward the past. Horace pays tribute to an eminent precursor within his own tradition and culture in the hope that some of the precursor's authority will rub off on him. Pope, however, finds himself unable to claim quite the same relation to Horace that Horace does to Lucilius. Indeed, Pope's point is not only that Grubstreet is further from the Roman *principate* than the *principate* from the republic but also that he stands in a more precarious relation to his own culture than Horace stood to his. Thus a certain amount of rue underlies Pope's boast to be "no Pimp of Pleasure." If he lives among the great, he wishes to imply, that is because the great are themselves disenfranchised from the seat of power in England.

What precedes this avowal of moral immunity is the famous self-portrait of Pope in the guise of *vir bonus*, beginning with "What? arm'd for *Virtue* when I point the Pen" (105) and culminating in the claim to be "To VIRTUE

ONLY and HER FRIENDS, A FRIEND" (121). Around the image of the poet as a refugee from the hurly-burly of public affairs, or what we might nowadays term the culture wars, Pope envisions a fraternity of the exiled and out-of-favor as a deliberate gesture of defiance to the Whig monopoly on high office.

> Know, all the distant Din that World can keep
> Rolls o'er my Grotto, and but sooths my Sleep.
> There, my Retreat the best Companions grace,
> Chiefs, out of War, and Statesmen, out of Place.
> There *St. John* mingles with my friendly Bowl,
> The Feast of Reason and the Flow of Soul:
> And He, whose Lightning pierc'd th'*Iberian* Lines,
> Now, forms my Quincunx, and now ranks my Vines,
> Or tames the Genius of the stubborn Plain,
> Almost as quickly, as he conquer'd *Spain*.
>
> (123–132)

The satiric model for this "retreat" is the seat of *otium* such as the Sabine farm mentioned not in Horace's Satire 2.1 but in 2.6.16–19 ("Ergo ubi me," etc.). The farm in Horace is clearly a refuge where the talk of the town on subjects such as legacy-hunting and dancing gains no admittance to the dinner conversation (see lines 70–76) and the company consists of friends who all remain strictly anonymous in the poem (with the exception of Horace's neighbor Cervius). Pope's grotto, on the other hand, supplies a place for public figures who have lost their principal employment: "Chiefs, out of War, and Statesmen, out of Place." They are men whose genius ill suits them for compromise with the culture of avarice that surrounds them. For such eminences, history as it is being written now, the history of the victors in the game of self-promotion, is not worthy of their participation. Those who rebel against such a history are out of step with their times in a positive sense.

Both Brean Hammond and Maynard Mack link the freedom with which Pope castigated Walpole (sufficient at least to permit the invocation of Bolingbroke and Charles Mordaunt, earl of Peterborough, as examples of virtue) during the years 1733–35, when these lines were written and published to the diminishment or disappointment of Pope's hopes for ingratiation with the government, with the momentary pall thrown over Walpole's political reputation circa 1733 due to his ill-fated Excise Scheme.[78] Both Hammond, who calls the passage "galling" from a government standpoint, and Mack, who goes as far as to detect "a tone that . . . blends ridicule with something almost like threat, and both with a parade of strength," bring out the taunting quality of the passage.[79] Such an emphasis perhaps consorts with the impression frequently given by the lines of an overt shift from a Horatian to a Juvenalian mode of satire. Yet mingled with the taunt is also a melancholic sense of the precariousness of the position of *viri boni* such as Bolingbroke, Peterborough, and, most of all, Pope. Pope's ambivalence about their air of moral superiority is suggested by his likening it to sleep, a sleep soothed by the world's din, however distant. The "retreat" provided by the grotto thus seems to hover somewhere in between triumph and defeat. The place of genius in such a world is clearly an unenviable one.

By the start of the *Epistle to Dr. Arbuthnot* (1735), the protection that the grotto offers genius, already sufficiently equivocal in Satire 2.1, has grown clearly inadequate.

> Shut, shut the door, good *John*! fatigu'd I said,
> Tye up the knocker, say I'm sick, I'm dead,
> The Dog-star rages! nay 'tis past a doubt,
> All *Bedlam*, or *Parnassus*, is let out:
> Fire in each eye, and Papers in each hand,
> They rave, recite, and madden round the land.
>   What Walls can guard me, or what Shades can hide?
> They pierce round my Thickets, thro' my Grot they glide,
> By land, by water, they renew the charge,
> They stop the Chariot, and they board the Barge.
> No place is sacred, not the Church is free,
> Ev'n *Sunday* shines no *Sabbath-day* to me:
> Then from the *Mint* walks forth the man of Ryme,
> Happy! to catch me, just at Dinner-time.
>   (1–14)

Reference to the malign influence of Sirius would seem to suggest a humoristic or physiological explanation for the effronteries of hireling scribblers who, in their quest for advancement, "rave, recite, and madden round the land." We might think the medical argument clinched here by the appearance in the next line of "Bedlam," London's foremost hospital for the mentally ill, but as we soon discover, "Bedlam" comes to be associated in the poem with another well-known London institution, and implicitly to take on some of its function. "Then from the *Mint* walks forth the Man of Ryme," writes Pope (13), naming the latest literary offender to be "let out." And again at a later point: "If want provok'd, or madness made them print, / I wag'd no war with *Bedlam* or the *Mint*" (155–156). The parasitic "man of Ryme" takes his cue from Horace's unwelcome companion on the Via Sacra in Satire 1.9 who wishes to ingratiate himself with the satirist in order to gain access to his patron and who identifies himself with the phrase "I am a scholar" ("docti sumus," 7). The poetaster who accosts Pope is more crass in his demands, and it is implied that the crassness is a sign of a malaise peculiar to the literary professionalism of the eighteenth century. Behind the needy presumption of the debtor who makes "the Mint" his home swells an ever-increasing army of sycophants and cultural delinquents.

> One dedicates, in high heroic prose,
> And ridicules beyond a hundred foes;
> One from all *Grubstreet* will my fame defend,
> And, more abusive, calls himself my friend.
> This prints my Letters, that expects a Bribe,
> And others roar aloud, "Subscribe, subscribe."
> (109–114)

Underneath the contempt for the talentless hireling we may detect a keener hostility toward the commercialism of a print culture that is increasingly drifting away from a patronage model, allowing more hacks to scrape by and dangerously accelerating the vulgarization of the calling.

This complication of course does not mitigate the contempt.

> Nine years! cries he, who high in *Drury-lane*
> Lull'd by soft Zephyrs thro' the broken Pane,
> Rymes e're he wakes, and prints before *Term* ends,
> Oblig'd by hunger and Request of friends.
> (41–44)

The line "Oblig'd by hunger and Request of friends" is particularly stinging. In a nice phrase describing the different deployment of the same verb in the portrait of Addison that occurs later in the poem ("And so obliging that he ne'er oblig'd," 208), Pat Rogers has pointed out that there "the overtones of 'obliging' are trapped and diverted in an unexpected direction by the end of the verse."[80] Here something subtler but no less pointed is going on. In a characteristic move, Pope pulls two incongruous nouns into the orbit of the same verb, but in so doing points up the oddity of their convergence. Notice that "hunger" and "request of friends" are not of the same order of urgency. The point is to make us recognize which is the more fundamental imperative. For what makes such requests consistently obliging is precisely not friendship but need. That Pope recognizes the irresistibility of the obligation does not signal any sympathy for the obliged. To the contrary, Pope regards their penury (hence their suggestibility) as symptomatic of an incompetence that predisposes such figures to a life of habitual turpitude.

Because of the unprecedented success of his translation of Homer and the status it gave him as one of England's first comfortably independent men of letters, Pope gets to have it both ways in his attacks on rivals. Not only do down-and-out Grubstreet flunkies feel his disdain but so do all who win the attention of patrons whose judgment happens to be less than fastidious, as we see from the sharp satire on the destructive patronage of Bufo (231–270). There the tone of the attack is set in the passage on the egregious neglect of Dryden by those who could have helped him while he was alive: "But still the Great have kindness in reserve / He help'd to bury whom he help'd to starve" (247–248). Here the compliment given in the first line by "great" and "kindness" is retracted by "help'd to starve" in the second. "Greatness" also comes under assault in the lament for Gay. Pope's frustrating inability to save his friend (an inability at least partly financial in nature) curiously places him on the same footing in the passage with Gay's aristocratic patroness, the duchess of Queensbury. The equivalence helps to amplify the Epistle's moral of the mutual responsibility of rich and poor. In a healthy state of society, the mutual cooperation of the classes would represent no more than the fulfillment of everyday expectation, and culture would be self-rejuvenating. But at the present time, Pope implies, the class structure has lost its center of gravity. The sense of the attack in the satire is of a plague on both houses: the seedy Baviuses who pander to the tasteless and the wealthy Bufos who reward the inept (250).

The affliction under diagnosis in the Epistle, that is to say, is economic rather than biological in origin, and the object of its attacks is the body politic. The "Dog-star," *canus major*, according to Sir Thomas Browne in the *Pseudodoxia Epidemica* of 1672, was regarded by the Egyptians as the source of the "great fertility of Egypt, the overflow of Nylus happening about the ascent hereof" and so provides the appropriate symbol for a Walpolean financial revolution that has brought prosperity at the expense of justice, threatening to transform the new Roman empire of England into a second Egypt. That the first minister, who was famed for the sway—shared with Queen Caroline—that he exerted over George II, bears responsibility for the increasing abuse of patronage and commercialism of print culture is strongly implied by the poem in the lines on Midas and his court.

> 'Tis sung, when Midas' Ears began to spring,
> (*Midas*, a sacred Person and a King)
> His very Minister who spy'd them first,
> (Some say his Queen) was forc'd to speak, or burst.
> (70–73)

Midas, we should recall, grows ass's ears due to his decision of a musical contest in favor of Pan rather than Apollo, a decision that provokes the god's wrath. The thrust of the parable, in which the "sacred Person" of Midas becomes a thing of amusement to both his "very Minister" and "Queen," is clear. And, indeed, throughout the Epistle Pope's bitterness at the impunity granted the Whig ministry is more than evident. "Any poem that spoke of a longstanding friendship with St. John," as Hammond has observed, "while mounting a virulent attack on Hervey must be opposition inspired."[81]

This attack on the system by which wealth was distributed under Walpole's leadership builds on Bolingbroke's description in "The Idea of a Patriot King" of the work of "corruption," or partisan self-preference: "The most incapable . . . wretches, invested with power, and masters of the purse, will be sufficient for the work, when the people are accomplices in it. . . . Want is the consequence of profusion, venality of want, and dependence of venality."[82] Bolingbroke's strategy was to enlist the popular interest in pressuring electors, as H. T. Dickinson has put it, "to reject candidates who were courtiers, placemen, moneyed men or stockjobbers and to vote instead for men of large landed estates who could be trusted to preserve their own integrity and the liberties of the subject."[83] Country ideology sought to mobilize opposition to the Walpolean ministry in the name of the landed gentry, those who had a propertied investment in the status quo (hence the idea of a "Country Party" that transcends party). Yet the theoretical premise that such opposition took shape in the name of "the liberties of the subject" gave the ideology radical implications: "The Country interest believed that Britain could enjoy the best system of government in the world if only the balanced constitution of King, Lords and Commons was safeguarded from the alarming threat posed to it by the growing patronage at the disposal of the executive."[84] As Dickinson adds, "it is ironic that it was attacks such as these [aimed at the 'threat' posed by Walpole's system of patronage], largely mounted by the Tories, that built up the most effective indictment of the executive authority and led the way to demands for constitutional change that were to be adopted by the radicals of the later eighteenth century."[85]

It is in the spirit of this doctrine that Pope persists in a critique of corruption that cuts across class boundaries:

> 'But why insult the Poor, affront the Great?'
> A Knave's a Knave, to me, in ev'ry State,
> Alike my scorn, if he succeed or fail,
> Sporus at Court or Japhet in a Jayl,
> A hireling Scribbler, or a hireling Peer,
> Knight of the Post corrupt, or of the Shire,
> If on a Pillory, or near a Throne,
> He gain his Prince's Ear, or lose his own.
> (360–367)

At the end, the queasy sense of chiasmus in the last two lines brings home the rapidity with which the social opportunist slides in and out of public favor and the flimsiness of the distinction between the two states, a flimsiness that points to the arbitrary nature of justice in such a corrupt society.

We might expect this argument to conclude in a tribute to the virtue of the landed peerage. Pope ends instead with a portrait of his father as moral exemplar that quietly displaces any sense of class allegiance.

> Born to no pride, inheriting no Strife,
> Not marrying Discord in a Noble Wife,
> Stranger to Civil and Religious Rage,
> The good Man walk'd innoxious thro' his Age.
> No Courts he saw, no Suits would ever try,
> Nor dar'd an Oath, nor hazarded a Lye:
> Un-learn'd, he knew no Schoolman's subtle Art,
> No Language, but the Language of the Heart.
> By Nature honest, by Experience wise,
> Healthy by Temp'rance and by Exercise:
> His Life, tho' long, to sickness past unknown,
> His Death was instant, and without a groan.
> Oh grant me thus to live, and thus to die!
> Who sprung from Kings shall know less joy than I.
>   (392–405)

In holding up his father as a picture of the good life, Pope accomplishes two aims. In the first place, he insistently reminds the reader of the anti-Catholic proscriptions on education, property, and place imposed by the official Church and, in the second place, he allows us an autobiographical glimpse of his own life beneath the palimpsest of his father's story. Erskine-Hill remarks that these lines "form an Horatian *topos* quite as well known as that of the poet trying to shake off the impertinent," namely the grateful tribute to the satirist's humbly born father for providing the satirist with moral tutelage in childhood (Satire 1.6.45–99).[86] What is new and different in Pope's use of the topos is the quiet suggestion that the virtuousness of the poet's father not only does not reflect back onto society but also throws into higher relief its inequity.

The tribute deviates even further from the topos when Pope introduces the figure of his mother. For Pope's nursing of his mother is presented as analogous to Arbuthnot's nursing of the queen and thus as analogous at a more remote level to the artist's nursing of the nation. When he vows that he will "with lenient Arts extend a Mother's breath / . . . Explore the Thought, explain the asking Eye" (410, 412), Pope's strategic abstractness regarding the nature of these duties prevents the reader from taking either "lenient Arts" or "Mother" in a strictly literal sense. Ultimately, this line of implication climaxes in the idea of the writer or satirist as healer. The idea is a late variant within a tradition that stretches back to the Greek conception of logos as a cure for misplaced emotion in Plato, with special force in Aristotle, and then in the later Hellenistic philosophers. By the time of the Romans, the idea has been familiarized to the point that logos no longer need be seen solely as an instrument of philosophy. Cicero in *De Oratore* argues that the orator must be like a careful physician in preparation ("sin id aut non erit aut erit obscurius," etc., 2.44.186). Horace also writes of the curative or therapeutic value of language, most notably in Epistle 1.1.34–35. ("sunt verba et voces," etc.).

In *Arbuthnot*, the possibility is raised that Pope already is familiar with the "nostrum" for the "plague" that has attacked the poet and his society at the beginning of the poem: it is none other than poetry itself. Yet the fiction of the satirist-as-surgeon in the eighteenth-century context works at a further remove from the political realities of its own time than from those of Greece or Rome. That Arbuthnot's service to the queen belongs to the historical past ("as when he serv'd a Queen," 417; note that the image occurs as a reminiscence) complicates any political reading of Pope's nursing of his mother. If she is a figure for Mother England, she is a figure for an England that already is dead. Just as Arbuthnot's position at the court vanished with Queen Anne, Pope's authority as satirist threatens to disappear under the advancing influence of the Walpolean financial revolution on print culture. All of this results from the fact that there no longer exists the kind of ruler whom the poet could in good conscience idealize as the moral parent of the nation. The impression conveyed is that Pope has been forced into a divided position between the impulse to confirm and to parody the classical image of the poet-satirist as therapist. That the history of Arbuthnot's past career and ailing life interposes itself between the image of Pope's nursing of his mother and the idea of the poet-as-therapist throws the whole chain of metaphor into jeopardy. Here the very possibility of satire as an effective instrument of change is itself subtly satirized.

Pope takes up the mythical theme of the founding of the nation and its authorization by a mother divinity at greatest length in the *Dunciad*. The importance to the poem of the mother figure of Dulness is signaled by the opening of the 1743 edition ("The Mighty Mother, and her Son . . . I sing"), which radically alters the opening of the Variorum of 1728 ("Books and the Man I sing"). Warburton's note to the 1743 line that "the *Mother*, and not the *Son*, is the principal Agent of this Poem" only serves to underline the change. A number of critics have noted that Dulness is an example of the Magna Mater archetype, the Great Mother of the gods, often identified in the classical mythology with figures such as Ceres and Minerva.[87] It is true, for instance, that "Dulness is the 'Great Mother' accompanied by opium poppies at A 1.33, and that her lands flowing 'with clenches and with puns' (A 1.252) are not just a parody of the Biblical 'land flowing with milk and honey' but an allusion to *alma Ceres*, mother, corn, goddess, and queen of bees, who is worshipped with 'Milk and Honey.'"[88]

Yet it is less often remarked how Pope's handling of the allusion transforms its character. On this score, Brookes-Davies's assertion is not quite true that "as a model [Spenser] invited [in Pope's eyes] burlesque and ridicule."[89] For Dulness fills the role not only of a Magna Mater figure but also of an Errour figure overtly in the Spenserian train. Consider the spectacle that Dulness surveys from her throne in "the Cave of Poverty and Poetry" and how it colors our first glimpse of her.

> Here she beholds the Chaos dark and deep,
> Where nameless Somethings in their causes sleep,
> 'Till genial Jacob, or a warm Third day,
> Call forth each mass, a Poem, or a Play:
> How hints, like spawn, scarce quick in embryo lie,
> How new-born nonsense first is taught to cry,
> Maggots half-form'd in rhyme exactly meet,
> And learn to crawl upon poetic feet....
>
> All these, and more, the cloud-compelling Queen
> Beholds thro' fogs, that magnify the scene.
> She, tinsel'd o'er in robes of varying hues,
> With self-applause her wild creation views;
> Sees momentary monsters rise and fall,
> And with her own fools-colours gilds them all.
>   (55–62, 79–84)

This "wild creation" monstrously parodies the fertility customarily ascribed to Magna Mater figures such as Ceres. That it is "her" creation and one that provokes "self-applause" turns the whole scene into a disfiguration of female sexuality. For rather than serving an ideal of cultural or social utility, this creation merely leads to deluded self-approbation. In this Pope is reappropriating the Spenserian paradigm. When the Redcrosse knight encounters Errour in her den, she spews a "vomit full of bookes and papers . . . / With loathly frogs and toades, which eyes did lacke, / And creeping sought way in the weedy gras" (*Fairie Queene* 1.1.20). This "fruitfull cursed spawne" (1.1.22) Spenser likens to the offspring of the river Nile when its floodwaters recede in the spring: "Ten thousand kindes of creatures, partly male / And partly female of his fruitfull seed: / Such ugly monstrous shapes elsewhere may no man reed" (1.1.21). The myth of abiogenesis, or spontaneous generation, that has one locus classicus in Ovid (*Metamorphoses* 1.416–437), with special reference to the Nile (1.422–429), leads to a vision of unproductive fecundity that represents a fear specifically of the corruption of learning in both Spenser and Pope.

Whereas in Spenser's tale, however, the Protestant knight at all times remains a mediating presence between the reader and Errour, no such figure intervenes in Pope's poem. Instead a curious sense of authorial identification or complicity with Dulness and her minions hovers over this scene, a feeling underscored by the appearance of "genial Jacob [Tonson]," one of Pope's occasional friends and infrequent publishers. The implication of the satirist in the very crimes he seeks to arraign will eventually lead to his destruction in the poem. For in the *Dunciad*, the vandalization of language leads to Dulness's delivery of the self-annihilating command "MAKE ONE MIGHTY DUNCIAD OF THE LAND," an utterance that will ultimately silence even itself in the process of drowning out all other discourses ("'Till drown'd was Sense, and Shame, and Right, and Wrong— / O sing, and hush the Nations with thy song!" 4.625–626). Yet the pessimism of this image of linguistic abuse only serves to reflect back, in an oblique manner, the idealized potential that Pope ascribes almost everywhere else in his writings to a measured and self-aware use of language.

As I have been presenting it, the British Augustan temperament takes for granted the idea, which may scandalize more modern dispositions, that what shapes moral choice is artistic or poetic skill in its barest state: an equipoise that grows out of a commitment to self-cultivation at the expense of self-interest, a commitment gradually solidified through repeated trial and error. This is an idea everywhere evident in Pope's writings. We may happen on the most generalized expressions of it in the letters, where, perhaps in order to keep up a studied rhetorical ease, he tends to content himself with merely advancing the first half of the idea, namely, the claim that artistic creation typifies ethical action. To his old friend John Caryll, for instance, he writes, probably in January of 1733, on the subject of Caryll's sixteen-year-old grandson, whose fledgling verses had been sent to Pope: "I would rather see him a good man than a good poet; and yet a good poet is no small thing, and (I believe) no small earnest of his being a good man."[90] With a slightly more emphatic air of confession, he says to Swift in a letter that apparently dates from the following February, "I . . . have nothing so much at heart, as to show the silly world that men of Wit, or even Poets, may be the most moral of Mankind."[91] In an odd way, the adverb "even" serves here both to moderate and to intensify the force of this avowal. That poets may represent a special breed of wits and also the most moral members of society is meant to sound like a more astute claim than the same allegation on behalf of either the general run of the "silly world" or the bureaucrats who wished to purchase its acquiescence.

3

Byron, Laughter, and Legitimation

If obliged to name the defining theme of Byron's poetry, a reader would have good reason to choose the problem of legitimacy or literary authority. The poet evokes the theme at the beginning of his career in the diatribe of *English Bards and Scotch Reviewers* (1809), where with all of a twenty-one-year-old's ham-fisted self-importance he declares: "But now, so callous grown, so changed since youth, / I've learned to think and sternly speak the truth." And he voices it at the end in "On This Day I Complete My Thirty-Sixth Year" (1824), where by laying claim to a "soldier's grave" in the fight for Greek independence he proposes to write his own epitaph and thus take authorship of the public record of his life.

I will start this chapter with the observation that Byron achieved his most daring response to the problem in his satiric masterpiece *Don Juan*, which, along with his earlier poems *Childe Harold's Pilgrimage* 4 and *Beppo*, suggests a reinvention of Augustan skepticism toward social convention. Taken together, these poems discredit the accepted interpretation of history in early nineteenth-century England and Europe. Moreover, they do so most convincingly at the moments when they deny having any privileged knowledge or objective truth-value of their own. It is by articulating bathetic, indecorous, or impertinent points of view that Byron's satires bring to light the repressions of "polite," bourgeois discourse and thereby begin to articulate something like a sustained political argument against the public sphere in which they participate. Significantly, they present this very polemic as a self-conscious modernization of the Augustan project, albeit in a highly idiosyncratic sense. For Byron may be said to interpret the enterprise as an effort of mediation between ancient and modern historical frames of reference in order to arrive at a new and more open horizon of social interchange. Yet, in undertaking the effort, his satires mockingly demonstrate the impossibility of such a synthesis. The loss of a certain foundation of cultural renewal enforces in turn a sharpened sense of the historicity of culture per se. Precisely because poetry no longer can affirm a unifying Pax Augustana, it helps to envision an ambivalent state of truce between rival moral vocabularies.

Recognition of the untimeliness of the Augustan cultural ideal thus entails for Byron acknowledging the fallibility of all narratives of rational progress, hence returning ironically to something like a Horatian stance of philosophical equanimity. We may see this point most vividly illustrated, curiously enough, by a passage not from one of the satires but from the fourth canto of his quintessentially Romantic quest epic, *Childe Harold's Pilgrimage*. While traveling through Italy, Harold berates himself for a schoolboy "impatience" (4.76) that rebelled in the classroom against the tedium of studying the Latin language:

> Then farewell, Horace; whom I hated so,
> Not for thy faults, but mine; it is a curse
> To understand, not feel thy lyric flow,
> To comprehend, but never love thy verse,
> Although no deeper Moralist rehearse
> Our little life, nor Bard prescribe his art,
> Nor livelier Satirist the conscience pierce
> Awakening without wounding the touch'd heart,
> Yet fare thee well—upon Soracte's ridge we part.
>
> (4.77)

This renunciation of Horace sounds a complex note. Much of our understanding of the gesture hinges on what connotations we assign to the key term "curse," one of the poet's favorite words. The larger tone of the passage appears to be one of melodramatically inflated regret, neither the high tragic sang-froid of Manfred when he exclaims "By the strong curse which is upon my soul" (1.1.47) nor the low comic exasperation of *Don Juan*'s narrator when he blusters "With one good hearty curse I vent my gall" (6.22). As with many of Childe Harold's pronouncements in the poem, the rhetoric flirts with self-parody without ever quite yielding to the impulse. The exaggeration, however, falls in a more subdued register than that of his megalomaniacal outburst in the third canto: "He who surpasses or subdues mankind / Must look down on the hate of those below" (3.45). That some latent hint of the absurd hovers over the image of the superhuman Harold swearing as he toils to memorize the basic Latin declensions and construe Horace's verse seems plausible; that it is anything more than latent seems doubtful.

At any rate, the overt self-indictment of the speaker's curse surreptitiously works to reaffirm the very classical virtues it ostensibly disclaims. The strategy is paradoxical insofar as the sustained deprecation of his own parochial, modern insensibility to Horace's subtleties keeps those subtleties in the reader's view with an urgency that acts of praise would be hard pressed to match. Beneath the surface of Harold's rhetoric we may detect an anxiety of regression that redeems the overall sentiment from the affected callousness of the valediction. Understanding without feeling and comprehension without love are made to look like botched or debased attempts at the sort of unprejudiced intelligence that a knowledgeable reader of Horace would recognize as the mentality of *nil admirari*. By comparison to the cultivated judiciousness that enables the Roman satirist to arouse "without wounding" his addressee's conscience, Harold is left with little more than chagrin at his own superficiality of knowledge, an embarrassment we see veering into self-hatred. Byron gives a sly parting twist to this comparison when he fixes the scene on the ridge of Mount Soracte (now Sant' Oreste), a location that figures in the opening of Horace's Carmen 1.9.

> Vide ut alta stet nive candidum
> Soracte, nec iam sustineant onus
> silvae laborantes, geluque
> flumina constiterint acuto.
>
> See how the deep snow whitens Soracte
> and the trees can no longer support the weight
> of that gelid burden, and the rivers
> are congealed by penetrating frost.[1]
>
> (1–4)

The lyrical evocation of the scene is colored by the speaker's projection onto the natural landscape of melancholy at his own advancing age. Although such a tactic may all too easily be made to serve the purposes of self-pity, the worldliness of the speaker lends credence to the poem's advocacy of a spirit of hedonistic opportunism. For Carmen 1.9 is an erotic ode in which the poet urges a young boy not to spurn the pleasures of "sweet love" ("nec dulcis amores sperne / puer," 15–16) but rather to seize what momentary gratifications he may while still in the bloom of youth. In this context, the snow-clad vista of Soracte provides a convenient symbol for the ode's implicit argument that, no less than geological or meteorological events, human experiences have their natural places and seasons. Horace's encouragement of youthful philandering therefore presumes a long view of the life well lived with respect to the use of one's abilities.

A more than casual irony suffuses Byron's invocation of the Horatian ode in the course of his diatribe against the historical apathy and myopia that constitute the modern conditions of knowledge. When Harold takes leave of Horace with the pronouncement "upon Soracte's ridge we part," we may surmise his words to be more telling than he himself realizes. To the Roman poet the mountain signifies the natural propriety of sustained intellectual, emotional, and moral self-cultivation. To the Romantic adventurer it represents a kind of cognitive or logical impossibility after the fashion of the sublime; it therefore fails altogether to signify. Byron's description of Soracte as a shape that "from out the plain / Heaves like a long-swept wave about to break" (4.75) clearly upholds a traditional association of the confounding terror of the sublime with the violence of the sea. The convention dates back at least to Longinus's illustration of such terror in the tenth chapter of *On the Sublime*. Longinus's handling of the topic crucially invokes the Homeric simile in *Iliad* 15.624–628 that likens Hektor's ferocity toward the Greeks to the ocean's stormy battering of a ship.

Childe Harold's apostasy from the classical Augustan (or at any rate Horatian) ideal of self-actualization thereby unexpectedly works to revitalize the modern Augustan ethos of radical epistemological uncertainty. Indeed, his pausing at Soracte and apostrophizing of Horace reinforce his consistent reading throughout the poem of ancient Rome's monumental traces (what he calls "the steps of broken thrones and temples" in stanza 78) as indications of the arbitrariness of historical change. With an almost Piranesian eye for the funereal, Harold views the ruins of Rome as mocking refutations of the myth of providential order espoused by modern commercial society. As I have shown in the examples of Dryden and Pope, a historical optimism justified on exclusively materialistic grounds was an article of faith that looked profoundly untrustworthy to the British Augustans. In a similarly wary mood, Harold's invective against his own lack of learning undermines any evolutionary narrative according to which Regency England may regard itself as culturally or politically superior to the Roman *principate*. In so doing, his "curse" elaborates a sense of history as a precariously accidental or irrational chain of events.

Byron's poetry thus recuperates the feeling of crisis that, as we know, James Noggle associates with the "skeptical sublime" of the Tory satirists. What Noggle says of Pope's posture in the *Dunciad* might well be said of Byron's in *Childe Harold's Pilgrimage*, that "in undertaking poetically to represent the gravity of the threat to . . . [his ostensible] values by indicating the impossibility of their survival, Pope himself lays hold of the power that he admits must destroy his own moralism, defying the promptings of epistemological perversion even as they speak through him."[2] Indeed, Harold's contemplation of Rome adopts the language of the *Dunciad* with startling felicity and much the same ironic grandeur.

> The Goth, the Christian, Time, War, Flood, and Fire,
> Have dealt upon the seven-hill'd city's pride;
> She saw her glories star by star expire,
> And up the steep barbarian monarchs ride,
> Where the car climb'd the capitol; far and wide
> Temple and tower went down, nor left a site:—
> Chaos of ruins! who shall trace the void,

> O'er the dim fragments cast a lunar light,
> And say, "here was, or is," where all is doubly night?
>
> The double night of ages, and of her,
> Night's daughter, Ignorance, hath wrapt and wrap
> All round us; we but feel our way to err:
> The ocean hath his chart, the stars their map,
> And Knowledge spreads them on her ample lap;
> But Rome is as the desert, where we steer
> Stumbling o'er recollections; now we clap
> Our hands, and cry "Eureka!" it is clear—
> When but some false mirage of ruin rises near.
>   (4.80–81)

Byron constructs an allegory of cultural catastrophe in these stanzas that inverts Horace's gesture in Carmen 1.9. Instead of finding in the workings of nature symbols of the necessity of human society, Harold alarmingly discerns signs of its futility. In its misogynistic representation of the threat to the masculine civic order by a feminized decadence, the human phenomenon of Ignorance reveals itself to be a cousin of Pope's Dulness, hence a potential relative of the classical figure of Fortuna as the chaotic nemesis of ordering virtue. J. G. A. Pocock's reminder that Machiavelli's adaptation of this figure to the analysis of Renaissance politics inspired in turn its reappropriation by eighteenth-century British political discourse is not without relevance to Byron's association of Ignorance with modernity.[3] Harold's emphasis on the "double" benightedness that Ignorance inflicts on the amnesia-prone consciousness of the present argues that historical shortsightedness results not in the confirmation but in the derivative, parodic simulation of nature. If we do not learn to read the historical signs, we doom ourselves to trip over our phantasmatic, mirage-like "recollections" and so, Harold implies, to further lose our bearings. Byron poetically underscores the moral through a beautifully gauged, subtly fatiguing use of alliteration ("star by star," "car climb'd the capitol," "temple and tower," "lunar light," "wrapt and wrap") that makes repetition per se seem a baleful force. In this light, the triumph of "barbarian monarchs" over Rome looks like a historical absurdity: an annihilating backlash of imperial violence with none of the Roman empire's beneficial aftereffects in the domains of civil administration or the arts and sciences.

This historically pessimistic picture provides the framing context for a bathetic confrontation between the poetic spokesperson and his classical precursor that belongs to the tradition of the Popean parody of Virgil in the *Dunciad*, book 3. Anchises' prophecy in *Aeneid* 6 of an *aurea saecula* in which Augustus Caesar would unite a Roman empire stretching as far to the east as

India and to the south as North Africa is stood on its head by Pope's Settle, when he foretells the Gothic sack of Rome:

> Lo! where Maeotis sleeps, and hardly flows
> The freezing Tanais through a waste of snows,
> The North by myriads pours her mighty sons,
> Great nurse of Goths, of Alans, and of Huns! ...
>
> See, where the morning gilds the palmy shore
> (The soil that arts and infant letters bore)
> His conqu'ring tribes th'Arabian prophet draws,
> And saving Ignorance enthrones by laws.
>
> (3.87–90, 95–98)

Eventually Pope conflates the barbarian impulses of the Germanic tribes responsible for the sack of Rome not only with the non-Western threat of conquest by "th'Arabian prophet" but also, and more important, with the banality of England's unrelentingly commercialized social order as governed by a House of Hanover "where Dunce the second rules like Dunce the first" (1.6). A threat of violence external to society, Pope seems to be saying, has been imported by the antiintellectual and mercenary forces internal to society. The epic language of heroic conflict gives way in these lines to the satiric language of corruption, which eloquently captures the debasement of a culture hostile to the interests of those authors who represent its best hope for renewal and for the expression of political dissent and who all happen to belong to Pope's coterie: "Gay dies unpension'd with a hundred friends, / Hibernian Politics, O Swift! thy fate; / And Pope's, ten years to comment and translate" (3.330–332). The satire's anxiety of ethical and intellectual decline culminates in the famous, apocalyptic vision of Dulness's victory over civilization:

> She comes! she comes! the sable Throne behold
> Of Night Primaeval, and of Chaos old! ...
>
> As one by one, at dread Medea's strain,
> The sick'ning stars fade off th'etherial plain;
> As Argus' eyes by Hermes' wand opprest,
> Clos'd one by one to everlasting rest;
> Thus at her felt approach, and secret might,
> Art after Art goes out, and all is Night.
>
> (4.630–631, 635–640)

The rhetoric of this passage resonates throughout the Byronic adaptation. Both Pope and Byron stress an epistemological darkness or blindness that coincides with a loss of historical memory. Both poets hint that the real danger of obscurantism consists in its efficiency of self-perpetuation, the ruthlessness with which it snuffs out the lights of knowledge "one by one."

Byron, who early in *Childe Harold's Pilgrimage* 4 makes reference to Austria's renewed subjugation of Venice as of 1814 ("the Suabian sued, and now the Austrian reigns," 4.12) and who in *The Vision of Judgment* revives to amusing effect Pope's defamatory association of Gothic brutality with the boorishness of the Hanoverian monarchs, may toy with the allegorical linkage between ancient Goths and modern Germans, but if so he keeps it at a practically subliminal level. Of more immediate interest is the insinuation behind Harold's use of the plural first person ("we but feel our way to err," etc.) that he himself belongs to the train of Ignorance, a message facilitated by the condemnation of his own incapacity to read Horace with greater ease. The notion that Harold himself may be a modern barbarian consorts with a certain idiom of self-deprecation that Byron employs most persistently and to greatest advantage in the satires. In *Beppo*, for example, he characterizes the writing as "rambling verse" (52) and in *Don Juan* describes his poem as "merely quizzical" (9.41). His satire relies, then, in important ways on the devices of self-satire to achieve its ends. Its author thereby lays claim to a kind of negative self-awareness—a sense of the limits of personal knowledge—that Noggle regards as exemplary of the British Augustan sensibility. As he puts it, the distinguishing feature of this sensibility is "a power to remain ironic, as it were, in the very insistence that the ironic distance between [the poet] and the satirized butt has collapsed. At this limit of ironic reflection and differentiation, the satirist has brought the typical sublime blending of object into subject into its uniquely Augustan register."[4] Yet Byron, it should be noted, collapses this "ironic distance" with such a vengeance that his revival of modern Augustan historicism seems to place the order of post-Napoleonic social relations under the gaze of a new extreme of skepticism. By impugning his own deficiencies of understanding, he throws into higher relief the effrontery of a cultural and political conservatism that grasps at absolute authority, which is by definition impossible.

Other readers have noticed the paradoxical, self-questioning ironies of Byron's satire without, I think, fully acknowledging their significance as forms of polemic or protest. Jerome McGann rightly declares that Byron's facetious "attack upon the Europe of Napoleon, Metternich, and Castlereagh is made possible because he agrees . . . 'to become what he beholds.'"[5] However, McGann's contention that the task undertaken by the poet is "to break free of language altogether in order to achieve an unmediated set of responses" and thereby "to translate its observations . . . into equivalent emotional signs" gives poetry an ontological weight that, as I shall attempt to show a bit later, Byron does not believe it possesses.[6] Worse, by so suppressing the interpretive nature of satire, McGann robs the mode of any possible moral or ethical burden beyond that of a sentimentalized journalism.

Jerome Christensen assesses more persuasively the iconoclastic value of the poet's mocking self-critique:

> In the wake of the public failure of traditional metaphors to fit and enlightened ones to be fully adopted [in early nineteenth-century England], a new figure emerged on the contemporary scene as the figure *of* the contemporary. That figure ... became the culturally dominant and economically profitable phenomenon called "Byron." ... In the aftermath of Waterloo Byronism took on an imperial dimension, which reached its fullest scope in *Childe Harold* IV. This empire conspicuously began to unravel with the publication of *Don Juan*, which, in apposition to Byronism, addressed a strong, ethical challenge to the murmurous complacencies of commercial society.[7]

Although I have tried to suggest that there is at least a moment in *Childe Harold's Pilgrimage* when that poem anticipates *Don Juan*'s increasingly radical contemplation of its own historical situation, Christensen is right that the shift of Byron's later poetry from a largely Romantic to a largely satiric mode represents an ideological turn against a commercial society in which the poet felt himself to have been implicated. The critic immediately retreats from the logical consequences of his own reading, however, assuring us that he does not wish to be understood as proposing "a new stage of development or a sudden access of consciousness that occurs between *Childe Harold* and *Juan*," because of the risk thereby of reaffirming Romanticism's "repeatedly embarrassed claims to transcendence."[8] Instead, he construes *Don Juan* as the enactment of a literary "circumstantial gravity," a sort of commodified zeitgeist that exposes the emptiness of the cultural marketplace and so ironically points out a horizon of potential resistance.[9]

In spite of its wording, Christensen's theory clearly implies that the poem's achievement of such an effect, sustained over the course of its serial publication, is not itself entirely accidental or "circumstantial" but deliberate; Byron's satire still must be reckoned with from the perspective of its ethical or political ramifications. James Chandler speculates that by complicating "the relation of intelligibility and causation" at those moments when "most involved with the topic or practice of explanation," *Don Juan* espouses a "principle of autonomy" that in the political domain aligns itself with "the liberal cause."[10] Yet Chandler concludes that it is precisely the satire's insistence on its freedom from dogma that in the end undercuts its own assertion of its ostensible political rationale: "The question of whether the case of *Don Juan* may be said to have a cause remains suspended in its contradictions."[11] Such a suspension represents in his eyes Byron's original contribution to the "casuistry" of Romantic historicism: the mystificatory reading of a historically specific event or "case" as exemplary of an explanatory general principle. In this light, Byron's satire may be regarded as casuistical in the perplexing sense of unmasking the fictive operations of such a principle.

All three of these readers, it seems to me, grapple at length with a fundamental peculiarity of his writing: namely, that his chief method of attacking the repressions or bad consciousness of the British and European monarchies in the period following Waterloo is to embrace a position of scandalous irrelevance or inutility to the cultural agenda of the modern, commercial nation-state. In a sense, the more his poetry admits its frivolity or lack of authenticity from the perspective of social orthodoxy, the more it calls into question the criteria and procedures of authentication by which that orthodoxy perpetuates itself. An eloquent, exemplary application of this rhetorical strategy occurs toward the beginning of the fourth canto of *Don Juan*:

> And if I laugh at any mortal thing,
>   'Tis that I may not weep; and if I weep,
> 'Tis that our nature cannot always bring
>   Itself to apathy. . . .
>
> Some have accused me of a strange design
>   Against the creed and morals of the land,
> And trace it in this poem every line:
>   I don't pretend that I quite understand
> My own meaning when I would be *very* fine;
>   But the fact is that I have nothing plann'd,
> Unless it were to be a moment merry,
> A novel word in my vocabulary.
>
> (4.4, 4.6)

The disavowal of any "strange design" in the writing of the poem refers to the charges of immorality and the atmosphere of controversy that greeted the publication of the poem's first two cantos. Byron's mixture in the poem of sexual innuendo, half-veiled lampooning of his legally separated wife, religious irreverence, and broadsides against figures central to the literary and political establishment of the day such as Southey and Castlereagh provoked consternation from his friends and priggish disapproval from the critics.[12] As is well known, anxieties ran so high within Byron's inner circle regarding the legality of the material that the publisher, John Murray, printed the initial run of the first two cantos without either the author's name or his own.[13] The poet's defense that he has no conscious hostility to the "creed and morals of the land" such as his critics accuse him of espousing raises the possibility instead that he might have an *un*conscious antipathy to the prevailing norms of the political consensus. The lines thus may be said to imply a version of the Juvenalian claim that indignation necessitates poetry ("facit indignatio versum," Satire 1.68). Byron sets up the Juvenalian pose when he alleges that his satirical laughter represents the creative sublimation of a deeper anguish over history's "mortal" conditions, a grief that otherwise would cause him to weep. Furthermore, by denying any premeditated meaning or intention he foregrounds poetry's general lack of seriousness (which he associates with the ideal of the "merry") and thereby undermines potential charges of libel or sedition. To write satire, he intimates, is necessarily to stand outside the law, hence to enunciate perspectives that the morality of the law considers to be intolerable.[14]

Here I want to resume a line of reasoning familiar from earlier observations. I have tried to suggest in what ways the cultural liberalism of Dryden and Pope both affirms and complicates Habermas's vision of a "bourgeois public sphere" emerging at the start of the eighteenth century where "the private people, come together to form a public, readied themselves to compel public authority to legitimate itself before public opinion."[15] My contention has been that the British Augustan satirists must be said to contribute to the formation of the public sphere in a highly ironic sense. That is, their very appeals to authority to justify itself call into question the universality of the rules of reason by which such justification is supposed to proceed. Byron gives this irony a yet more radical turn. Positively avowing the incommensurability of human passions to such rules, he posits the very task of justifying or legitimating authority as an ideological mystification and, as such, irretrievably corrupt. In this light, his example may be seen to prefigure Habermas's argument in *The Structural Transformation of the Public Sphere* that, beginning in the nineteenth century, the institutions and practices of the public sphere are transformed by capitalism "so that precisely their remaining in private hands in many ways threatened the critical functions of publicist institutions."[16] Rather than providing a forum for the synthesis of diverse private interests into a genuine political consensus, the public sphere then becomes a machine for the manufacture of conformity. The philosopher further diagnoses this transformation in *Legitimation Crisis*, where he argues that the advance of capitalism since the nineteenth century "not only frees the economic system, uncoupled from the political system, from the legitimations of the socially integrative subsystems, but enables it, along with its system integrative tasks, to make a contribution to social integration. With these achievements, the susceptibility of the social system to crisis certainly grows, as steering problems [i.e., difficulties in systemic decision-making] can now become *directly* threatening to identity."[17] Byronic satire, it seems to me, may be read in the spirit of Habermas's theory of crisis as an early analysis of the effects of the failure of legitimating norms on the identity of the nation or "social system."[18]

Beppo certainly invites such a reading. The poem depicts Venice as a society in which the cultural heterogeneity of the disguises worn by the reveling populace during Carnival manifests a fluidity or instability of identity that Byron comically implies is the everyday state of affairs resulting from a paucity of regulating rules.

> And there are dresses splendid, but fantastical,
>   Masks of all times and nations, Turks and Jews,
> And harlequins and clowns, with feats gymnastical,
>   Greeks, Romans, Yankee-Doodles, and Hindoos;
> All kinds of dress, except the ecclesiastical.
>   (stanza 3)

Even the taboo hinted at in the final line against insulting the clergy reveals its emptiness in the following stanza when the poetic narrator warns that any such sacrilege will result in dire punishment at the hands of the authorities, "unless you paid them double." The running joke of such passages consists in the narrator's unperturbed pleasure in an urban physiognomy in which appearances and realities never quite coincide and social purposes and roles can be changed or revised at a whim. On this reckoning, it should come as no surprise that the poem persistently resorts to metaphors of dress to advance its satiric project. This tactic is evident in local elements such as the witty description in stanza 19 of the celebrated Venetian gondola as an object that looks "like a coffin clapt in a canoe." Byron quickly shows that this association is as temporary and changeable as the "livery" of funeral mourners:

> And up and down the long canals they go,
>   And under the Rialto shoot along,
> By night and day, all paces, swift or slow,
>   And round the theatres, a sable throng,
> They wait in their dusk livery of woe,
>   But not to them do woeful things belong,
> For sometimes they contain a deal of fun,
> Like mourning coaches when the funeral's done.
>   (stanza 20)

Gondolas capture the spirit of Venice by embodying not some indigenous picturesque quality but rather a sort of ironic pragmatism with respect to social forms that in fact precludes a naive or fetishizing overvaluation of appearances. The narrator's casual linkage of gondolas and "theatres" subtly reinforces the message.

The same tactic of focusing on the overdetermined surfaces of Venetian experience in order to suggest the instability of the supposed depths or reserves of identity beneath pervades the elaboration of *Beppo*'s central narrative. This comic tale recounts the eponymous hero's return to Venice to reclaim "wife, religion, house, and Christian name" (stanza 97) after several years of living on the sea as a castaway turned Turkish pirate. All three of the central characters—Beppo, his wife, Laura, and her lover, the Count—are presented as virtuosi of social manipulation. Much of the story's drollery derives from the contrast between their proficiency and the anticlimactic lack of recognition that greets Beppo's appearance at the end (stanzas 87–90). This incomprehension is not what we might expect from characters that are such emphatically visual creatures. Laura's description when she and the Count attend a masked ball is telling in this regard:

> Laura, when drest, was (as I sang before)
> A pretty woman as was ever seen,
> Fresh as the Angel o'er a new inn door,
> Or frontispiece of a new Magazine,
> With all the fashions which the last month wore,
> Coloured, and silver paper leav'd between
> That and the title-page, for fear the press
> Should soil with parts of speech the parts of dress.
>   (stanza 57)

The language of this stanza resuscitates the Popean trick of encouraging a hedonistic fascination with the spectacle of bourgeois society to the point at which the feeling approaches its limits and hints at something like jadedness. Laura has been made to look appealing but inhuman in the manner of a street sign or magazine advertisement. The parallelism in the last line smartly captures the homogeneity of a world in which both language and clothing have been reduced to utterly fetishized commodities. When she makes her entrance at the dance hall, her self-presentation alters according to expectation with mechanical efficiency:

> Now Laura moves along the joyous crowd,
> Smiles in her eyes, and simpers on her lips;
> To some she whispers, others speaks aloud;
> To some she curtsies, and to some she dips.
>   (stanza 65)

Laura's dexterity at gauging the interest of others as she makes her way through the multitude recalls the famous depiction of Belinda in Pope's *Rape of the Lock*: "Favours to none, to all she Smiles extends, / Oft she rejects, but never once offends" (2.10–11). As a marriagable member of eighteenth-century England's Catholic moneyed class, Belinda's impersonal coquetry in the end serves her interest of finding a suitable match and thereby the larger aim of perpetuating the institution of the bourgeois nuclear family. (Although Pope smilingly assails her virginal reserve with respect to the Baron's advances, her place in the libidinal economy as the poet depicts it seems preordained.) In contrast to Belinda, Laura's "airs and triumph" at the Ridotto, where "well-drest males still kept before her filing, / And passing bowed and mingled with her chat" (stanza 69), upholds no such program, since, as Byron amusingly remarks, she already possesses not only a husband but also a "vice husband" (stanza 29), thus enjoying "a *second* marriage which corrupts the *first*" (stanza 36). The very idea of marriage is evacuated by the infinite regress of admirers vying for her attention, suitors who together with Laura and the other women in the throng incarnate a system of amoral, free-floating desire.

This uniquely Venetian economy points up the hypocrisy of England's own sexual marketplace, which, while lacking devices such as the *cavalier servente* for satisfying the libido's anarchic promptings, nonetheless provides the same sort of public forum as the Ridotto for their voyeuristic excitation. As the narrator tells us, Venice's favored ballroom is exactly "(on a smaller scale) like our Vauxhall" (stanza 58), that is, a space ruled by "the demagogues of fashion" (stanza 60). Fashion, on his view, is the domestic guise of none other than "Fortune" (stanza 61), that capricious divinity who, determining "the present, past, and all to be yet, / . . . gives us luck in lotteries, love, and marriage" (stanza 62). Byron thus identifies the social function of institutions such as the Ridotto and Vauxhall with the familiar allegorical icon that, I already have observed, may supply the model for the figure of Ignorance in *Childe Harold's Pilgrimage* 4. As we know from Pocock's authoritative analysis, however, eighteenth-century writers associated Fortune chiefly with the figure of Credit in order both to deplore and to defend England's commercial revolution under the early years of Hanoverian rule.[19] Byron's reinterpretation of the metaphor seems to suggest that the corrupting influence of this sort of modern consumerism has advanced to the point of invading our very sexual being. One may confront this disquieting fact either with pragmatism, as the Venetians do, or with blindness.

If there is one personage in the poem who seems less worried about the legitimation or rationalization of his actions than the always matter-of-fact Laura, it is the inexhaustibly adaptable Beppo, who is capable both of passing for a "Turk, the colour of mahogany" (stanza 70) and of resuming his place in Venice as casually as if merely putting on a fresh set of clothes.

> His wife received, the patriarch rebaptized him,
>   (He made the church a present by the way);
> He then threw off the garments which disguised him,
>   And borrowed the Count's small-clothes for the day.
>   (stanza 98)

Beppo's ability to mobilize wife, church, and even his chief rival in support of his reintegration into Western society appears to represent a further instance of the cheerful unconcern with scruples that allows him to survive after being cast away at sea. As the narrator tells us, Beppo dramatically reverses his misfortune, turning an encounter with pirates to his distinct advantage: "He joined the rogues and prospered, and became / A renegado of indifferent fame" (stanza 94). His eventual recovery of comfortable, bourgeois respectability with his return to Venice thus is predicated on a capacity to operate successfully outside the boundaries of "civilized" morality and law. Moreover, since his conduct does not affirm the expected cultural codes, his identity in the poem becomes a function strictly of context or situation. The narrator thus is free to refer to Beppo as "the Mussulman" (stanza 87) and "the Turk" (stanza 88) until the moment in the narrative when he reveals his history to Laura and the Count.

The thought that the individual's increasingly mutable social character may reflect a modern crisis in our basic principles of linguistic exchange and historical self-imagination provides Byron with one of *Don Juan*'s central themes. In the course of Byron's epic comedy, the hero encounters a cast of characters whose modernity is reflected in their differences of nationality, race, and sexual practice. The experience exposes the presumption of regarding the standards of European society as universal norms. Juan's farcical encounter in canto 6 with the seventeen-year-old harem girl Dudù is an exemplary moment. After Juan has been sold at Constantinople into the service of Gulbeyaz, the sultana, he is dressed as a female slave in order to deceive the jealous eye of the sultan and assigned during the night to bed with the other women in the seraglio, where he is paired with Dudù. The narrator describes her beauty in terms that suggest a familiar narrative of the encounter between modern European commerce and the relics of an ancient, orientalized Greek culture.

> A kind of sleepy Venus seemed Dudù
>   Yet very fit to 'murder sleep' in those
> Who gazed upon her cheek's transcendant hue,
>   Her Attic forehead, and her Phidian nose. . . .
> She looked (this simile's quite new) just cut
>   From marble, like Pygmalion's statue waking,
> The Mortal and the Marble still at strife,
>   And timidly expanding into life.
>   (6.42–43)

Dudù's Venus-like aspect, "Attic forehead," and "Phidian nose" signify the naive aesthetic harmony of a classical sculpture inviting the consumeristic gaze of the nineteenth-century European connoisseur. She represents a fetishized "marble," as she is labeled a moment later, to the Lord Elgin–like narrator. Yet while her interpolation into the Pygmalion myth assigns her the role of the objectified and subjugated female artwork in a banal male fantasy of erotic wish-fulfillment, the motif also hints at the possibility of her "waking" into intellectual and sexual autonomy, upsetting the assumed distinctions between the material and the transcendent, the natural and the artificial, the primitive and the civilized.

Indeed, the narrator undermines his initial work of depiction a few stanzas later when he tells us that Dudù's natural consistency of proportion makes her artistically unrepresentable. The narrator explains that she possesses "the most regulated charms of feature, / Which painters cannot catch like faces sinning / Against proportion" (6.52). In the next stanza, we learn that such "charms" do not belong to art but to nature, as Dudù's attributes are likened to "a soft Landscape of mild Earth, / Where all was harmony and quiet, / Luxuriant, budding" (6.53). The line of reasoning that has resulted in this reversal of terms leads the narrator to a complicating, ironic conclusion:

> And therefore was she kind and gentle as
>   The age of Gold (when Gold was yet unknown,
> By which its nomenclature came to pass;
>   Thus most appropriately has been shown
> "Lucus a *non* Lucendo," *not* what *was*,
>   But what *was not*; a sort of style that's grown
> Extremely common in this age, whose metal
> The Devil may decompose but never settle;
>
> I think it may be of "Corinthian Brass,"
>   Which was a Mixture of all Metals, but
> The Brazen uppermost).
>   (6.55–56)

A sense of clashing historical and cultural horizons pervades the narrator's perception of Dudù as the embodiment of worldliness or civilized hospitality. She herself exemplifies a long-lost, Eastern urbanity of manners that in its antique strangeness or alterity abashes the "brazen" falsehood of "this age," which the narrator clearly associates with the modernity of the post-Napoleonic West. The claim that Dudù is "kind and gentle as / The age of Gold" thus implies the confrontation of a sophisticated, foreign *ancienneté* by a European mind that experiences its own comparative youth as a bathetic cultural shallowness or barbarity. By invoking Saint Paul's mockery of the self-importance of the uncharitable in Corinthians 1:13 ("Though I speak with the tongues of men and of angels, and have not charity, I am become as sounding brass"), the narrator moreover aligns the modernity of the West with a "brazen" parochialism that, like the Christian believer prior to the enlightenment of conversion, "spake as a child." The overall impression, it seems to me, is of an irreconcilability of cultural perspectives that ultimately presents Dudù to the reader as a sort of psychological paradox or enigma.

The self-mocking depiction of the poet's present day as an Age of Bronze renews the typically British Augustan avowal of a thwarted desire to share the Roman confidence in a fated *aurea saecula*. Byron's skepticism regarding England's place in world history in this sense may be seen to emulate his favorite writers, but with a radical twist. By positioning the formulaic drama of imperial decline and fall against the backdrop of advancing modern confrontation between East and West, the poem reinterprets Augustan historical pessimism from a Byronic perspective that, as Saree Makdisi points out, the satirist first articulated in *Childe Harold's Pilgrimage*:

> Harold's arrival in the East represents a passage across a multidimensional "border" into the space and time of the Orient, a space-time that . . . is a discrete spatio-temporal sphere, different from that of the West which Harold leaves behind. . . . Byron conceives the historical relationship between East and West in synchronic, rather than diachronic, terms. Indeed, he could conceive of the Orient as a spatial alternative to Europe precisely because he sees European and Oriental histories as distinct—as synchronic *histories*, rather than as one diachronic *History* narrated and controlled by Europe.[20]

This fragmentation of History into histories has severe consequences for the public sphere in the Habermasian sense. Because the boundaries of public discourse are being expanded and renegotiated, the problem of political consensus has been exacerbated to the point of crisis. The challenge to modern society is to adapt to the historical proliferation of cultural horizons without sacrificing the capacity for judgment that makes social and political action possible. It is in Byron's revisionist account of the siege of Ismail in cantos 7 and 8 that he composes for us his fullest portrait of imperial Europe's incapacity to meet this challenge. The incapacity, as he points out at the beginning of canto 7, grows out of a general coarsening of sensibilities.

> They accuse me—Me—the present writer of
>   The present poem—of—I know not what,—
> A tendency to under-rate and scoff
>   At human power and virtue, and all that;
> And this they say in language rather rough.
>
> (7.3)

Readers misconstrue both "the present writer" and "the present poem," perhaps taking too much at face value Byron's profession of epic intention, an aim he both affirms and ridicules a moment later when he defines his central theme as "fierce loves and faithless wars," travestying Spenser, who advertises his own subject in the *Fairie Queene* as "fierce warres and faithfull loves." Do not expect the conventional epic celebration of empire, Byron seems to be warning us. In fact, a lapse in taste has resulted in the public's inability to recognize *Don Juan* as a serious work of poetry.

Byron, it should be noted, is teasing his readers in a subtle manner here. The main sources on which cantos 7 and 8 draw are not so much mythic or poetic paradigms as historical reportage, specifically Gabriel Marquis de Castelnau's *Essai sur l'histoire ancienne et moderne de la Nouvelle Russie* (1820). The poet is rubbing his critics' noses in their expectations of a comfortably familiar fantasy. He will turn the tables on them by showing that facetiousness is far more innocent than candor, that human brutality is more likely to be exposed by the urge to unblinking historical realism than to irreverence. The real risk is not of underrating or scoffing at power and virtue but of blindly accepting a received idealization of human worth. This warning has a definite political or ideological edge. For it cuts against a reverential or idolatrous attitude with respect to the existing institutions of society, urging instead an attempt at critical engagement. In Byron's case, this engagement commences in the satirizing of his source material. Castelnau delivers an approving report of the attack by the Russian army in the name of the Empress Catherine on the Turkish city of Ismail beginning on November 30, 1790. The monarchist sympathies of Castelnau's history are sharply on display in a number of passages that Byron chooses to incorporate directly into his poem. Yet the poet's rehabilitation of the source material supplies him with occasion for pronounced sarcasm.

The roll call in the *Essai* of the French emigrés and volunteers who fought in support of the Russian troops led by Aleksandr Suvorov identifies only the prominent members of the nobility and reverts to an insistently propagandistic or hyperbolic set of descriptive terms.

> On ne tarirait pas si on voulait rapporter tout ce que les Russes firent de memorable dans cette journée; pour contrer les hauts faits d'armes, pour particulariser toutes les actions d'éclat, il faudrait composer des volumes. Parmi les étrangers, le prince de Ligne se distingua de manière à meriter l'estime générale; de vrais chevaliers français, attirés par l'amour de la gloire, se montrerent dignes d'elle: les plus marquants etaient le jeune duc de Richelieu, les comtes de Langeron et de Damas.[21]

Byron reappropriates this account in a manner that initially appears to promise an exact or close translation of French prose into English verse but instead rapidly moves to something more like an aggressive travesty of the original.

> "If" (says the historian here) "I could report
>   All that the Russians did upon this day,
> I think that several volumes would fall short,
>   And I should still have many things to say;"
> And so he says no more—but pays his court
>   To some distinguished strangers in that fray;
> The Prince de Ligne, and Langeron, and Damas,
> Names great as any that the roll of Fame has.
>
> This being the case, may show us what fame *is*:
>   For out of these three "*preux Chevaliers*," how
> Many of common readers give a guess
>   That such existed? (and they may live now
> For aught we know). Renown's all hit or miss;
>   There's Fortune even in fame, we must allow.
> 'Tis true, the Memoirs of the Prince de Ligne
> Have half withdrawn from *him* oblivion's screen.
>
> But here are men who fought in gallant actions
>   As gallantly as ever heroes fought,
> But buried in the heap of such transactions
>   Their names are rarely found, nor often sought.
> Thus even good fame may suffer sad contractions,
>   And is extinguished sooner than she ought:
> Of all our modern battles, I will bet
> You can't repeat nine names from each Gazette.
>   (7.32–34)

The last line of stanza 32 pays out a compliment in the spirit of Castelnau's flattery of the nobility that the following verses immediately retract. The narrator of the poem wickedly collapses the patronymics "Prince de Ligne," "Langeron," and "Damas" into the generic "three 'preux Chevaliers,'" as if to demonstrate the ease with which family and personal histories may be dismantled and reduced to empty titles, thus denying the bearers any share of honor specific to their exploits. Even the memorial operation of the versified "roll of Fame" is undercut by the narrator's parenthetical reminder at the fourth line of stanza 33 that some of the participants may not yet belong to history—and, indeed, at the time of composition in 1822 both the Comte de Langeron and the Comte de Damas were still alive. All of these deflating gestures are moralized by the movement of the rhyme words in stanza 34 down a diminishing scale of praise from "actions" to "transactions" to "contractions," a movement exemplary of the rhetorical impetus of the passage as a whole and that humiliatingly results in the implied relegation of Castelnau's *Essai* to a position no better than that of a "gazette."

Castelnau's disillusioning fall within the poem from the status of a prestigious source of history to that of mere tabloid journalism indicates a shift in the direction of political revaluation that is founded on a growing skepticism toward the ostensible "facts" of Castelnau's history. To approach dissent in *Don Juan* is thus also to approach the project of fictive invention. Byron presses the point as he catalogs the Russian soldiers who participated in the siege.

> The Russians now were ready to attack;
>   But oh, ye Goddesses of war and glory!
> How shall I spell the name of each Cossacque
>   Who were immortal, could one tell their story?
> Alas! what to their memory can lack?
>   Achilles' self was not more grim and gory
> Than thousands of this new and polished nation,
> Whose names want nothing but—pronunciation.
>
> Still I'll record a few, if but to encrease
>   Our euphony—there was Strongenoff, and Strokonoff,
> Meknop, Serge Lwow, Arseniew of modern Greece,
>   And Tschitsshakoff, and Roguenoff, and Chokenoff,
> And others of twelve consonants a-piece;
>   And more might be found out, if I could poke enough
> Into gazettes; but Fame (capricious strumpet)
> It seems, has got an ear as well as trumpet,
>
> And cannot tune these discords of narration,
>   Which may be names at Moscow, into rhyme.
>
>   (7.14–16)

Something of the same energy galvanizes Byron's worrying of the Russian names into comic deformations as those passages in Pope or Swift in which a mock-heroic roll of "real life" personages widens to encompass the names of classical or invented moral icons. We might recall the passage in the *Dunciad*, for instance, where Dulness challenges her minions to a competition of noise-making, and they reply with

> chatt'ring, grinning, mouthing, jabb'ring all
> And Noise and Norton, Brangling and Breval,
> Dennis and Dissonance, and captious Art,
> And Snip-snap short, and Interruption smart,
>
>   (2.237–240)

or we might compare how Swift in "On Poetry" (301–310) runs together Virgilian nonce-names (Bavius, Maevius) with the names of his own contemporaries (Cibber, Gay, Pope, Young).

Whereas in Pope or Swift, however, the effect is to make a historical situation conform to a recognizable narrative pattern where the wit or novelty resides in the unexpectedness of the juxtaposition, the effect in Byron is quite different. Here the joke is to take the foreign-sounding names of actual Russian soldiers (Meknop, Serge Lwow, and Arseniew are all mentioned in the *Essai*, as are Strogonov and Chicagov) and, by turning them into vulgar English epithets ("rogue-enough," etc.) that in phonologically impressionistic terms sound Russian, to highlight the meaninglessness of the Russian language to an English ear, thus transforming the canonical paradigm into an object of parody. After a certain point, the Russian names grow to sound so strange that the narrator unthinkingly reshapes them into something more familiar.

By running together authentic and counterfeit Russian names, Byron throws into question the groundedness of the whole list in historical particulars, as if the punning intralingual confusion, underscored by the rhyme between "Chokenoff" and "poke enough," were meant to dissolve the social and cultural bonds of language itself. It is as though the multiplication of fake names were meant to demonstrate that there is no existing vocabulary that can adequately encompass the historical catastrophe of a world in which every foot soldier is a potential Achilles. Yet by the same token, the figurative return of Achilles through the bloody deeds of the Russians suggests that present-day reality does not disappoint because it fails to live up to the paradigm given by a classical fiction but because it does so all too well. This is much in line with Pope and Swift's condemnations of their own sordid modernity for both repeating and outdoing the classical vices.

Clearly, the problem of imperial violence or national conquest is linked in Byron's mind to a sense of the increasing incompatibility of our fracturing historical narratives. It is evident that Byron sees a discrepancy between an idea of History that may be equated with "the roll of Fame" and the histories, or "discords of narration," that cannot be made to harmonize with such a unifying recitation. Byron goes to even greater lengths to moralize this dichotomy when he rehearses Prince Potemkin's terse command to Suvorov to take Ismail at any price.

> "Let there be light!" said God, and there was light!"
> "Let there be blood!" says man, and there's a sea!
> The fiat of this spoiled child of the Night
>   (For Day ne'er saw his merits) could decree
> More evil in an hour, than thirty bright
>   Summers could renovate, though they should be

> Lovely as those which ripened Eden's fruit,
> For war cuts up not only branch, but root.
>
> (7.41)

Of course, the anaphoric parallelism that organizes the first two lines only serves to throw emphasis on the desecratory nature of the reappropriation of God's word by man. The repetition represents at once a historical step forward and sideways, the transition from "light" to "sea" signaling the progression from the first to the third day when God divided dry land from water, thus bringing into being the seas and oceans. Yet the nature of the agent and the action have changed so drastically that the departure from the original Word outlined here by Byron cannot be said to stand for an incremental, cosmological advance but rather for a rupture or break with linear historicity and a concomitant plunge into human error. To lapse from divine to mundane time means to fall from logos to languages, from an edenic monolingualism to a debased heteronomy; and it is precisely this scenario that Potemkin's "fiat" endorses.

The principal interest of Byron's allusive engagements not only with literary predecessors but also with the current events and personages of his day is not so much historical as historiographical. It is in a self-consciously polemical mood that Byron's poetic commentary confronts the reader. As much as his portraits of imperial heroes such as Suvorov, for example, may draw on histories and lives that prop up a conservatively patriotic ideal through fulsome idealizations of the nobility, Byron gives the renderings his own inimitable spin.

> Suwarrow chiefly was on the alert,
>   Surveying, drilling, ordering, jesting, pondering,
> For the man was, we safely may assert,
>   A thing to wonder at beyond most wondering;
> Hero, buffoon, half-demon and half-dirt,
>   Praying, instructing, desolating, plundering;
> Now Mars, now Momus; and when bent to storm
> A fortress, Harlequin in uniform.
>
> (7.55)

At least two of Byron's editors (Coleridge and McGann) name Tranchant de Laverne's *la Vie de Souvaroff* as a possible source for the emphasis on the restlessness of the man. Byron, however, is sliding into his own voice here, as we might gather from the phrase "half-demon and half-dirt," which mimics his own characterization of Manfred as "half-dust and half-deity" (1.2.40). Yet the comic incongruities of this passage sound most like they derive from

Pope (as Claude Rawson points out, the lines also smack of Dryden's portrayal of Zimri in *Absalom and Achitophel* as "Chymist, Fidler, States-Man, and Buffoon"[22]). The bathetic insistence of catalogs such as "hero, buffoon, etc." and "praying," where the series of terms is ordered in descending arc, harkens back to the comic descriptions in *An Essay on Man* on the vanity of man.

> Then shall Man's pride and dulness comprehend
> His action's, passion's, being's, use and end;
> Why doing, suff'ring, check'd, impell'd; and why
> This hour a slave, the next a deity.
> (3.65–68)

Suvorov, that "Harlequin in uniform," certainly represents a more menacing object of ridicule than Pope's "glory, jest, and riddle of the world," but in calling him "A thing to wonder at beyond all wondering" Byron may be recalling the moment in the *Essay* at which Pope apostrophizes man as "wond'rous creature."

Pope's *Essay* constructs an abstract argument about the moral nature of human being that descends at various points to historical examples (such as "Why then a Borgia or Catiline?"). In *Don Juan*, the drama unfolds at the level of historical particularity to rise at various points to moral abstraction. The basic strategy, in other words, is one of exaggeration, but in a peculiar sense. We are never unaware of Byron's exaggeration as editorializing, of his pushing the rhetoric of praise beyond the limits of etiquette to points at which the terms spill over into blame (Suvorov is made to encompass so many moral extremes that he reveals an amorality indistinguishable from immorality). This is to say that Byron does not aim to translate so much as to traduce. Historical observations will not be converted into poetic analogues but inverted or wrenched into a separate, apocryphal meaning.

> La nuit était obscure, un brouillard épais ne nous permettait de distinguer autre chose que le feu de notre artillerie, dont l'horizon était embrasé de tous côtés: ce feu, partant du milieu du Danube, se réfléchissait sur les eaux, et offrait un coup d'oeil très singulier. A peine eut-on parcouru l'espace de quelques toises au-delà des batteries, que les Turcs, qui n'avaient point tiré pendant toute la nuit, s'apercevant de nos mouvements, commencèrent de leur côté un feu très-vif, qui embrassa le reste de l'horizon; mais ce fut bien autre chose lorsque, avancés davantage, le feu de la mousqueterie commença dans toute l'étendue du rempart que nous apercevions. Ce fut alors que la place parut à nos yeux comme un volcan dont le feu sortait

de toutes parts. Un cri universel d'*allah*, qui se répétait tout autour de la ville, vint encore rendre plus extraordinaire cet instant, dont il est impossible de se faire une idée.[23]

The narrator is the duc de Richelieu and the narrative taken from the diary that forms the basis of Castelnau's *Essai*. The atmospheric details subtly allegorize the story of the encounter between the Russian forces and the Turks, who are made to seem a natural part of the catastrophic forces of nature on display here.

They are hostile, alien, primitive; their musket fire, suggestive of subterranean energies, transforms the walls of Ismail into the sides of "un volcan." Their "cri universel d'allah" hovers indeterminately in a register somewhere between the voice of nature and of civilization (the cry reverberates—"se repetatait"—about the city, but it is not certain whether it originates from it). The mirroring of the fire in the Danube suggests the narcissism of a drama in which the confrontation with the "extraordinaire" or sublime will confirm the humanity and, at a further remove, the judgment of the spectator over and against the primal opacity of the Turks, even as it brings him to a state beyond the limits of language ("dont il est impossible"). Here, in other words, the sublime proves the narrator's responsiveness (Richelieu is both a participant in and recounter of the events) and thus the reliability of the narrative. The avowal of the ineffability of the experience strikes a note of firsthand or eyewitness realism.

Byron apes something of this moral structure of a standoff between opposites that ultimately confirms the supremacy of one side, but by driving this logic to absurd lengths shows up the self-serving piety of the argument and repudiates the perspective altogether.

> The night was dark, and the thick mist allowed
>   Nought to be seen save the artillery's flame,
> Which arched the horizon like a fiery cloud,
>   And in the Danube's waters shone the same—
> A mirrored Hell! The volleying roar, and loud
>   Long booming of each peal on peal, o'ercame
> The ear far more than thunder; for Heaven's flashes
> Spare, or smite rarely—Man's make millions ashes!
>
> The column ordered on the assault scarce passed
>   Beyond the Russian batteries a few toises,
> When up the bristling Moslem rose at last,
>   Answering the Christian thunders with like voices;
> Then one vast fire, air, earth and stream embraced,
>   Which rocked as 'twere beneath the mighty voices;

While the whole rampart blazed like Etna, when
The restless Titan hiccups in his den.

And one enormous shout of "Allah!" rose
    In the same moment, loud as even the roar
Of War's most mortal engines, to their foes
    Hurling defiance: city, stream, and shore,
Resounded "Allah!" and the clouds which close
    With thick'ning canopy the conflict o'er,
Vibrate to the Eternal name. Hark! through
All sounds it pierceth "Allah! Allah! Hu!"

The columns were in movement one and all,
    But of the portion which attacked by water,
Thicker than leaves the lives began to fall,
    Though led by Arseniew, that great son of Slaughter,
As brave as ever faced both bomb and ball.
    "Carnage" (so Wordsworth tells you) "is God's daughter:"
If *he* speak truth, she is Christ's sister, and
Just now behaved as in the Holy Land.

                                                    (8.6–9)

The landscape presents Richelieu with a site for the proper encounter with an epistemologically confounding spectacle of the Other (note the emphasis on the visual in "coup d'oeil" and "nos yeux") and thus with an occasion for meeting the demands of historical narrative. The same vista presents Byron with an occasion for meeting the demands of mock-epic so thoroughly as to leave the epic paradigm in shambles in his aftermath. The contrast drawn in stanza 6 between the canonical trappings of war, "Heaven's flashes," and the modern innovations that make "millions ashes" looks back to a tradition of celebrating, whether earnestly or derisively, the advances of the latest military technology over the past, a tradition that has its roots in classical epic and achieves a satiric revival of peculiar harshness in Swift's depictions of modern warfare in *Gulliver's Travels*.

Byron's blasé disgust at the ease and the scale of wholesale slaughter in his day—the brevity of the protest apparently conceding the unremarkable nature of the crime—is something original, however, and probably finds its most sympathetic later resonance in Auden's lyric satires. Consider, for instance, his feigned approval in "Fleet Visit" of American gunboats that look "certainly worth every cent / Of the millions they must have cost," where a chill sets in when we realize "millions" does not refer to a unit of currency. We might recall in a similar light the flatness of his description of "A million eyes, a million boots in line / Without expression, waiting for a sign" in "The

Shield of Achilles." Auden looses his anger on capitalist regimes that in the wake of the World War II persist in justifying oppression through appeal to national self-interest; Byron pins his indignation at the outcome of the French Revolution and Napoleonic Wars on different targets, but a similar sense of helplessness turned to outrage with respect to the bureaucracy of the modern state is at work.

The jibe at the excessiveness of modern cruelty occurs in the middle of a group of stanzas that describe the struggle between Turk and Russian in the spiritualized accents usually reserved for genuine epic. The Danube's reflection of the artillery fire has become a "mirrored Hell," the siege of Muslim by Christian has become (albeit in a slapstick register) the imprisonment of the primitive, titanic Enceladus under Aetna by Zeus the lawgiver, and the fall of casualties in the fighting has attached itself to a topos that reaches back through Dante's association of the souls of the damned with "foglie" in the third canto of the *Inferno* to the speech by Glaukos in book 6 of the *Iliad* in which he likens the cycle of generations to the failure and renewal of leaves in a forest.

The reply to the "Christian thunders" of Suvorov's army by the Muslims' "enormous shout of Allah" is the most sustained allusion in the passage, echoing the account in book 2 of Milton's *Paradise Lost* of the response by the army of fallen angels to the recess of the devilish cabinet.

> The Stygian Council thus dissolv'd; and forth
> In order came the grand infernal Peers:
> Midst came thir mighty Paramount, and seem'd
> Alone th'Antagonist of Heav'n. . . .
>
> Then of thir Session ended they bid cry
> With Trumpet's regal sound the great result:
> Toward the four winds four speedy Cherubim
> Put to thir mouths the sounding Alchymy
> By Herald's voice explain'd: the hollow Abyss
> Heard far and wide, and all the host of Hell
> With deaf'ning shout, return'd them loud acclaim.
>   (2.506–509, 514–520)

With this inarticulate ("deaf'ning") clamor, the throng disintegrates from an organized body into a rioting mass of contestants engaged in a group of menacing exercises: "As when to warn proud Cities war appears / Wag'd in the troubl'd Sky, and Armies rush / To Battle in the Clouds" (2.533–535). The echoing of the cherubic trumpets by the roar of the demons strikes a martial note that is amplified in these lines by the deployment of the epic simile and inaugurates skirmishes among the troops that both in their destructive enormity and material inconsequence look ahead to the battle between the hosts in book 6.

When it deploys such devices, Milton's poem succeeds as epic in spite of itself. *Paradise Lost* both satisfies expectations of heroic action by mounting the spectacle of a larger-than-life struggle between opposing ethical forces and pacifies qualms about the morality of modern warfare by sanitizing the violence through cartoonishly fantastic effects, such as Satan's instantaneous healing on being "shear'd" in two by Michael.[24] The echoing in *Don Juan* of the Russian artillery's "long booming" by the Turkish war cry, on the other hand, heralds the outbreak of hostilities that cannot be rehabilitated within the customary poetic framework. Yet the poem's consciousness of its failure on this score implies a certain rebellion against not only brutal, modern truth but shopworn metaphor as well.

The argument is sharpened by the snipe at Wordsworth's "Thanksgiving Ode," a poem written to celebrate the defeat of Napoleon at Waterloo. Byron is making the point that Wordsworth's sycophantic encomium to the government represents an abdication not so much of the basic moral obligations of a citizen but more scandalously of his responsibilities as a poet. Precisely by translating the version of history that holds greatest currency with the English public into the idealizing terminology of poetry, and by performing this act of translation with a literalism impinging on grossness, Wordsworth has discredited the office. The epithet given to Arseniew neatly inverts the Wordsworthian hyperbole in order to remind the reader that the original figure glosses over the historical particularity of suffering and the conviction such anguish arouses that a specific name and face ought to be attached to deeds of war. The final couplet of the octave draws out the figure to its logical conclusion in order to show the obscenity of the proposition, in and of itself, that "Carnage," the butchering of humans by humans, could be assigned the same metaphysical genealogy as Christ the son, the primary figure who represents to the western world the ideal par excellence of self-sacrificial charity.

Reprimanding Wordsworth in this canto for his praise of empire, Byron enlarges on a theme first broached as early as in the dedication. There a set of tongue-in-cheek remarks disparaging *The Excursion* for its length and dullness (Byron dubs the poem "vasty" and exclaims "I think the quarto holds five hundred pages") rises into a more serious excoriation of the poet for turning a poem and poetics that claim to be about the virtues of autonomy into a philosophy of self-gain.

> 'Tis poetry—at least by his assertion,
>   And may appear so when the dogstar rages;
> And he who understands it would be able
>   To add a story to the Tower of Babel.

You, gentlemen! by dint of long seclusion
    From better company have kept your own
At Keswick, and through still continued fusion
    Of one another's minds at last have grown
To deem as a most logical conclusion
    That Poesy has wreaths for you alone;
There is a narrowness in such a notion
Which makes me wish you'd change your lakes for ocean.

I would not imitate the petty thought,
    Nor coin my self-love to so base a vice,
For all the glory your conversion brought,
    Since gold alone should not have been its price.
You have your salary—was't for that you wrought?
    And Wordsworth has his place in the Excise.
You're shabby fellows—true—but poets still,
And duly seated on the immortal hill.
                        ("Dedication," 4–6)

What begins as a complaint about style rapidly advances to incorporate a suspicion regarding the implication of the professional artist in the corruption of public affairs that in its general outlines is familiar from the works of writers for whom the question of patronage and its decline is somewhat more pointed, namely Dryden and Pope. In their satires the question of patronage is explicitly tied up with a defense of the Horatian theory of the arts: the need to reach a sense of earned intellectual autonomy acquires new urgency in the face of the unfamiliar and changing consciousness of writing as a profession. Byron's specific imputation regarding the incomprehensibility of *The Excursion* is that the poem's difficulty is not a symptom of true complexity so much as a sign of a banal deferentiality, linked to the fact that the dedicatee of the poem, William Lowther, earl of Lonsdale, was the patron who obtained a sinecure for the poet as collector of stamps for Westmoreland. The echo of Pope's *Epistle to Dr. Arbuthnot* in the reference to the "dogstar" suggests that the poem's banality is a function of its being written for the ulterior motive of profit.

Byron, it should be noted, runs a quirky variation here on the usual Augustan impertinence with regard to class boundaries. The reference to "better company," set up by the sarcastic use of the term "gentlemen," carries no hint of defensiveness yet still manages to draw attention to the inverse snobbery of the seclusion into which the Lake Poets have withdrawn, while recalling to the reader Byron's own superiority in title. His raillery against avarice is not disingenuousness, insofar as he himself inherited no money with his baronage.

The insult thus conforms nicely to the rhetoric of such class-protective hauteurs as the celebrated swipe at Southey's manhood, where the laureate is likened to a "flying fish" that falls "for lack of moisture, quite adry, Bob!" As has been shown, the ascription of (literal and figural) impotence to Southey imitates Rochester's put-down of Dryden, a bit of locker-room bawdry designed to isolate and humble the upstart social climber.[25] In context, however, Byron's sarcasm seems pointed somewhat differently, as it reprimands a "narrowness" or illiberality that, by avoiding a show of social intercourse with "better company" while surreptitiously accepting the offered perks, masquerades as a refusal to compromise moral and creative independence. The assault on Wordsworth ultimately recalls Rochester's contempt of social inferiors less than Pope's scorn for hack competitors, as voiced in the *Dunciad* and the Horatian imitations.

Attacks on poetic adversaries in *Don Juan* fall within a larger pattern of complaints against the willing complicity of bad writers with worse statesmen, against the symbiotic relation between the technologies of civilization and of domination. The complicity is perhaps summed up best in canto 7 by a bathetic bit of wordplay when the narrator asks "if a man's name in a *bulletin* / Can make up for a *bullet in* his body?" (7.21). The punning reminds us that for the foot soldier there is no difference between getting his name in the paper and getting shot. The verbal play gives the impression of being of a piece with the "God's daughter / Christ's sister" parody of the Wordsworth formula and with the irrepressible recitation of phony Russian names, an impression that I take to be the poem's method of suggesting that the exploitativeness of the papers, the proselytizing of the bad poet, even the provincial habit of mishandling foreign names represent abuses of language that belong to related moral orders.

Language per se seems to be in danger of corruption as a result of its support of the traffic in bodies and bodies politic, its contribution to the excesses of the "brain-spattering, windpipe-slitting art" of war (9.4). We may suspect Byron to be protesting the complicity of the publishing industry and the business of empire in the same economy, a suspicion confirmed at one point by the narrator's plea to the reader: "Think how the joys of reading a Gazette / Are purchased by all agonies and crimes" (8.125). Even (or perhaps especially) the reader's pleasure is heavily implicated in the violence. It is this pleasure that motivates the mistranslation of sales into slaughter, "bulletin" into "bullet in." The violence, we are reminded, may come back to hurt us close to home: "Read your own hearts and Ireland's present story, / Then feed her famine fat with Wellesley's glory" (8.125).

By alluding to the famine in Ireland that England cannot ameliorate because of war debts, Byron enlarges on the sensationalism of the propaganda supporting the military effort. This sensationalism is on display earlier in the canto in the anecdote about a Russian officer whose foot, as he stepped over "a dying Moslem," was bitten by the expiring man and not released until after the officer had decapitated his cannibalistic assailant. We might expect the moral of the story to be something involving the civilized-versus-savage distinction in representations of the relation between occidental and oriental cultures, but Byron is making a different point. The real issue is about how such an event gets appropriated and redeployed by the publishing industry. To this story the narrator will append the sanctimonious moral "But then a fact's a fact—and 'tis the part / Of a true poet to escape from fiction / Whene'er he can" (8.86). Here the appetite for lurid fact, implicitly opposed to the "appetite for lies" explicitly associated by the stanza with "poetic diction, " finds a repellent literalization in the battlefield feeding of savagery on itself.

Like Pope's castigations of writers gone bad such as Colley Cibber and John Dennis, Byron's jabs at professional scribblers may be understood as driven by a more or less suppressed fear of the potential for corruption of the self. Byron's satires stand in the Augustan tradition that regards poetry as most powerfully able to balance its Horatian functions of delighting and instructing when it confronts its own reflection in the distorting mirror of false art, thus exposing poetasters, dunces, and hirelings for what they really are.

We may see the anxiety involved in such self-confrontation coming to the surface most directly perhaps in the episode of Juan's failed romance with Haidee following his shipwreck on Lambro's island in Greece. As they are in the story of Juan's service to Gulbeyaz and confinement in a Turkish harem, confusions of identity are a significant part of the experience of this canto, as evidenced plainly by Haidee's dream in which Juan metamorphoses into Lambro (4.36) and by the uncanny mirroring between father and daughter as they face one another in a standoff over Juan at which the narrator remarks "'t was strange / How like they looked" (4.44).

The confusions of identity extend to the multivalent narrative evocations of the *Odyssey* in the episode. What structural parallel to the Homeric original is being drawn: Juan's shipwreck to Odysseus' landing on Skheria and encounter with Nausikaa, or Lambro's return home to Odysseus's disguised homecoming on Ithaka? The answer is both, which means the reconfiguration of the Homeric allusion poses us a further question: who is the protagonist of the narrative, Juan or Lambro? It has been pointed out by Peter Manning that in light of this reconfiguration (which implies a precise congruence between the erotic triangles Lambro-Haidee-Juan and Odysseus-Penelope-suitors), the competition between the younger and older man for the leading role in the story and for the loyalty of Haidee quite explicitly sketches out an Oedipal drama. A comment by the narrator at Lambro's first appearance, "An honest gentleman at his return / May not have the good fortune of Ulysses" (3.23), makes recollection of the *Odyssey*'s denouement inevitable, a thought that interprets "Juan's love for Haidée as a rivalry for the wife of an older man, thereby confirming that the symbolic importance of daughters in Byron's writings is a displacement of conflicts over the father with the mother."[26] While the psychoanalytic interest of such an interpretation ought to be evident, it might be less clear at first glance how the Oedipal paradigm also furthers the aims of Byron's political argument.

Strong hints abound in the text, as many commentators have noted, that the character of Lambro was molded not only after literary models but at least one flesh-and-blood original in the Albanian ruler Ali Pasha, whom Byron met in Yannina on his travels in 1809. (To cite two examples: the "classical profiles" and "large black eyes" of children on Lambro's island echoes Byron's own description of the "large black eyes & features perfectly regular" of Ali's grandsons, and the poem's portrait of the feast at which are displayed "sherbet cooling in the vase . . . The orange and pomegranate nodding o'er," brings to mind Ali's frequent plying of Byron with "almonds & sugared sherbet, fruit and sweetmeats."[27]) If we admit the proposal we get a significant clue as to the ideological light in which the poet means us to view Lambro, since in a letter of November 12, 1809, to his mother Byron referred to Ali as "a remorseless tyrant, guilty of the most horrible cruelties, very brave & so good a general, that they call him the Mahometan Buonaparte."[28] However long the poet harbored a sentimental enthusiasm for the actual Napoleon past the point at which such an attachment could have been defended on the basis of support for the spread of liberal constitutionalism, the proximity here of the categories "tyrant" and "Buonaparte" spell out a certain anxiety behind the apparently complimentary epithet.

Even if we do not take the characterization of Ali in the letter to reflect back on Lambro directly, we may begin to see how Haidée's "piratical papa" (3.13) might be made to conform to the conventional image of a tyrant and the test of wills between Lambro and Juan refigured as a conflict between the forces of patrician order and of revolution.

> Now in a person used to much command—
> To bid men come, and go, and come again—
> To see his orders done too out of hand—
> Whether the word was death, or but the chain—
> It may seem strange to find his manners bland;
> Yet such things are, which I can not explain,
> Though doubtless he who can command himself
> Is good to govern—almost as a Guelf.
>
> (3.47)

"Guelf," Byron's favorite name for the House of Hanover recalling its descent from the German royal line of Guelph, seals the comparison between Asian and European governments to the detriment of the latter and, in the process, the narrative of conservative versus radical. Lambro is as much a ruler as either George III or George IV (whose accession took place in January 1820, the month Byron completed revisions on the manuscript of this canto) and, the interjection nudges us to recognize, a good deal more endowed with self-control than his English counterparts. Moreover, the comparison is moralized by the relative antiquity of the cultures in accordance with the allegory of generational rivalry that, as I have noted, structures the erotic relationships of the episode. The Asiatic patriarch holds claim to the throne of a nation substantially more *ancien* than any European *régime*. It could be argued that the competition in *Don Juan* between an old Eastern dictatorship and a young Western republicanism recapitulates in certain respects the theme of the "adolescence of the colonizing mind," as Sara Suleri has called it.[29] According to Suleri, this figural adolescence inevitably entails an admission, whether deliberate or not, of the "disempowering impropriety of colonialism" in the face of a colonized foreignness that stands as a sublime "locus of all things ancient, a backdrop against which the colonizing presence cannot but be startled by its own novelty."[30]

Suleri's powerful deconstruction of the Oedipal anxieties underlying colonialist discourse demonstrates that the terms of the narrative are at once untenable and unavoidable for the Western mind, at least at certain points in history. Yet the antimonarchist polemics of Byron's tale complicates any reading of the poem as a mystifcation of colonialist ideology. As Marilyn Butler has observed, "in . . . [the] period of Napoleon's decline and fall, when European old regimes were being reinstated, it was widely expected that the Ottoman empire would soon break up: it appealed to the radicals, then, as the likeliest site for a hoped-for replay of the French Revolution."[31] The very possibility of extending revolutionary significance to the Orient thus necessitates dismantling of the East-West opposition. Byron, however, will go a step further in questioning the appropriateness of any attempt at communication with the East that does not aspire to a liberalizing of society.

Butler proceeds to explicate the politics of Byron's poem *The Giaour*, another story in which a triangular relationship between a tyrannical, oriental husband (Hassan), his beautiful wife (Leila), and her young, occidental lover (the Venetian "Giaour") self-destructs, in this case ending with the death of all three. In Butler's reading, none of the religious afterlives associated with the different characters in the poem (including Christian heaven, Moslem paradise, and even the supernatural limbo of vampirism) offers any viable place for "the body of the defeated people" represented by Leila. The promise of "human fidelity" or "cameraderie" (Butler's words) offered by the Giaour is finally no more effective for the specific characters but at least is different in kind from the absolutism of the religions. Insofar as the crosscultural romance between Leila and the Giaour is figured not simply as doomed but tragically doomed, it becomes an argument on behalf of liberal, republican revolution over and against all other ideological movements that might compete for the reader's sympathies. "Written in the year when Parliament was brought to allow 'missionizing' in India [1813]," Butler moreover reminds us, the poem "questions the claims to progressiveness of proselytizing Christians."[32] Pondering the relevance of Butler's reading to the orientalist narrative of *Don Juan* specifically in canto 3, we might note that one of Byron's sources for the plot was an anecdote involving (and told by) Muchtar Pasha, Ali Pasha's eldest son.

Within the context of Byron's views regarding the relation between East and West, we may find it easier to recognize the import of the plot of the *Don Juan* episode. A high emphasis is placed on the youthfulness and primitivism of the two lovers: Juan is a "boy" (2.174), a "young flower snapp'd from the stalk" (2.176), while Haidee is both "Nature's bride" and "Passion's child" (2.202). The language placing Haidee and Juan in absolute figurative continuity with their natural island paradise ("Amidst the barren sand and rocks so rude / She and her wave-worn love had made their bower," 2.198) suggests a state of nature à la Rousseau in which spontaneity of feeling is the sign of authentic human being, a sign that the corrosive forces of civilization conspire to eradicate or, at a minimum, to distort. (Juan, the young Spanish aristocrat who has been shipwrecked on the island, is not a solidly practical Crusoe whose struggle to survive necessitates the reinvention of civilization but rather a kind of sentimentally volatile Émile who receives his initiation into the natural world not from a Rousseauvian narrator but from Juan's own emotional twin, Haidee.) The poem advances this argument most explicitly in the stanzas describing their first kiss on the beach where Juan has washed up:

> A long, long kiss, a kiss of youth and love,
>   And beauty, all concentrating like rays
> Into one focus, kindled from above;
>   Such kisses as belong to early days,
> Where heart, and soul, and sense, in concert move,
>   And the blood's lava, and the pulse a blaze,
> Each kiss a heart-quake. . . .
>
> They fear'd no eyes nor ears on that lone beach,
>   They felt no terrors from the night, they were
> All in all to each other: though their speech
>   Was broken words, they *thought* a language there, —
> And all the burning tongues the passions teach
>   Found in one sigh the best interpreter
> Of nature's oracle—first love,—that all
> Which Eve has left her daughters since her fall.

> Haidee spoke not of scruples, ask'd no vows,
>   Nor offer'd any; she had never heard
> Of plight and promises to be a spouse
>   Or perils by a loving maid incurr'd;
> She was all which pure ignorance allows.
>   (2.186, 189–190)

The kiss seals a social commitment that is the antithesis of the ceremonial or sanctified. Spontaneous, sentimental, such a bond operates outside the formal exchange of vows, relying instead on the transmutation of "the blood's lava" into "the burning tongues of passion," an exchange that we might see as the ideological opposite of Richelieu's metamorphosis of the foreign body politic into an inhuman natural force: it is rather the spilling over of an all-too-human nature into an ad hoc social cooperation. About this narrative there is something of a revolutionary implication.

Indeed, the poem makes the implication more explicit when Lambro, having discovered Juan and Haidee asleep together, demands that Juan surrender his sword and, on being refused, menaces Juan with the cocking of a pistol. Juan's defiant reply to Lambro, "Not while this arm is free," gives voice to an emphatically revolutionary attitude that is taken up as well by Haidee when she intercedes between the men to shield Juan from the threatened violence of her father; there the narrator tells us "She stood as one who championed human fears" (4.43). Here the paradigm of the rebellion of human nature against the conventions of civil society is being given a clearly political valence, with Lambro, the despotic pseudo-"Guelf," representing the interests of conservative authority. The equation here of strong emotion with social radicalism is couched in language that recalls the hymn to freedom sung as an entertainment by the court poet at Juan and Haidee's feast in canto 3. We are prepared to understand in political terms the generational struggle that divides Juan and Haidee from Lambro by the historical argument propounded by the modern Greek poet's song.

> And where art thou,
>   My country? On thy voiceless shore
> The heroic lay is tuneless now—
>   The heroic bosom beats no more!
> And must thy lyre, so long divine,
> Degenerate into hands like mine? . . .
>
> Must we but weep o'er days more blest?
>   Must we but blush?—Our fathers bled.

> Earth! render back from out thy breast
> A remnant of our Spartan dead....
>
> (3.86.5, 7)

To sympathize with the indignation behind this call to arms is to admit that our "fathers," having "bled," were possessed of convictions of which we seem incapable, given that "the heroic bosom beats no more." A hardening of sensibility has warranted our acquiescence to a slavery our ancestors died to avoid. Meanwhile, the ironic rearticulation of Oedipal tensions here is unmistakable. Are we prepared, the poet demands, through rebellion to prove ourselves against the example of our fathers?

In the end, Lambro overwhelms and expels Juan from the island by force. On seeing her lover overcome, Haidee faints, only to reawaken in Juan's absence, sicken, and eventually die. The pathos of this tragic conclusion will be increased by the narrator's revelation that, at her death, she is carrying a child, "A second principle of life, which might / Have dawn'd a fair and sinless child of sin" but instead "went down to the grave unborn" (4.70). The curious formulation "might have dawn'd" interprets the "sinless child of sin" as a heavenly apparition, a sun who is also a son, and reveals the religious role that might have been played by the child of Haidee's union with Juan, the offspring of a conjugal mingling of East and West. Haidee's death during pregnancy symbolizes not one more among the natural sequence of human mortalities but rather the stillbirth of an epochal savior.

If the revolutionary momentousness of the union between Juan and Haidee and of their disobedience to Lambro is revealed under the auspices of a failed epiphany, we might wonder over what occasion presides the sculpture of the Madonna that ornaments the Norman Abbey in the English Cantos of *Don Juan*. The statue in its integrity throws into relief the marks of historical adversity that surround it and that disfigure the overall design of the house and its precincts.

> Within a niche, nigh to its pinnacle,
>   Twelve saints had once stood sanctified in stone;
> But these had fallen, not when the friars fell,
>   But in the war which struck Charles from his throne,
> When each house was a fortalice—as tell
>   The annals of full many a line undone—
> The gallant Cavaliers, who fought in vain
> For those who knew not to resign or reign.
>
> But in a higher niche, alone, but crown'd,
>   The Virgin Mother of the God-born child,

> With her son in her bless'd arms, look'd round,
>   Spared by some chance when all beside was spoil'd;
> She made the earth below seem holy ground.
>   This may be superstition, weak or wild,
>   But even the faintest relics of a shrine
> Of any worship, wake some thought divine.
>
> (13.60–61)

Praising the "gallant Cavaliers," Byron reminds us that his Scottish ancestors fought in the service of the Stuart line. In light of this reminder, it is difficult not to perceive the nostalgic tribute in the following stanza to "relics" that "wake some thoughts divine" as an affirmation of the divine right of kings and thus as a verbal thumbing of the nose at the House of Hanover and George IV. We should bear in mind that this gesture of defiance is not meant to be read as a comprehensive declaration of the poet's ideological opinions, for he looks on the relics with a rather jaundiced eye, admitting that they might as well belong to "a shrine / Of any worship," hence that they do not belong to the shrine of *his* worship, whatever that may be. At the same time, we should not simply overlook the fact that in these verses Byron is taking on the rhetoric of Jacobite loyalism and, as a result, the standing of the Hanoverian dynasty's ancient enemy. Such a posture is not conservative in any typical sense of the word. Instead it is a taboo stance that profanes the totemic order of the ruling house; as Malcolm Kelsall has observed, "the recognition of the religiously empowered force of the Hanoverian monarchy is extremely strong even in the antagonistic discourses of English eighteenth-century philosophical radicalism."[33] Kelsall aligns the writings of both Pope and Byron with these expressions of radicalism while pointing out that their satires acquire a special authority precisely because of their iconoclastic views and tactics: "Between them they define the Hanoverian epoch."[34] In the case of Byron's *Vision of Judgment*, for example, the poem's capacity to antagonize may be measured through the unpacking of a single word: "Byron's verses foreground the personal role of the king, and they suggest an arbitrary tripwire—the word 'liberty'—which is taboo. Speak the forbidden word and all hell (or heaven!) breaks loose."[35]

On the premises of the Norman Abbey, the "crown'd" figure of the Virgin Mother consecrates ground "spoil'd" by the civil wars that ended in Charles I's execution. As I have noted already, the appeal in *Don Juan* to maternal authority as a possible sponsor of social and historical reform carries out the dictates of an imaginative refusal of the law of the father. It would not be pursuing the thought too far to suppose that the statue may represent a sort of tacit memorial to the dead Queen Caroline, whose infidelities to George IV, general popularity, and Whig connections all conspired to make her into a living symbol of revolution at the time of George's accession. Although this monument to female sexuality may encode a recollected disappointment over the outcome of Caroline's attempt to return to London in 1820, however, it nevertheless aims to picture for us the basis of a potential future renovation of the patrilineal status quo—to "wake some thoughts divine."

The final cantos outline for us a nascent bedroom farce in which Juan piques the erotic interest of three of the women staying at the abbey: Lady Adeline Amundeville, Aurora Raby, and the Duchess Fitz-Fulke. Surveying a morning breakfast scene at the end of the poem, the narrator tantalizes the reader with hints that the Duchess Fitz-Fulke, last seen visiting Juan in his room at midnight while dressed as the "Black Friar," the abbey's legendary resident ghost, in fact has acted on her whims with our hero. The narrator gives no explicit details ("I leave the thing a problem, like all things," 17.13), but his rhetorical nudging and winking makes the situation clear. The domestic economy that supplies the foundation of the civil order is being comically subverted here under the sign of a redemptive maternity. Small wonder that during Juan's visit, then, his host, Lord Henry, is driven to ask himself, "Could he quit his king in times of strife?" and to imagine what it would be like to "cut through and through (oh! damnable incision!) / The Gordian or the G*eor*di-an knot, whose strings / Have tied together Commons, Lords, and Kings" (16.24).

Given such a vision of household disorder and its consequences, we may understand better why the very architecture of the abbey seems to suggest to the narrator a metaphor for political change.

> There was a modern Goth, I mean a Gothic
>   Bricklayer of Babel, called an architect,
> Brought to survey these grey walls, which though so thick,
>   Might have from time acquired some slight defect;
> Who, after rummaging the Abbey through thick
>   And thin, produced a plan whereby to erect
> New buildings of correct conformation,
> And thrown down old, which he called *restoration*.
>
> The cost would be a trifle—an "old song"
>   Set to some thousands ('tis the usual burthen
> Of that same tune, when people hum it long)—
>   The price would speedily repay its worth in
> An edifice no less sublime than strong,
>   By which Lord Henry's good taste would go forth in
> Its glory, through all ages shining sunny,
> For Gothic daring shown in English money.
>   (16.57–59)

Behind these stanzas, of course, stands a long line of panegyrics to the English country house, of which Jonson's poem *To Penshurst*, Marvell's poem *Upon Appleton House*, and Pope's poem *To Burlington* comprise only the most celebrated examples. Associated with this topos is a more or less obligatory argument in praise of the landed gentry and its interests, an ethic that by Pope's time came to see itself as directly opposed to both the rise of a new moneyed class and the development of a new bureaucratic order to serve this group. But the stress Byron places on the word "restoration" makes manifest the radical valence of this celebration of the country estate. The stanzas ask for no less than a social revolution from within the aristocracy, and they work hand-in-hand with Lord Henry's hypothetical project of cutting the "Geordian knot." At the same time that they praise the ancient families for developing a sense of "good taste" through the proper use of riches in the past, they urge that those resources be deployed in the present toward the overthrow of the current ruling house.

As I see it, this idealized description of the "restoration" of the Norman Abbey does not so much contradict as qualify Nicola J. Watson's claim that, at the end of *Don Juan*, "[the] installation of a scandalous heterogeneity in the place of the paternal . . . translates into a definite distaste for the general process of Restoration that governed Europe in the post-Napoleonic era."[36] The image of the abbey's repaired edifice is a projected one and points up the sorry disarray of the existing social structure. There is both an aspect of pathos and an aspect of triumph inherent to the position that Byron adopts here, as he interprets the affairs of early nineteenth-century Europe in the English Cantos. Despite all of his brilliant excavation and reconstruction of the past, no ready paradigm for restoration of the present has fully come to light. So he will have to make up his own. In the end, it is the ironic designs of the satirist that sustain the promise of a restored house.

4

Auden in the Polis of the Absurd

Auden's notorious dictum that "poetry makes nothing happen" can be construed as the motto of a self-excusing complacency, a readiness to accommodate bourgeois philistinism that to some eyes may make the poet look like a "licensed jester."[1] Such a reading fastens to the exclusion of all else on his efforts to debunk Romantic illusions regarding art's prophetic authority and, dismayingly, does so with his frequently expressed approval.[2] This assessment, however, risks missing a larger point behind Auden's insouciance, which becomes clearer if we restore the assertion from the poem "In Memory of W. B. Yeats" to its original context:

> Mad Ireland hurt you into poetry.
> Now Ireland has her madness and her weather still,
> For poetry makes nothing happen: it survives
> In the valley of its making where executives
> Would never want to tamper.[3]

Poetry on this reckoning has an analytic, historical value; it registers the conditions of Ireland's "madness," even if it cannot effect a cure. Furthermore, the memory of the author's discomfort at such conditions is preserved by poetry in precincts of language beyond the jurisdiction of bureaucratic or corporate power, "where executives would never want to tamper." Art thus implicitly performs a chastening function, the significance of which should neither be exaggerated nor denied. The work of art resists the efforts of authority to regulate all human initiative according to a utilitarian calculus of costs and benefits and thus to reduce individual expression to mere, unwitting validation of the existing social "contract."

Auden's boldest declaration of this view occurs in his 1962 essay "The Poet and the City," where he writes: "In our age, the mere making of a work of art is a political act. So long as artists exist, making what they please . . . they remind the Management of something managers need to be reminded of, namely, that the managed are people with faces, not anonymous members, that *Homo Laborans* is also *Homo Ludens.*"⁴ In the final clause of this sentence, the extension of human nature from the realm of labor to that of play pointedly evokes and revises the language of Hannah Arendt's book *The Human Condition* (1958), which Auden reviewed shortly after its publication and described as giving him "the impression of having been written especially for me."⁵ Arendt's book expounds the significance of two major shifts in our conception of the human since the advent of modernity. The first is the triumph of the active life, or *vita activa*, over the reflective life, or *vita contemplative,* in Western society, a victory that reverses the classical privileging of intellectual over corporeal experience. The second is the promotion of the figure of *animal laborans* over that of *homo faber* within the modern account of the active life. This development, which can be attributed in part to the introduction of mass production and consumption, threatens to destroy our very capacity to identify ourselves as humans:

> The last stage of the laboring society, the society of jobholders, demands of its members a sheer automatic functioning, as though individual life had actually been submerged in the over-all life process of the species and the only active decision still required of the individual were to let go, so to speak, to abandon his individuality, the still individually sensed pain and trouble of living, and acquiesce in a dazed, "tranquilized," functional type of behavior.⁶

The abandonment of the "still individually sensed pain and trouble of living" that signals the surrender of political personality to a purely functionalist or behaviorist outlook means, in an ultimate sense, the eradication of consciousness itself and thus of culture, too. For if we accept the ruthless commodification of social relations, we give up our capacity to be hurt into poetry, as the elegy for Yeats phrases it. Arendt seeks to put in critical perspective the triumph of capitalist mass society by opposing the production of consumable goods through labor to the fabrication of durable objects through work. Auden seeks to do the same, but by opposing labor to play. His revision of the philosophical dialectic betokens an idea of culture more thoroughly aligned with the irrational, hedonistic, and erotic impulses than Arendt, for all the importance she grants our "pain and trouble," seems willing to sustain. Her anxiety at the loss of the goal of permanence in human activity as a result of the downfall of *homo faber* goes hand-in-hand with a residual nostalgia for the classical ideal of the polis as a public space in which words and deeds achieve a lasting historical importance, hence come to represent a "guarantee against the futility of individual life."⁷

Auden's satiric corrective to such nostalgia is to promote a sense of culture's value as residing in its expression of our most perishable, tenuous, and whimsical thoughts and experiences. His poetry always "proves the child ephemeral," to invoke a phrase from one of his most plangent lyrics. According to Barbara Everett, his project is one of "momentary tasks and purchasable needs."⁸ As she finely observes, what his writings early and late "have in common, beyond their alteration from the 'attractive' to the 'honest' or the 'exciting' to the 'true,' is a shared understanding that existence is always askew from where it ought to be or might be.... It is a poetry of fragments and splinters, always changing styles and doxologies."⁹ Such restless experimentalism is more than a merely stylistic principle. As an avowal of the ludicrous idiosyncrasy of our desires, it is an ethical credo. At his best moments, in other words, Auden achieves in theory and in practice an art that debunks the masquerade of egomania as high seriousness and the monolithic historical narrative that such a posture presumes. His writing ironizes history by registering its narrative or logical incoherence, thereby restoring to view perspectives that have been excluded from the official canons of cultural progress.

In his satiric ekphrases, for example, which I discuss at various points throughout this chapter, a distinct impression arises that the poem not only enables the idealized pictorial or plastic work to "speak out" but also disparages its obeisance to a consumerist conception of art. The attitude of scorn is worthy of Theodor Adorno, who would have aligned its targets with what he and Max Horkheimer contemptuously labeled "the culture industry."¹⁰ In Auden's oeuvre, the locus classicus of such a moral polemic occurs in *Musée des Beaux Arts*, where the poem ascribes to Brueghel's "Fall of Icarus" a neutrality of feeling toward the historical event of Icarus's drowning that the poem itself cannot share. To speak of feeling in this manner is to raise a question of sympathy, to ask for whom the poetry is written—who is capable of maintaining the proper critical acumen in the face of civilization's disheartening silence? Auden answers the question in a number of poems over his career when he speaks of the citizens of an imaginary, ideal polis (sometimes called the Just or Holy City), a community of the forgotten and overlooked who are united only in their defiance of the dehumanizing power of the modern bureaucratic state. He represents these personalities as the potential agents of an emancipating political critique when he characterizes them in "September 1, 1939," for example, as "ironic points of light" whose "affirming flame" resists the benightedness of fascism (*SP* 89).

By exposing the linguistic incompatibility of rival historical theses, then, his poetry dramatizes the clash between entrenched authority and vulnerable individuality. In "The Fall of Rome," this strategy achieves a kind of apocalyptic explosiveness as different periods of Roman antiquity (both the heyday of the republic and the decadence of the late empire), exhausted capitalist modernity, natural or cosmological time, and the threatened ahistoricism of a barbarian Dark Age all collide with one another. The complex interplay between these horizons ultimately reveals the inadequacy of each perspective in turn when it comes to reconciling hostile ethical and political interests. The poem's description of scene begins with a series of small surprises that escalate, as the conceit develops, into ever-larger shocks.

> The piers are pummelled by the waves;
> In a lonely field the rain
> Lashes an abandoned train;
> Outlaws fill the mountain caves.
>
> Fantastic grow the evening gowns;
> Agents of the Fisc pursue
> Absconding tax-defaulters through
> The sewers of provincial towns.
>
> (*CP* 332)

A reader looking at the initial quatrain for the first time might well conclude on the evidence of the feature of the "abandoned train" that the poem will proceed to explore the bankruptcy of industrial society and means its title to be taken in a strictly allegorical sense. The first line of the second stanza seems to keep the account rooted in the twentieth century, but references to the "agents of the Fisc" and "provincial towns" in the following lines abruptly resituate the action in an ancient, imperial setting.

As the imagery proliferates in the third stanza, the forms of civilization's discontents will grow increasingly sinister: from the apparent narcotizing of "temple prostitutes" to the escapism of "the literati," who without exception retreat into some manner of relationship with "an imaginary friend" (*CP* 332). In the three subsequent quatrains, the anachronisms and shifting points of view crowd on one another to compose a disorienting collage of historical indicators. The moral oratory of "cerebrotonic Cato," whose writings actually date back to the republican era some six hundred years before the collapse of the empire, contrasts with the forceful rebellion of evidently modern, "muscle-bound Marines" against the neglect of a state that has terminated their "food and pay." Caesar luxuriates in his warm "double-bed," while an anonymous clerk "writes I DO NOT LIKE MY WORK / On a pink official form" (*CP* 333). Eventually, the picture widens to include details from the natural environment surrounding the city, visual cues that connote the introduction of a nonanthropocentric model of time. An alarming prospect then emerges of a multitude of small birds seated on "speckled eggs" who, without quite giving away whether they are disease-carriers or scavengers, remorselessly "eye each flu-infected city." Finally, the last quatrain arrives with a sublime vision of impending doom.

> Altogether elsewhere, vast
> Herds of reindeer move across
> Miles and miles of golden moss,
> Silently and very fast.
>
> (*CP* 333)

The reindeer, of course, are creatures of a northern clime. They are being displaced by the movements of the Germanic tribes who will destroy the Roman Empire with the invasion and sacking of the capital. The "herds" of reindeer thus form a metonym, or accidental sign, of the onslaught of the Gothic hordes; that the animals move "silently and very fast" terrifyingly suggests the same of the human troops following behind them. The poem's own refusal to name the cause of the reindeer's stampede brilliantly emblematizes the feat of historical erasure that will be accomplished with the triumph of barbarian lawlessness.

Indeed, what distinguishes "The Fall of Rome" as a genuinely disquieting and original work of satire is its trick of making all the various mythologies of civilization it invokes reveal their illusory procedures, so that their violent disproof at the hands of those who never have been granted a role in such fictions seems at once grievous and necessary. There is, moreover, a sense in which the poem's suppression of the historical record in its final stanza, the Goths' imminent obliteration of the ancient city, and the clerk's trivial deed of vandalism against the protocols of corporate administration are all of a piece. Each of these gestures represents a revolt against the conviction that a realistic political theory might be premised on the supposed universality of an abstract idea of the human. The verse structure further underlines the moral insofar as each quatrain forms a self-contained grammatical unit, as if, through the avoidance of enjambment across stanzas, to accentuate the atomized conditions of personal experience and the incapacity of language to bind those fragments into a synthetic whole.

Wherever the claim to abstract universality is made, Auden's poetry implicitly argues, a persecutory phobia of the unfamiliar cannot be far behind. Art risks subservience to this peculiar form of bad faith whenever it surrenders the voice of open-ended, historical querulousness for that of prophetic authority. The poet advances the argument in "Secondary Epic" by satirizing the propagandistic homages of classical Augustan literature to its imperial patron. Auden specifically takes Virgil to task for the ekphrasis in *Aeneid* 8.626–732 that details the shield wrought by Vulcan for Aeneas. On the shield, the history of Rome is illustrated from Romulus's founding of the city to Augustus's triumphant return in 29 B.C. after triple victories abroad in Dalmatia, at Actium, and in Egypt. The gift of the shield, conveyed to Aeneas by his mother Venus, is meant to sanction and consecrate the hero's mission by foretelling the consequences of his actions. But the prophecy, Auden nudges us to remember, is a selectively incomplete summary of Roman history, one that ends just as the golden age of Augustus's reign is commencing and projects the events of the "future" with the full benefit of Virgil's hindsight.

> No, Virgil, no:
> Not even the first of the Romans can learn
> His Roman history in the future tense,
> Not even to serve your political turn;
> Hindsight as foresight makes no sense.
>
> (*CP* 598)

The negative apostrophe of the opening line strikes a conversational note that bespeaks the familiarity of an intimate and keeps the quarrel with Virgil from seeming academic or overly polite.

Auden, clearly thinking of the shield's romanticized depiction of the battle of Actium (rather than the celebration on Augustus's return to Rome two years later), demands of his predecessor "how was your shield-making god to explain / ... why he didn't foresee / The future beyond 31 B.C.?" He amplifies the question in the following lines with a damning reinterpretive flourish:

> Why a curtain of darkness should finally drop
> On Carians, Morini, Gelonians with quivers
> Converging Romeward in abject file,
> Euphrates, Araxes and similar rivers
> Learning to flow in a latinate style,
> And Caesar be left where prophecy ends,
> Inspecting troops and gifts for ever?
> Wouldn't Aeneas have asked—"What next?
> After this triumph, what portends?"
>
> (*CP* 599)

The "curtain of darkness" dropping on the scene cunningly echoes the last lines of the *Dunciad*: "Thy hand, great Anarch! lets the curtain fall / And Universal Darkness buries all" (4.655–656). In the previous chapter, I observed the influence of the finale of Pope's grand historical satire on Byron's melancholy description of Roman ruins in *Childe Harold's Pilgrimage* 4. Auden eschews Pope's mock-epic technique of misapplying the ancient devices of heroic idealization to bathetic modern circumstances. The twentieth-century poet's rereading of the rhetoric of imperial Roman self-glorification through the lens of a modern awareness of the empire's demise instead assumes a historical vantage closer to that of Byron's rueful retrospection. Yet the catalog of tributaries to the might of Augustus in the next lines subtly but significantly travesties the terms of the Virgilian original, thus making good on the satiric aspirations signaled by the evocation of Pope. The Carians, Morini, and Gelonians are all constituents of the class of *gentes victae,* or conquered people, whom Virgil mentions as part of the grandiose procession commemorating Augustus's foreign victories. Auden's memory of the *Aeneid* is sharp enough to recall that the members of the last group indeed are pictured in the poem as still outfitted with their quivers when they march past the *princeps* (they are *sagittiferos Gelonos*). Such precision makes it all the more glaring when he revises Virgil's description of the procession's "long line" ("longo ordine," 8.722) to an "abject file" and changes the undulation of the Euphrates "with softer waves" ("mollior undis," 8.726) to the act of flowing "in a latinate style." Auden's sardonic alterations sharply ironize the imagined curiosity of Aeneas with respect to Rome's fortunes "after this triumph."

To this point, "Secondary Epic" has managed its distortions of the classical ideal with such care that the irreverence has never quite risen to outright parody. As the next verse paragraph advances, however, Auden begins to toy with a revolutionary counterfiction that reflects back in a grotesque light on the *Aeneid*'s conditions of production. (To paraphrase Marx's *Eighteenth Brumaire,* the strategy might be said to demonstrate that Augustan imperialism, like historical dialectic, occurs twice: first as epic, then as satire.) Inspired by the ingenuity of the Virgilian model, the modern poet gleefully imagines "a continuation / To your Eighth Book, an interpolation" thrown together by "a down-at-heels refugee rhetorician / With an empty belly, seeking employment" from Rome's enemies in the day when barbarian feudalism has brought the *imperium* to its knees (*CP* 599). This scathing indictment of a literary art that is totally conciliatory catches some of the knowing, acid tone of Byron's lampoon of the "sad trimmer" of a poet who sings for Juan and Haidée in *Don Juan,* a hack who "lied with such a fervour of intention— / There was no doubt he earn'd his laureate pension" (3.80). Like Byron, who mingles swipes at Southey with both comic self-condemnation and despairing cynicism at the decline of literary aura in an increasingly commercial print culture, Auden blends caricature and self-caricature so thoroughly that his castigation of depoliticized pastiche begins to look like the disgusted impatience of a solipsist ready to turn his back on art altogether.

The addendum "scrawled at the side of a tattered text" of Virgil's epic will introduce into the description of Aeneas's shield a glamorized portrait of the sack of Rome by the Visigoth Alaric in 410 A.D., a mock-ekphrasis shrewdly fashioned for the riotous entertainment "of some blond princeling whom loot had inclined / To believe that Providence had assigned / To blonds the task of improving mankind" (*CP* 599). Edward Mendelson has interpreted "Secondary Epic," written during the height of the Cold War in

1959, as "a poem that obliquely questions what later writers called the 'Pax Americana'" through its insistence on the futility of imperial aspirations.[11] However, Auden's chillingly indistinct designation of the hireling rhetorician's employer as "blond" brings to mind another historical parallel, namely that between the conquering Germanic tribes who overran Rome and the Nazi dictatorship of the German Third Reich. This simile, of course, is facilitated by the ominous identification of the politico's self-prescribed mission as that of "improving mankind." The broadness of the poem's caricature of aggressive, flaxen-haired egomania gives the impression of a general exposé of Western barbarity toward what it perceives as foreign cultures, a description of authoritarian tendencies that unhappily applies to a variety of historical circumstances.

In the lines immediately following, "Secondary Epic" lives up to its own title as it enacts the poetic description of Aeneas's literally vandalized shield through a remarkable feat of stylistic impersonation.

> Now Mainz appears and starry New Year's Eve
> As two-horned Rhine throws off the Latin yoke
> To bear the Vandal on his frozen back;
> Lo! Danube, now congenial to the Goth,
> News not unwelcome to Teutonic shades
> And all lamenting beyond Acheron
> Demolished Carthage or a plundered Greece:
> And now Juturna leaves the river-bed
> Of her embittered grievance—loud her song,
> Immoderate her joy—for word has come
> Of treachery at the Salarian Gate.
> Alaric has avenged Turnus.
>
> (*CP* 599)

Auden's rhetoric in this passage is a tour de force of mimicry. When he calls the Rhine "two-horned," he echoes Virgil's epithet for the river, "bicornis" (8.727). Yet the ironic backward glance serves only to highlight the modernizing reversals and overturnings of the heroic order as the natural world shrugs off its "Latin yoke" and the dialectical process of Rome's ruination is set in motion. Indeed, the resonance of this description of frozen northern rivers bearing Gothic marauders southward to Italy ultimately has very little to do with any precedent from the Latin literature. The barbarian "interpolation" is in fact an exuberant pastiche of lines we already know well from one of the most celebrated of English Augustan poems.

> From Hyperborean skies
> Embody'd dark, what clouds of Vandals rise!

> Lo! where Maeotis sleeps, and hardly flows
> The freezing Tanais thro' a waste of snows. . . .
>
> See Alaric's stern port! the martial frame
> Of Genseric! and Atilla's dread name! . . .
>
> See Christians, Jews, one heavy sabbath keep,
> And all the western world believe and sleep.
>   (*Dunciad* 3.85–88, 91–92, 99–100)

Pope's vision here of the gradual disintegration of classical civilization beneath the waves of invaders issuing from "Hyperborean" regions signals the poem's general anxiety regarding the corruption of both politics and culture by the enemies of learning. Auden reshapes the passage to warn readers that when absorbed in a spirit of self-approval, learning becomes a mechanism of denial or avoidance, thus facilitating its own destruction. His allusions to "demolished Carthage" and "plundered Greece" and his recasting of Alaric as Turnus's avenger bespeak his sense of Rome's responsibility for the hatred of those who will destroy the empire. The satiric inversion of the political ideology of the *Aeneid* brings to light the involvement of the work of art in the social brutalities from which it supposedly distances us. The contrast between Virgilian encomium and Popean censure perhaps serves to underline the point. At any rate, Auden's pessimism regarding the autonomy of culture again brings to mind Adorno in the mood of revulsion that prompted his notorious remark that "to write poetry after Auschwitz is barbaric."[12]

After spinning out this mock-ekphrastic conceit, Auden indulges in his own work of retrospective prolepsis, one that glorifies neither the Roman nor the barbarian perspective but impartially savors an irony of history that looks too pointed to be accidental. In so doing, he tacitly points out how a poetics grounded in satire may help to redeem art for the purposes of ideological critique.

> No, Virgil, no:
> Behind your verse so masterfully made
> We hear the weeping of a Muse betrayed.
> Your Anchises isn't convincing at all;
> It's asking too much of us to be told
> A shade so long-sighted, a father who knows
> That Romulus will build a wall,
> Augustus found an Age of Gold,
> And is trying to teach a dutiful son
> The love of what will be in the long run,
> Would mention them but not disclose

> (Surely, no prophet could afford to miss
> No man of destiny fail to enjoy
> So clear a proof of Providence as this)
> The names predestined for the Catholic boy
> Whom Arian Odovacer will depose.
>
> (*CP* 600)

Auden's corrective to Virgil is really a corrective to the Western fantasy of domination as a means to enlightenment, the sword as necessary harbinger of the torch. Hegel incorporated this fable into the very foundations of his dialectical method when he famously referred to history as a "slaughter-bench, upon which the happiness of nations, the wisdom of states, and the virtue of individuals were sacrificed" in order for Spirit to progress toward its world-historical destiny, which is consciousness of its own freedom.[13] By disabusing readers of such illusions, satire may set the record straight on behalf of Clio, the betrayed muse of history whose weeping we hear beneath Virgil's sonorities.[14] Auden dedicated another of his neoclassicizing poems from the 1950s, "Homage to Clio," to this divine patroness and here at the close of "Secondary Epic" gives her the satiric last laugh. The joke consists in the fact that the name of the last emperor of Rome in the West, deposed and exiled in 476 A.D. by the German commander of the imperial guard mentioned in the last line, is "Romulus Augustulus." Alluding to the "Catholic Boy" by invoking his namesake predecessors but at the same time withholding any explicit reference from the reader, Auden rectifies the historical account by memorializing Arian Odovacer while maintaining a stunning reticence with respect to the identity of the ruler whom he vanquishes.

Like "Secondary Epic," the Horatian epode entitled "Forty Years On" insists in its title and central fictive premise on its posterior condition, framing its hermeneutic confrontation with the reader in terms of the poem's own historicity. Even the metrical form, which consists of distichs pairing an initial, accentual hexameter line with a subsequent trimeter line, presents itself as a sort of pictogram of decline or diminishment, casting an ironic light on its own ostensible neoclassicism. Written in 1968, the epode is a sardonic, self-elegizing monologue delivered by Autolycus, the roguish pickpocket and ballad-monger of Shakespeare's *The Winter's Tale* whose name, Frank Kermode tells us, belonged in Greek mythology to "the son of Hermes, under one aspect the god of thieves."[15] At once a child of the messenger of the gods and a dissembling outlaw, Autolycus embodies the duplicity of the humanistic arts. In "Forty Years On," he represents a parody of the modern ideal of self-cultivation, a caricature of the individual as rational agent. The poem thus delicately satirizes the plight of bourgeois society, a milieu in which a petty criminal reaps the rewards of prosperity and respectability for greasing the wheels of business. The title suggests how much time has elapsed since the close of the play.[16] As the epode commences, Autolycus gives a disheartening glimpse of the advance of consumerism and industrialization into the pastoral landscape of Shakespearean romance.

> Except where blast-furnaces and generating-stations
>   have inserted their sharp profiles
> or a Thru-Way slashes harshly across them, Bohemia's contours
>   look just as amiable now
> as when I saw them first (indeed, her coast is gentler,
>   for tame hotels have ousted
> the havocking bears), nor have her dishes lost their flavor
>   since Florizel was thwacked into exile
> and we and Sicily discorded, fused into rival amalgams,
>   in creed and policy oppugnant.
>
>   (*CP* 782–783)

The qualifications and caveats of this sentence belie its placatory rhetoric. So phrased, however, the modernizing of a familiar topos acquires a subdued, almost unconscious shock value. Shakespeare's Bohemia provides an image of nature as an idealized, sensual economy in some of the most affecting and justly celebrated language in his late plays. Polixenes introduces the idea when he characterizes nature as a principle that "make[s] conceive a bark of baser kind / By bud of nobler race" (4.4.94–95), but Perdita gives it sumptuous immediacy when she rehearses the local flora:

> Daffadils,
> That come before the swallow's dares, and take
> The winds of March with beauty; violets, dim,
> But sweeter than the lids of Juno's eyes,
> Or Cytherea's breath; pale primeroses,
> That die unmarried, ere they can behold
> Bright Phoebus in his strength (a malady
> Most incident to maids); bold oxlips, and
> The crown imperial; lilies of all kinds
> (The flow'r-de-luce being one).
>
>   (4.4.118–127)

The intrusion of the "sharp profiles" of "blast-furnaces" and "generating stations" into Perdita's edenic garden has accomplished the violent transformation of a biological into a commercial economy. The "Thru-Way" that "slashes harshly across" the face of the land is a symbol of the human drive to technological domination of the earth that recalls one of Auden's earlier satiric portraits of the will to power, "Et in Arcadia Ego" (1964), where "the autobahn / Thwarts the landscape / In godless Roman arrogance" (*CP* 725). Autolycus's disclosure of the civil strife arising between the two monarchies united by marriage at the end of *The Winter's Tale* and leaving them "in creed and policy oppugnant" suggests that the costs of the ascendancy of modern mass culture have been both psychic and political. Civilization's discontents have come to coincide with capitalism's dialectical self-contradictions.

We therefore may regard Autolycus's reassurances regarding the inviolateness of Bohemia's innocence as a form of repression or false consciousness. His testimony that "her coast is gentler / for tame hotels have ousted / the havocking bears," for instance, encodes an unacknowledged ambiguity. The comparative adjective "gentler" connotes the domestication and cultivation of a potentially threatening wilderness (*OED*, sense 4), thus unmistakably echoing Polixenes's explanation to Perdita of the art of husbandry: "You see, sweet maid, we marry / A gentler scion to the wildest stock" (4.4.92–93). Yet the adjective also hints at an elevation of social status (*OED*, sense 2) with an insinuation of the commodification or gentrification of a previously less marketable locale. The civilizing of a feral environment thus comes to seem synonymous with its prostitution at the hands of a ruthless profiteerism. The expulsion of the "havocking bears" by the hotel trade strikes a decidedly ominous note. Autolycus reminds us of the animal that in act 3, scene 3, of *The Winter's Tale* chases and kills Antigonus, the Sicilian lord who, obeying the bidding of the psychotically jealous King Leontes, has sailed to Bohemia to abandon Perdita, the daughter of Leontes and his persecuted wife, Hermione. The fatal encounter between Antigonus and the bear is the first inkling we have in the play that on occasion death may be a consequence of the natural order rather than of human murderousness. Ironically, because the animal knows nothing of cruelty, it may be said to further the aim of social reparation. By upholding the rule of nature, the bear avenges the victims of Leontes' patriarchal rage, the women and children whom he has killed or silenced. Paulina, Hermione's lady-in-waiting, is the *dramatis persona* who pleads for such redress. When Hermione apparently dies as a result of Leontes' abuse, Paulina proclaims: "the Queen, the Queen, / The sweet'st, dear'st creature's dead; and vengeance / Not dropped down yet" (3.2.198–200). Fulfilling the threat latent in these words, however unwittingly, the bear realizes Paulina's wish for restitution. The animal's wrath falls on the lord who happens not only to be the king's instrument in the abandonment of Perdita but Paulina's husband.

The bear's intervention in the action deflects the course of the drama from the tragic toward the comic. Because the bear dwells in the middle ground between comedy and tragedy, and because it plays havoc with the dealings of a tyrannous society, it assumes in the eyes of a clown who witnesses Antigonus's death the figure of a fellow satirist. This witness tells the shepherd who adopts Perdita that the bear, "roaring louder than the sea or weather," has "mocked" the hapless Antigonus to pieces (4.1.101–102). The association of feminine outrage with the offices of satire that logically follows from the clown's conclusion reflects, I think, Shakespeare's intuition that satire is always the recourse of those for whom the institutional avenues to justice are closed, that satire inevitably excoriates an otherwise inured and unrepentant power. To the extent that the bear stands for natural law, Antigonus's sacrifice looks like the miraculous restoration of a lost moral equilibrium.

Autolycus asserts in "Forty Years On" that the mercenary exploitation of Bohemia's resources has had a propitious outcome. Yet the gentrification of its coast evidently has gone hand-in-hand with the undoing of the comic resolutions that the play had maneuvered to secure. The marriage between Sicily's Princess Perdita and Bohemia's Prince Florizel has collapsed into "rival amalgams," now that Florizel has been "thwacked into exile." Unsettlingly, Autolycus's report that Florizel has been "thwacked into exile" returns us to the opening of Shakespeare's drama, where Hermione playfully claims that if Polixenes, Bohemia's visiting monarch, avows his yearning to see his son, "We'll thwack him hence with distaffs" (1.2.37). The queen's cartoonish image of expulsion accidentally presages the forced flight of Polixenes from Sicily to escape Leontes' bloodthirsty jealousy. A reader who hears Autolycus reappropriating her words in "Forty Years On" must conclude that the whole cycle of violence has started over among the members of the younger generation. The fable that Autolycus initially propounded of Bohemia as a suburban utopia where commerce makes nature "gentler" has revealed itself as a paradigm of alienation, a decadent, mutilated conglomeration of rapacious consumerism, neurotic resentments, and political feuding.

Autolycus is not the sort of character whom we might suppose capable of developing any critical consciousness regarding these historical conditions. He himself readily volunteers that he never had the "schooling" to be a "useful technician" (nor, for that matter, the "*Sitz-Fleisch*" to be a "bureaucrat"), only "the courtier's agility / to adapt my rogueries to the times" (*CP* 784). Disclaiming any esoteric, technical competence and avowing only a "courtier's" understanding of human behavior, he briefly seems to assume the aspect of that early modern archetype of liberal judgment, the Renaissance humanist. Rather than espousing the civic ideals of Elyot's governor or Castiglione's *cortegiano*, however, Autolycus professes an ethos of self-gain more appropriate to the protagonists of Hobbes's or Smith's theories. The language of a humanist rapidly gives way to that of Economic Man:

> I survived and prosper
>   better than I ever did under
> the old lackadaisical economy.

> ... A pedlar still, for obvious reasons
>   I no longer cry my wares,
> But in ill-lit alleys coaxingly whisper to likely clients.
>
> (*CP* 784)

Until now he always has been able to turn the needs of others to his own profit, as he avouches at the end of the song Auden gives him in parodic tribute to the peddler's song from Shakespeare's romance ("Lawn as white as driven snow"). "Believe me, I know all the tricks," sings Auden's peddler, "There is nothing I can't fix." Having benefited from the country's economic expansion and having sailed in the political winds with a "courtier's agility," Autolycus is not without his share of responsibility for Bohemia's present circumstances.

Neither is he without some uneasiness with respect to those circumstances, however. "Only to the ear is it patent something drastic has happened," he admits, expressing a former street-singer's sensitivity to popular rhetoric. Exactly what event this "something drastic" represents is unclear, even to the experienced listener. The change nevertheless has an undeniable effect on those who endure its aftermath: "But how glib all the faces around me / seem suddenly to have become / and how seldom I feel like a hay-tumble." Autolycus finishes his soliloquy by rehearsing a fantasy that has troubled him recurrently in his sleep.

> For three nights running
>   now I have had the same dream
> of a suave afternoon in Fall. I am standing on high ground
>   looking out westward over
> a plain, run smoothly by Jaguar farmers. In the eloignment,
>   a-glitter in the whelking sun,
> a sheer bare cliff concludes the vista. At its base I see,
>   black, shaped like a bell-tent,
> the mouth of a cave by which (I know in my dream) I am to
>   make my final exit,
> its roof so low it will need an awkward duck to make it.
>   "Well, will that be so shaming?"
> I ask when awake. Why should it be? When has Autolycus
>   ever solemned himself?
>
> (*CP* 785)

The dreamer fears an impending judgment, a "shaming," that will coincide with his "final exit." Casting himself in the role of a Dantean pilgrim, he faces the start of a forbidding quest that will take him across a plain inhabited by "Jaguar farmers" and through a portal shaped to ensure the humiliation of whoever seeks the next life. The farmers' unusual choice of livestock conjures up the leopard, "una lonza leggiera e presta molto," of *Inferno* 1.32, an allegorical beast generally taken to symbolize lust. The association suggests that Autolycus's anxiety originates in some sort of sexual guilt. This implication is strengthened if we bear in mind a point that Mendelson presses in his reading of the last line: "Auden's daily readings in the *Oxford English Dictionary* would have reminded him that the verb 'to solemn' means *to celebrate a marriage*, which Autolycus has never done."[17] Auden portrays Autolycus, in other words, as a frivolous hedonist whose sexual and mercenary appetites have blinded him to political reality. On another level, his unmarried state clearly marks him as something of an outsider in relation to the bourgeois domestic economy. By focusing on Autolycus's sustained bachelorhood, Auden may be acknowledging tacitly his own plight as a gay man in heterosexist society. The unspoken assumption of such a society that the topic of gay desire is supposed to be handled tacitly or covertly is, in fact, an aspect of this plight. The final question Autolycus poses at the end of "Forty Years On" thus may be regarded as an example of what Richard R. Bozorth has identified as its author's chief rhetorical strategy in writing about his erotic life, that is, a tendency to "make a social game out of the open secret of [his] own sexuality."[18] A form of ambivalence governs the end of the poem, then. Autolycus's confession of his dream may be said to satirize his own egocentrism, to expose the irresponsibility of his narcissistic pursuit of gain. Yet this very pursuit of an unattainable satisfaction bespeaks the pathos of the individual in a commodity culture, where social relations that do not obey market imperatives are veiled or erased. If Autolycus has never "solemned himself," in the sense that he has never refused to prostrate himself before authority, his self-declaration mockingly reflects the brutality of the society that has taught him to be so pliant.

As noted earlier, "Et in Arcadia Ego" resembles "Forty Years On" in rebuking the technocratic instrumentalism of capitalist modernity. Even more sharply than the Shakespearean pastiche, however, "Et in Arcadia Ego" questions the historical justification of this phenomenon as a sign of "progress." Auden's argument again bears comparison to Arendt's critique of the triumph of *animal laborans*, an event implying the establishment of a machine society that "guides the body's labor and eventually replaces it altogether" and prompting Arendt to remark: "The question therefore is . . . whether machines still serve the world and its things, or if, on the contrary, they and the automatic motion of their processes have begun to rule and even destroy world and things."[19] Auden's poem may be said to ridicule the perversion of an earlier, humanist ideal of culture into this domain of laboring machines. In so doing, it casts into doubt the supposed rationality or logic behind the ascendancy of mass consumption as the organizing social principle of the modern day.

The Latin phrase that gives the poem its title comes from an inscription originally depicted in an allegorical scene of two shepherds pondering a death's head encountered in the woods, a painting completed in the early seventeenth century by Giovanni Francesco Guercino. From Guercino's picture, the text eventually found its way in 1769 into a double portrait of two women, Mrs. Bouverie and Mrs. Crewe, by Sir Joshua Reynolds. In Reynolds's painting, the two female subjects are shown sitting in front of a tombstone and contemplating its inscription: "Et in Arcadia ego" ("and even in Arcadia am I"). In an essay on the elegiac tradition, Erwin Panofsky recounts a conversation between Reynolds and Samuel Johnson concerning the meaning of the formula, an exchange that ensued on the latter's first-time inspection of the picture. Johnson, an expert Latinist, asked what the inscription purported and added that it seemed "very nonsensical—I am in Arcadia."[20] Reynolds answered that the king, George III, who had visited the painter the day before, had comprehended the Latin tag immediately and had exclaimed, "Oh, there is a tombstone in the background: Ay, ay, death is even in Arcadia."[21]

The substance of this anecdote, which Panofsky misses, is not that Dr. Johnson somehow failed to comprehend the grammar of the phrase but that he did not connect the sentence to the idea of death as a menacing reality that underlies the literary fantasy of an inexhaustibly self-replenishing nature in which all needs have been magically satisfied. Panofsky declares that the "royal rendering" of George II "represents a grammatically correct, in fact the only grammatically correct, interpretation" of the sentence, but the question of grammar is irrelevant to understanding Johnson's hesitancy; indeed, the learned Doctor's paraphrase proves this point.[22] His blindness to the symbolism instead seems related to a question of critical perspective, as the king's observation of the tombstone's position "in the background" makes clear.[23] Perspective, on this reckoning, is less a matter of spatial location than of rank, knowledge, and authority. The comparison between Johnson and George III constitutes a parable about the sort of worldliness requisite to the penetration of culture's fundamental illusions. The king, of course, is more accustomed than the scholar to looking for death where we have been told it has no place.

"Et in Arcadia Ego" begins by proposing a cartoonish myth of the foundation of culture:

> Who, now, seeing Her so
> Happily married,
> Housewife, helpmate to Man,
>
> Can imagine the screeching
> Virago, the Amazon,
> Earth-Mother was?

> Her jungle-growths
> Are abated, Her exorbitant
> Monsters abashed,
>
> Her soil mumbled,
> Where crops, aligned precisely,
> Will soon be orient.
>   (*CP* 724)

The process of mastering the earth and yoking its resources to human purposes farcically reinterprets the cliché male fantasy of conquering the Amazon warrior, the figure of female sexual sovereignty par excellence. The disciplining of the earth's "exorbitant monsters" may be meant to call to mind the allegorization in Aeschylus's *Oresteia* of the establishment of Athenian law as the transmutation of the chthonic, murderous Erinyes into the civilized Eumenides. At any rate, the poem represents Western civilization as an explicitly comic, patriarchal resolution to a war of the sexes between Man and Nature. The seemingly cozy marriage between these protagonists gradually divulges a more frightening actuality beneath the surface, as the poem turns to examine the other member of the partnership and asks "As for him / What has happened to the Brute / Epics and nightmares tell of?" (*CP* 724). The comic insistence on harmony is uneasily sustained with the sense of a barely suppressed recollection of past violence, as the poetic narrator assures us that "no bishops pursue / Their archdeacons with axes" and approvingly notes that, in an abandoned hideaway of thieves, "sightseers picnic / Who carry no daggers" (*CP* 725).

The final stanzas of "Et in Arcadia Ego" dispel the historically optimistic view of mass society as the fulfillment of the longstanding dream of an enlightened, humane polity:

> I well might think myself
> A humanist,
> Could I manage not to see
> How the autobahn
>
> Thwarts the landscape
> In godless Roman arrogance,
> The farmer's children
>
> Tiptoe past the shed
> Where the gelding knife is kept.
>   (*CP* 725)

In the autobahn, the symbol of modern German affluence and efficiency, the speaker discerns the sign of an ancient, world-dominating ambition. If the public realm is ruled by "godless Roman arrogance," the private is ruled by a "gelding" or castrating law of the father. The violence apparently pacified in the earlier stanzas returns with a vengeance in the patriarchal sadism of the household glimpsed in the final stanza and gives a chilling twist to the larger domestic theme with which the poem opens. The speaker disclaims the blitheness of mind that would allow him to take a celebratory, "humanist" view of this picture; death is all too apparent in contemporary Arcadia. It should be noted, however, that in a deeper sense the very terms used by the speaker to assess the scene belie the dismissal of learning. A healthy degree of bildung, or acculturation, is necessary to recognize the significance of the earth's metamorphosis from "Amazon" to "helpmate" and the autobahn's imperial peremptoriness. Only because of the humanist perspective he wishes to disown can the speaker *not* "manage not to see" what has taken place. In this sense, he may be said to align himself with a concern for history and critical acuity that is closer to Dr. Johnson's interests than the king's.

It would be a mistake to regard Auden, on the evidence of poems such as "Forty Years On" and "Et in Arcadia Ego," as a cultural reactionary who is nostalgic for some sort of premodern social idyll. However self-mockingly, his poetry consistently articulates the hope of a revolutionary reorganization of society that finally will allow the requirements of its weakest and least productive members to be met. One of the earliest expressions of this hope occurs in the untitled sonnet of 1929 that begins "Sir, no man's enemy" and concludes with a call for "new styles of architecture, a change of heart" (*SP* 7). One of its later enunciations appears in "Prologue at Sixty," a poem written in 1967 that culminates in a prayer "for an Eighth Day, / when the created Image shall become the Likeness" (*CP* 831). The desired ethical and political reawakening will build on the insight that, as the poet puts it in "New Year Letter," "all real unity commences / In consciousness of differences" (*CP* 241). The form of community that he envisions, in other words, is a free and peaceful meeting ground for diverse ways of life. Its ideal is tolerance, and Auden's favorite image for it is the modern city. The chastening tone he adopts in articulating this model of civic association might be said to harken back to St. Augustine's description of the *civitas Dei* in language meant to chastise the paganism of Rome at the time of the barbarian invasions:

> Accordingly, two cities have been formed by two loves: the earthly by the love of the self, even to the contempt of God; the heavenly by the love of God, even to the contempt of self. . . . In the one, the princes and the nations it subdues are ruled by the love of ruling; in the other, the princes and the subjects serve one another in love, the latter obeying, while the former take thought for all.[24]

Auden's indebtedness to the Augustinian conception of the *civitas* is most obvious in the free-verse panegyric "Encomium Balnei" from the lyric sequence entitled "Thanksgiving for a Habitat," where the speaker anticipates the moment when the "Holy City" will be realized and "all military hardware / already slighted and submerged" (*CP* 703).

Unlike St. Augustine's City of God, however, the Holy City imagined by Auden is an ideal to be fulfilled on this earth, through political action. His insistence on the city's political character and identification of this character with the open-minded embrace of "differences" is what gives the ideal its modernity. Although not restricted to any particular national or geographic affiliation, this *locus amoenus* unites those individuals to whom the inhuman bureaucracy of the state, while depending on their exertions, denies the fundamental rights of membership. The vision of a cosmopolitan plurality of views linked by a sense of estrangement from the apparatchiks of corporate conformity is a defining feature of that phase of the modern within which a self-conscious modernism emerges, as Raymond Williams once observed in a classic statement.

> Within the new kind of open, complex and mobile society, small groups in any form of divergence or dissent could find some kind of foothold, in ways that would not have been possible if the artists and thinkers composing them had been scattered in more traditional, closed societies.... Thus the key cultural factor of the modernist shift is the character of the metropolis: in these general conditions, but then, even more decisively, in its direct effects on form.... The most important general element of the innovations in form is the fact of immigration to the metropolis, and it cannot too often be emphasized how many of the major innovators were, in this sense, immigrants.... Liberated or breaking from their national or provincial cultures, ... the artists and writers and thinkers of this phase found the only community available to them: a community of the medium; of their own practices.[25]

To perceive how thoroughly Auden's project substantiates Williams's definition of "the key cultural factor of the modernist shift," one need only ponder how the poet articulated his identity as an immigrant in "Prologue at Sixty": "Who am I now? / An American? No, a New Yorker" (*CP* 831).

"Grub First, Then Ethics" is a Pindaric lyric also included in "Thanksgiving for a Habitat." Its title translates one of Brecht's slogans from his *Threepenny Opera* ("Erst kommt das Fressen, dann kommt die Moral," part of the refrain of the song closing the second act). The poem pictures Auden's ideal City as a sanctuary where "banausics can be liberals, / a cook a pure artist." Like the reference to *homo laborans* in "The Poet and the City," the term "banausics" recovers one of Arendt's key terms from *The Human Condition*. *Banausoi*, she reminds us, was the Greek term for the laboring class of artisans "whom Solon still described as sons of Athena and Hephaestus . . . that is, men whose chief interest is their craft and not the market place."[26] Arendt further points out that Aristotle, who regarded the kind of labor assigned to the *banausoi* as demeaning on account of its wearing demands on the body, argued in his *Politics* against extending citizenship to such workers. Auden's poem helps to clarify the identities of the citizens who comprise his ideal City.

> The houses of our City
>   are real enough but they lie
>   haphazardly scattered over the earth,
>   and her vagabond forum
> is any space where two of us happen to meet
>   who can spot a citizen
> without papers. So, too, can her foes. Where the
>   power lies remains to be seen,
> the force, though, is clearly with them: perhaps only
>   by falling can She become
> Her own vision, but we have sworn under four eyes
>   to keep Her up—all we ask for,
> should the night come when comets blaze and meres break,
>   is a good dinner that we
>   may march in high fettle, left foot first,
>   to hold her Thermopylae.
>   (*CP* 706)

The oath taken by the speaker in the poem's peroration balances nicely between epic grandeur and farcical absurdity, with its evocations on the one hand of disastrous cosmic portents and on the other of phalanxes of liberal gourmets marching into battle "left foot first." The lyric revolves around a curious mix of motifs, opening with the conceit of "the shade of Plato" visiting the modern world and appearing "anxious to know / how *anthropos* is." The argument then proceeds to the reimagination of "do-it-yourself America" as "New Cnossos," a municipality of domestic "engines" that feed "Jew, Gentile or Pigmy" until the apocalyptic day when the Epicurean inhabitants must "hold her Thermopylae" (*CP* 704–706). Auden's fantastical synthesis of ancient and modern images of the household envisions polis life from the viewpoint of idiosyncratic private needs rather than of monumental public actions. The effect is to suggest the novel idea of a civilization in which even banausic labors such as the preparation of a good meal can be granted moral dignity.

The poem cunningly appropriates the fundamental political language of Western culture, in other words, on behalf of those whom the culture traditionally has neglected or concealed. By making the Greek city-state the central metaphor on which this ideological reinterpretation hinges, the poet radicalizes a gesture that he first discovered in his 1948 essay "The Greeks and Us": "The historical discontinuity between Greek culture and our own, the disappearance for so many centuries of any direct influence, made it all the easier, when it was rediscovered, for each nation to fashion a classical Greece in its own image. There is a German Greece, a French Greece, an English Greece—there may even be an American Greece—all quite different."[27] In "Grub First, Then Ethics," it might be said, Auden endeavors to fashion a kitsch Greece. We should recall that "Thanksgiving for a Habitat," the sequence in which the poem appears, is in fact a series of twelve lyrics elaborating the mundane topos of the house, each of which is devoted to a different room within the structure. As its title suggests, "Grub First, Then Ethics" celebrates the domain of the kitchen and, through an insistence on the quotidian familiarity of this realm, approaches the type of effect that Marcel Duchamp made famous in the domain of the plastic arts by exhibiting ready-made objects such as a bottle rack or urinal. Like Duchamp's ready-mades, the ode attempts to rescue everyday experience from the idealizing mystifications of aesthetics. In the manner that we might read certain types of conceptual art into a genealogy of kitsch, so too might we construe Auden's vision of Greek civilization as a kind of scullery. Indeed, the poem leads the way on this score when it imagines the *anthropoi* who inhabit the poet's notional polis teasing the ghost of Plato about his metaphysical seriousness: "'Look!' / we would point, for a dig at Athens, 'Here / is the place where we cook'" (*CP* 704).

To speak of the poem as kitsch is to acknowledge as well that its inversion of the customary privileging of male-identified public deeds over female-identified domestic labors problematizes the sexual stereotypes on which Western civilization has been premised. Mendelson notes that the first stanza of "Grub First, The Ethics" overtly "rejects the Greek model of heroism as masculine, aggressive, and self-assertive." He then proceeds to read the lyric in the context of its author's overall intellectual curriculum at the moment of the poem's composition:

> Auden at this time was self-consciously taking lessons from feminine nurture and the feminine imagination. In his introduction to Phyllis McGinley's collection of poems *Times Three*, written probably in late 1959 or early 1960 . . . he dismissed any idea that masculine and feminine imaginations were mutually exclusive—"the hundred-per-cent male and the hundred-per-cent female are equally insufferable"—but proceeded to describe the kind of poetry that each might write if it ex-

isted in isolation. The faults of the masculine sound very much like the ones he saw in his earlier life and work; the virtues of the feminine imagination sound much like the ones he was now trying to achieve in his poems.[28]

Mendelson's sense of the manner in which the poet moralizes the antithesis between "masculine and feminine imaginations" in this essay clarifies on what basis "Grub First, Then Ethics" undertakes to revise by satiric means the self-image that Greek culture traditionally has supplied to the Western mind. This antithesis between male and female principles recalls another opposition between sexual types drawn by the poet in "The Greeks and Us," one that bears more directly on the themes of "Grub First, The Ethics":

> Even within a single country different Greeces coexist. For instance here are two English caricatures:
> Professor X. Reade Chair of Moral Philosophy. 59. Married. Three daughters. . . . Politics: Conservative. . . . Does not notice what he eats. . . .
> Mr. Y. Clasical Tutor. 41. Unmarried. . . . Has private means and gives wonderful lunch parties for favorite undergraduates. . . . Hobbies: travel and collecting old glass. Dislikes: Christianity, girls, the poor, English cooking. Current worry: his figure.
> To X, the word Greece suggests Reason, the Golden Mean, emotional control, freedom from superstition; to Y it suggests Gaiety and Beauty, the life of the senses, freedom from inhibitions.[29]

The contrast between stuffy, straight Professor X who "does not notice what he eats" and histrionic, gay Mr. Y who "gives wonderful lunch parties for favorite undergraduates" captures in a rudimentary form the tension animating "Grub First, Then Ethics" between the warrior ethos of the Greek polis and the hedonist spirit of Auden's city of gourmets. (Although Mr. Y's dislike of "the poor" also bespeaks a dandyish callousness that is quite different from the poem's attitude toward *banausoi*.) That the Pindaric lyric does not require us to decode this tension as a contest between heterosexist and gay-friendly cultures confirms the poem's status as a kitsch object in a specific sense. Kitsch, as Eve Kosofsky Sedgwick has written, represents a debased version of the feminized category of "the sentimental."[30] The defining quality of kitsch is its ambivalence between denial and cynical acceptance of its stigmatized or marginal condition, as opposed to the attitude of camp, which Kosofsky Sedgwick claims "involve[s] a gayer and more spacious angle of view."[31] José Esteban Muñoz reinforces this claim when he declares that "the word camp is integral to what Esther Newton calls the 'gay world' of homosexuality, whereas kitsch's usage seems to be less tied to any specific group."[32] Indeed, Auden's project in "Grub First, Then Ethics" ought to be understood as compatible with, but not restricted to, a queer critique of Western patriarchal society, precisely because this society has suppressed or ignored the concerns of a range of social groups, including, but not exclusive to, those of gay men.

Auden's poetry, in other words, celebrates personal eccentricity as a sign of political freedom and satirizes mass society's efforts to alienate such idiosyncrasy out of existence. In this light, it becomes clear precisely why Auden regarded Arendt's analysis of modernity in *The Human Condition* as the work of a kindred intelligence. Arendt defines the modern rise of the social as an eruption into the public domain of the activities of "housekeeping" or economics that classical civilization consigned to the private.[33] The classical outlook regarded the fiercely agonistic space of the polis as the realm of freedom, where all participants were free individuals performing unique and memorable deeds. The private site of the household, or *oikia*, was the domain of inequality, where all members labored to meet the momentary demands of necessity, thus enabling the patriarchal ruler of the *oikia* to participate in the polis. The irony of modernity is that it has done away with this invidious distinction at the price of diminishing, and perhaps ultimately destroying, the very concept of the individual. It has replaced the ancient equality of political agents with a "modern equality, based on the conformism inherent in society and possible only because behavior has replaced action as the foremost mode of human relationship."[34] What Arendt means by "behavior" is the utilitarian reduction of all human activities to statistical patterns of effects. The problem with such an emphasis on behavior is that it regards any variance from the pattern as a sign of error: "The unfortunate truth about behaviorism and the validity of its 'laws' is that the more people there are, the more likely they are to behave and the less likely to tolerate nonbehavior."[35] The freedom of the modern state in other words imposes on all individuals a view of human existence as consisting of nothing more than labor in the service of the accumulation of wealth, that most quantifiable measure of value. This is a condition the ancients would have regarded as a form of slavery and which they identified with the *animal laborans*.[36]

We are now in a position to recognize that the central satiric task Auden assigned to himself was to deplore this reduction of modernity to a utilitarian calculus of gains and losses. Instead of criticizing the behaviorism of modern society by appeal to the classical distinction between public and private, however, he engages in a more synthetic and idiosyncratic effort. Although he gives definition to his dream of community by appeal to the image of the city, the picture he offers is unrecognizable, strictly speaking, as a polis from the standpoint of classical philosophy. For what the poet espouses as an alternative to the numbing materialism of bourgeois, twentieth-century society is an urbane forum of the affections. This is what he means when he writes of "the *polis* of our friends" in "New Year Letter" (*CP* 224). As I will show, this notion of a cosmopolitan aggregation of individuals whose disparate interests are bound together by ties of love and sympathy is closely related to the image of private individuals united in their liberal resistance to fascist totalitarianism in "September 1, 1939." In Auden's stirring commemoration of the date of Poland's invasion by Germany, the act of political defiance is given a human motive when the poet appeals to the compassion of his readers with the ringing declaration "We must love one another or die." Much has been made of the poet's disowning of the sentiment in later life due to his feeling that it falsely presents love as an impersonal drive or instinct.[37] The line may be read, however, not as a reassuring fiction about the abstract universality of humanity's better, more loving nature but, to the contrary, as an acknowledgment of humanity's dividedness between the impulses of compasssion and cruelty. Precisely because of our sadistic inclinations, we must find a way to treat one another with mercy and compassion. There is a quasi-religious force to this injunction that recalls the language of Saint Paul when, for example, he exhorts the members of the church at Ephesus, "And be ye kind to one another, tenderhearted, forgiving one another, even as God for Christ's sake hath forgiven you," and tells them furthermore to "walk in love, as Christ also hath loved us" (Ephesians 4:32, 5:1). The moral commandment of Auden's poem, however, balances against an overwhelming sense of the propensity of human beings to cruelty, a view that is almost Hobbesian in its pessimism: "Those to whom evil is done / Do evil in return" (*SP* 86). In the poet's eyes, the individual performs acts of love or kindness against high odds and through not insignificant exertions of will. Love, in guises that range from friendship to marriage, is an improbability, as Auden tells us in his moving epithalamium "In Sickness and In Health": "All chance, all love, all logic, you and I / Exist by grace of the Absurd" (*CP* 319).

In an attempt to determine precisely the source of Byron's appeal to the reader, Auden remarks in the essay "Don Juan" that "the more closely his poetic *persona* comes to resemble the epistolary *persona* of his letters to his male friends . . . the more authentic his poetry seems" and proposes a moment later that "the authentic poet in Byron is Byron the Friend."[38] Auden's stress on "persona" tells us that his idea of friendship presumes a shared enthusiasm for the ludic artifice of language as an enabling condition of personal trust. His emphasis on the rhetorical encoding or performance of private feelings as the hallmark of their "authentic" status may be seen to consort with a kitsch reading of his poetry in a distinctive sense. For Auden proposes that the bond of friendship requires not only the presence of strong emotions but also the self-consciousness to treat such emotions as metaphors at the service of an ongoing conversation between social and intellectual equals, between individuals who understand intuitively each other's struggles with history and circumstance.

> Between two friends their first concern is not to bore each other. If they are persons of heart and imagination they will take for granted that the other has beliefs and feelings which he takes seriously and problems of his own which cause him suffering and sorrow, but in conversation they will avoid discussing them or, if they do discuss them, they will avoid the earnest note. One laughs with a friend; one does not weep with him (though one may weep *for* him).[39]

Here it seems the ability to amuse or divert stems from a quasi-Horatian equanimity, a skeptical self-command that presumes the transformation of a variety of experience into active judgment and a critical wariness toward self-pity ("the earnest note"). The final sentence seems to recast the claim in *Don Juan* that constitutes Byron's *ars saturae*: "And if I laugh at any mortal thing, / 'Tis that I may not weep" (4.4). I have noted in the previous chapter that Byronic laughter signifies an anguish or indignation that is granted no legitimacy by society at large and therefore cannot be articulated within the public sphere. Auden's insistence that we may laugh with or weep on behalf of a friend but never weep at a friend's bidding similarly implies that certain ethical or psychological burdens cannot be consoled by their mere publicizing. Such griefs instead must be addressed through more ironic, mediated responses (such as satiric laughter or private mourning) that bring the sympathizer to assume a critical relation to the rule of the depersonalized popular will, what Arendt would have called "behaviorism."

Resistance to the mass market of opinion is the rallying cry of the poet's "Letter to Lord Byron," which the essay "Don Juan" clearly reflects back on. Auden's only large-scale attempt at comic light verse, the poem was written for the most part on an excursion to Iceland during the summer of 1936 and published in the collection entitled *Letters from Iceland*, which also included a number of writings by the poet's traveling companion over the last month of the trip, Louis MacNeice. The central conceit of the "Letter" is Auden's epistolary elucidation of the effects of the Industrial Revolution and of the emergence of consumer society for the benefit of his ghostly addressee. The poem, originally published in five parts that were reduced to four in later reprintings, opens with a clear signal of its author's cynicism regarding the new apparatuses of cultural production when it invokes another satiric predecessor whose example antedates Byron's:

> I can't improve on Pope's shrill indignation,
> But hope that it will please his spiteful ghost
>   To learn the use in culture's propagation

> Of modern methods of communication:
> New roads, new rails, new contacts, as we know
> From documentaries by the G.P.O.
>
> (*EA* 169)

Given both Pope and Byron's derisive view of the publishing business in their respective epochs, Auden's sustained critique of modern technocracy and bourgeois acquiescence in the "Letter" should come as no surprise (as, for example, when he sarcastically declaims, "Hail to the New World! Hail to those who'll love / Its antiseptic objects, feel at home," *EA* 175). To the torpid, mediocre sameness of commodity culture the poet opposes the ideal of a "spiteful" noncompliance exemplified by cultural rebels such as Pope and Byron and the members of Auden's homosocial coterie of literary *enfants terribles* of the 1930s such as Stephen Spender, Christopher Isherwood, and MacNeice (all of whom the poem mentions at various points in its argument). Richard R. Bozorth sharply observes, in his study of the poet's gay sexual politics, how the "Letter" reinterprets the traditional association of art with pleasure or entertainment as a plea for libidinal and social freedom under the conditions of modernity.

> Clearly much of the "Letter" seeks to entertain friends. Just as clearly, it addresses a wider audience, and much of the fun comes from playing with [Auden's] friends' peculiarities and his own—especially sexual ones. In the various meanings of "peculiar" lies the problem with poetry as a vehicle for recovering community: what is particular to Auden is also what is odd.... "Letter to Lord Byron," however, posits eccentricity itself as the source of art's political value in the modern age—what a more recent critical vocabulary would term "difference" or "alterity." In inviting readers—*any* readers—to hear his "confession," Auden proposes that reading itself is an activity of consciously realizing our own peculiarities by discovering the writer's.[40]

The poem, in other words, mounts a scathing critique of ideological propriety and embraces a pluralist social vision. The only positive view that the "Letter" seems to advance is that life will be less contentious if we adopt a tolerant approach toward one another and a self-ironic attitude toward ourselves.

This advice holds true even (or especially) for life in the *civitas* of literary artists, Auden argues late in part 1:

> Parnassus after all is not a mountain,
>   Reserved for A. 1. climbers such as you;
> It's got a park, it's got a public fountain.
>   The most I ask is leave to share a pew

> With Bradford or with Cottam, that will do:
> To pasture my few silly sheep with Dyer
> And picnic on the lower slopes with Prior.
>
> (*EA* 173)

Although he invokes the arcadian imagery of classical allegory, Auden's description of "Parnassus" ultimately suggests a modern culture very much ruled by human usage. The landscape, with its civic landmarks of "park" and "public fountain" (which substitutes for the archetypal, Ovidian reflecting pool), has less in common with the pastoral world of ancient myth than with the metropolitan purgatory of airports, quays, and suburbs that appears at the start of "In Memory of W. B. Yeats," where "snow disfigured the public statues" (*CP* 247). At any rate, the key to the harmony of this society seems to be the skeptical self-deprecation of the modern artist; the ability to enjoy picnicking on the lower slopes with Prior, while fully acknowledging the silliness of one's own sheep. Such honesty stands in contrast to the mentality of "the average poet," whom Auden faults for being politically naive or susceptible—"A slick and easy generalization / Appeals too well to his imagination" (*EA* 171)—and describes as "unobservant, immature, and lazy," especially by comparison to real *auteurs* such as Jane Austen, whom the poet praises for exposing "so frankly and with such sobriety / The economic basis of society" (*EA* 171). Auden thus espouses a sort of liberating noncredulity that by working consistently to debunk the self's mystifications and denials of its own neuroses learns to penetrate the ideological coercions of mass culture, which he identifies with the conformist ideal of Normality.

> Goddess of bossy underlings, Normality!
>   What murders are committed in thy name!
> Totalitarian is thy state Reality,
>   Reeking of antiseptics and the shame
>   Of faces that all look and feel the same.
> Thy Muse is one unknown to classic histories,
> The topping figure of the hockey mistress.
>
> From thy dread Empire not a soul's exempted:
>   More than the nursemaids pushing prams in parks,
> By thee the intellectuals are tempted,
>   O, to commit the treason of the clerks,
>   Bewitched by thee to literary sharks.
>
> (*EA* 193)

As the poet tells us in a preceding stanza, the threat that contemporary society with its modern methods of communication poses to the individual is "of straightening out the kinks in the young mind" (*EA* 193). The worst betrayal of modernity is therefore that of the intellectuals who turn into apologists for the status quo, thus reducing culture to nothing more than a pool of "sharks" or predatory machines of consumption. As an alternative to such an ethos, Auden proposes the motto "Let each child have that's in our care / As much neurosis as the child can bear" (*EA* 193) and extols the benefits of education as a means to sexual and social self-awareness when he proudly recalls that "My first remark at school did all it could / To shake a matron's monumental poise: / 'I like to see the various types of boys'" (*EA* 192).

In its comic assault on conventionality and insistence on the untameable individuality of the libido, "Letter to Lord Byron" argues in quasi-psychoanalytic terms for the importance of self-interrogation as a means to liberation from the forces of emotional repression and thus of false consciousness. Recounting Auden's tutelage at the impressionable age of twenty-one by "a chap called [John] Layard" in a crank pyschological theory compounded of the ideas of Homer Lane, D. H. Lawrence, and André Gide, the poem paints a facetious but affectionate portrait of the youthful poet's happy freedom from inhibition while pursuing Layard's ideal of "the Pure-in-Heart": "He's gay; no bludgeonings of chance can spoil it, / The Pure-in-Heart loves all men on a par, / And has no trouble with his private toilet" (*EA* 195).[41] Yet the difficulty of achieving such self-emancipation becomes apparent in a remarkable passage in part 2 when Auden, having abandoned for the moment the plight of the "average poet," ruminates on the plight of the "average man," or in a somewhat equivocal salute to Walt Disney, "The little Mickey with the hidden grudge."

> "I am like you," he says, "and you, and you,
>   I love my life, I love the home-fires, have
> To keep them burning. Heroes never do.
>   Heroes are sent by ogres to the grave.
>   I may not be courageous, but I save.
> I am the one who somehow turns the corner,
> I may perhaps be fortunate Jack Horner.
>
> "I am the ogre's private secretary;
>   I've felt his stature and his powers, learned
> To give his ogreship the raspberry
>   Only when his gigantic back is turned.
>   One day, who knows, I'll do as I have yearned.
> The short man, all his fingers on the door,
> With repartee shall send him to the floor."

> One day, which day? O any other day,
>   But not to-day. The ogre knows his man.
> To kill the ogre—that would take away
>   The fear in which his happy dreams began,
>   And with his life he'll guard dreams while he can.
> Those who would really kill his dream's contentment
> He hates with real implacable resentment.
>
> (*EA* 179)

Anthony Hecht reads this passage as an expression of egregious class snobbery and describes the tone as "hostile and little short of cruel" to the "average man."[42] Such an interpretation, however, ignores the pathos of the poem's mousey protagonist when he says that he has to keep the "home-fires" burning as "heroes never do." Although the average man may be fearful, there is something tenacious in his surviving in order to "save." Whom does he save? He saves himself, of course, but potentially those as well in his family or community who are even weaker and more defenseless than he, those for whom he keeps the home fires stoked. What is debased about "the little Mickey" is his fantasy life; it seems clear that his secret wish of playing David to the ogre's Goliath will never amount to anything more than a daydream. Yet the evil that demands the reader's indictment does not reside so much in the average man's weakness as in the ogre's manipulation of it. As Auden says, "the ogre knows his man." If the poem censures the average man with the assertion that "without his bondage he'd be all at sea" and the observation that all the ogre need do is raise his voice "to make this man, so lovable, so mild / As madly cruel as a frightened child," the word "child" nevertheless implies a sharp counterargument regarding the morality of the struggle between master and slave. Auden is a writer who always sides with the small, the defenseless, the abandoned, and the overlooked against the abusers of power, and his poems are rife with examples of where his sympathies lie, from the haunting figures of "weeping anarchic Aphrodite" and Thetis crying out "in dismay" that end "In Memory of Sigmund Freud" and "The Shield of Achilles," respectively, to the martyred German theologian Dietrich Bonhoeffer in "Friday's Child" who suffers "[a] death reserved for slaves," to "the little children [who] died in the streets" in "Epitaph on a Tyrant."

Where then are we to turn for consolation, if we are no surer of ourselves than children? The answer must be sought from a source that is common to all yet teaches a different lesson to every individual.

> Yet though the choice of what is to be done
>   Remains with the alive, the rigid nation

> Is supple still within the breathing one;
>   Its sentinels yet keep their sleepless station,
>   And every man in every generation,
> Tossing in his dilemma on his bed,
> Cries to the shadows of the noble dead.
>
> (*EA* 181)

The "rigid nation's" example is "supple still" precisely insofar as the dead prompt the living to recognize that they have access to the past only through the work of critical analysis or reflection, that our lost objects of desire necessarily confront us as "shadows" or hermeneutic enigmas. By painfully coming to terms with the reality principle of loss, in other words, we learn to admit the contingency or eccentricity of our attachments and their roles in our fantasy life. As Bozorth puts it, "'Letter to Lord Byron' presents itself as a confession: a guilty revelation of the personal. . . . It is also an act of identification with Byron . . . [an] homage to a queer uncle—and the meanings of this gesture involve Auden's reception as a leftist and homosexual writer in the 1930s."[43] Byron is to be remembered and honored because he championed a performative ideal of social action and expression and therefore understood the falsehood of any claims to essential superiority. Auden praises the Romantic poet because "you liked to be the centre of attention, / The gay Prince Charming of the fairy story," who, in appropriately heroic fashion, upheld the rights of the defenseless against the oppressive force of the modern political order: "You never were an Isolationist; / Injustice you had always hatred for" (*EA* 180). Although Byron's love of the grandiose may have led him farther afield in pursuit of political causes than was necessary ("Nearer than Greece were cotton and the poor"), he fought on the side of freedom, and that is why Auden hazards that today his lordship "might indeed / have walked in the United Front with Gide" (*EA* 180).

In part 3, Auden relates the history of the arts since the end of the seventeenth century. The turning point for him is the "Industrial Revolution," which transformed the Western nations into consumer societies and gave such economic power to the bourgeoisie that it made possible "a new class of creative artist," poets "on whom the pressure of demand was let up" and who did not have to cater to "patron's taste or public's fickle mood." (Amusingly, Auden informs us that these artists owed their existence to "[Thomas] Savoury and [Thomas] Newcomen and [James] Watt," all inventors of various types of steam engine.) The heady taste of freedom enjoyed by the artist that at first inspired exciting literary innovations ("Brilliant the speeches improvised, the dances, / And brilliant, too, the technical advances") has in the meantime soured, while the artists ("the Poet's Party") have sickened themselves through self-indulgence.

How nice at first to watch the passers-by
  Out of the upper window, and to say
"How glad I am that though I have to die
  Like all those cattle, I'm less base than they!"
  How we all roared when Baudelaire went fey.
"See this cigar," he said, "it's Baudelaire's.
What happens to perception? Ah, who cares?"

Today, alas, that happy crowded floor
  Looks very different: many are in tears:
Some have retired to bed and locked the door;
  And some swing madly from the chandeliers;
  Some have passed out entirely in the rears;
Some have been sick in corners; the sobering few
Are trying hard to think of something new.
                    (*EA* 187)

The poets are guilty of succumbing to a feeling of belonging to an entirely different order than their fellow humans, of being "less base" than the masses. Auden prompts us to remember that the poets are not entirely to blame for the condition of their isolation from the masses: "In fact, of course, the whole tureen [of society] was salt. / The soup was full of little bits of snobs." The larger indifference of society has supplied the artists with enough rope to hang themselves: "The common clay and the uncommon nobs / Were far too busy making piles or starving / To look at pictures, poetry, or carving." Yet it is the artists who have chosen to tie the rope into a noose, whose response to their condition has been less than courageous. Their negative example, in combination with the positive example of Byron, nonetheless has helped Auden in his maturity "come only to the rather tame conclusion / That no man by himself has life's solution" (*EA* 196).

The lesson is underscored by the ending of the poem in which a number of false solutions that would only lead to social complacency are rejected. The first of these is to stay in Mother England, with whom the native son's relationship is in danger of lapsing into "an Oedipus fixation." Auden does not so much as say that the atmosphere of England is too confining for him, but he makes the society seem unhealthy along lines reminiscent of the Poet's Party, and despite his optimism regarding the state of British letters ("Cheer up! There're several singing birds that sing") his dissatisfaction with the class system is comically evident: "Mother looks odd today dressed up in peers, / Slums, aspidistras, shooting-sticks, and queers" (*EA* 198). The second false hope is "[t]he Great Utopia, free of all complexes" which will remain a dream as impossible "as that of being both the sexes." Those who support such a dream have a naive picture of human nature (what would it mean to be "free of all complexes?") and thus indulge in the complacency of "intolerant certainty," the belief that if we can just get everybody to conform to our idea of what is human, society will be cured. The final lines of the "Letter" reveal the poem to be an elaborate joke on the deadness of the addressee: "I hope you don't think mail from strangers wrong / As to its length, I tell myself you'll need it / You've all eternity in which to read it" (*EA* 199). The epistolary conceit works here to emphasize the distinction between the poem's addressee and its modern readership. The problems that Auden confronts in writing the "Letter" are not Byron's problems, so the latter can read the missive at his leisure, appreciating its wit without sharing its sense of urgency. By contrast, we the living are not so lucky. Byron may not have to worry about the spread of fascism or the decline of the arts, but we do. We must wrestle with these problems as Auden does.

The "Letter to Lord Byron" may be thought of as a satire of the bad faith that wishes to avoid the burdens of historicity—that wishes to change places with the dead rather than to examine the past for critical perspective on the present. The "Letter" represents an attempt on Auden's part to make light of the uncertainty he felt during the poem's composition, uncertainty about the future and what it held in store both for himself and for Europe. About a year before embarking for Iceland, he quit his job as a schoolteacher, which had been his full-time employment since the summer of 1930. In the autumn of 1935, he began to work for the newly formed film unit (that mostly produced documentaries) attached to England's General Post Office, but by February 1936 he had quit this job as well. Auden then traveled restlessly (visiting between early 1936 and the end of 1938 Portugal, Spain, Paris, China, and Brussels in addition to Iceland) and decided to rely only on his writing for income. In January 1937, while attempting to join an ambulance unit on the Republican side of the war in Spain, he was witness to the ban on church activities in Barcelona imposed by the Republican government. Later he would name this moment as his first instance of doubt as to the validity of his then atheistic outlook. In November of the same year, he received an English literary award, the King's Gold Medal. His acceptance was perceived by some (Stephen Spender among them) as an abandonment of the leftist politics that were de rigueur for the literati of his generation. At the beginning of 1939, Auden set out for America with Christopher Isherwood in tow. Some time late in 1940, he returned to the Anglican Communion of his childhood, attending service in New York City in the Episcopal Church.

Auden's career during these years might superficially look like an antithetical shift from political concerns to religious. Yet even in as expressly religious a poem as *For the Time Being*, which he began writing at the end of 1941, he adopts an actively political rhetoric, portraying Herod as a failed liberal bureaucrat, and echoing in a choral section ("Alone, alone, about a dreadful wood / Of conscious evil runs a lost mankind") his own protest against Nazi imperialism, "September 1, 1939" ("Lost in a haunted wood / Children afraid of the night"). For Auden, the religious and the political were continuous rather than discrete domains of experience; in effect, the religious was an enrichment or fulfillment of the political. In the first long poem he wrote after settling in New York, which was also the second great verse epistle of his career, he refines this feeling into an allegorical double vision of the polis as both a spiritual and secular community with responsibilities simultaneously in both realms. *New Year Letter* satirizes the bad faith that attempts to engineer unity on earth through the repression and elimination of difference and that, in an evident reference to the horrors of *Krystallnacht*, makes "a little crowd smash up a shop, / Suspended hatreds crystallise / In visible hostilities" (*CP* 200). Such self-aggrandizing brutality represents an irrationality that is also a form of sin in its denial of the fact that "order never can be willed / But is the state of the fulfilled" (*CP* 200).

"Doubledness" is the very essence of the poem. Written in octosyllabic tetrameter couplets, *New Year Letter* makes up the centerpiece to the 1941 collection entitled, at least in the U.S. edition, *The Double Man*.[44] The poem, dated January 1, 1940, celebrates a point in time that is a double occasion: the end of the old year and beginning of the new. The title derives from some words attributed to Montaigne by the theologian Charles Williams in his book *The Descent of the Dove*: "We are, I know not how, double in ourselves, so that what we believe we disbelieve, and cannot rid ourselves of what we condemn."[45] Williams points out the skepticism that Montaigne used as a foil for his own faith and calls it "belief-in-disbelief." According to Williams, Montaigne saw Christianity as a hypothesis, a conjecture to be tested rationally, and thus as a readiness "to admit that some other possibility may exist." The division of the modern mind between rational disbelief and irrational faith that Williams ascribed to Montaigne was one Auden shared. In a sermon he gave in Westminster Abbey in 1966, Auden declared: "It is almost a definition of a Christian that he is someone who *knows* he isn't one, either in faith or morals."[46] What Auden meant by this was that we must recognize that our salvation depends on grace, that this salvation, as Paul Tillich asserts, is "independent of any moral, intellectual, or religious precondition: it is not the good or the wise or the pious who are entitled to the courage to accept acceptance but those who are lacking in all these qualities and are aware of being unacceptable."[47] Such a position derives from the Lutheran emphasis on God's forgiveness as the origin of grace, but Auden revises the sentiment by arguing that the recognition of "being unacceptable" prepares us for ethical action, because it prepares us to forgive one another in the earthly, immediate present.

The embodiment in the poem of the self-deluding wish to conceal ethical uncertainty is the Devil, the "Spirit-that-denies" who has "no positive existence" but is only "a recurrent state / Of fear and faithlessness and hate"

(*CP* 209). The epithet, as Auden points out in a note to the 1941 edition of the poem (the notes would be dispensed with in subsequent editions), derives from the moment in Goethe's *Faust* when Mephistopheles, on being asked for his name by Faust, replies "Ich bin der Geist, der stets verneint!" (1.1338). The allusion is important because we know from *Faust 2* that Mephistopheles cannot, in the long run, succeed in corrupting virtue (he denies so much that he undercuts his own ends). Goethe may have called his play a *Tragödie*, but its ending, with the heavenly reunion of Faust and Gretchen, plays like a divine comedy. In the figure of Mephistopheles we have an archetypal example of the inability to live with the "belief-in-disbelief" that sees moral decision as a continuous struggle—a dialectic between absolute and relative values—rather than as an act of blind faith.

> [T]orn between conflicting needs,
> He's doomed to fail if he succeeds,
> And his neurotic longing mocks
> Him with his self-made paradox,
> To be both god and dualist.
> For, if dualities exist,
> What happens to the god? If there
> Are any cultures anywhere
> With other values than his own,
> How can it possibly be shown
> That his are not subjective? ...
> And yet to show complete conviction,
> Requires the purpler kinds of diction
> And none appreciate as he
> Polysyllabic oratory.
> (*CP* 213–214)

Mephistopheles' problem is that he is "torn between conflicting needs," divided between the desire to annihilate order on the one hand and to supplant it on the other. While he is "the great schismatic who / First split creation into two" (*CP* 213), the supreme disrupter of unity, he is also the would-be source of law, an apostate who aspires to the throne of creation. He wishes, in a fit of self-contradiction, "to be both god and dualist."

Although we human beings are also in some sense "torn between conflicting needs," we can learn to live with our partiality or incompleteness and to pursue solidarity through social engagement. In this hope lies the redemption of "the wish to be / Diversity in unity" inspired by the Devil (*CP* 213). The lesson is to shun solipsism in favor of tolerance or open-mindedness. Real artistic achievement (as opposed to the nonsense of "polysyllabic oratory") in this way presents us with an image of the individual will's proper fulfillment in social communion.

> To set in order—that's the task
> Both Eros and Apollo ask:
> For Art and Life agree in this
> That each intends a synthesis,
> That order which must be the end
> That all self-loving things intend
> Who struggle for their liberty,
> Who use, that is, their will to be.
> (*CP* 200)

Art provides us with an apt metaphor for the synthesis that ideally results from each individual's pursuit of the "liberty" of his or her self-interest, because it represents an order not of similarity but rather of diversity: "The symmetry disorders reach / When both are equal each to each, / Yet in intention all are one" (*CP* 200). The true work of art provokes a sense of the agonistic struggle toward ethical understanding, the active "symmetry" of particular "disorders," by challenging the beholder to overcome the limits of a strictly personal view and to acknowledge his or her obligation to the historical, cultural, and, therefore, political Other. Standing the Devil's "schismatic" work on its head, Auden resonantly asserts toward the end of the poem that

> All real unity commences
> In consciousness of differences,
> That all have wants to satisfy
> And each a power to supply.
> We need to love all since we are
> Each a unique particular
> That is no giant, god, or dwarf,
> But one odd human isomorph;
> We can love each because we know
> All, all of us, that this is so:
> Can live since we are lived, the powers
> That we create with are not ours.
> (*CP* 241)

The admonition that "all have wants to satisfy / And each a power to supply" recapitulates the argument regarding the universal necessity of love at the end of "September 1, 1939": "No one exists alone; / Hunger allows no choice / To the citizen or police" (*CP* 88). Auden, in Edward Mendelson's words, "later recoiled from this view of love as involuntary mutual need rather than as voluntary mutual forgiveness."[48] As I have suggested already, however, nothing in the poetry supports Auden's self-condemnation for propounding a false dichotomy. The very preoccupation of both poems with questions of ethical agency, with the truce between "the citizen" and "the police" or the interdependence of "wants" and the "power to supply," implies a conception of love closer in spirit to a moral or religious imperative than to a biologically predetermined impulse. Recognizing that our animal craving for compassion is universal, we directly confront the consequences of denying to others our care and sympathy. Yet each individual faces this ordeal under different circumstances and thus must devise a separate solution. Because the "machine" of mass society has "now destroyed / The local customs we enjoyed," as Auden maintains in *New Year Letter*, we may see "the secret that was always true / . . . Compelling all to the admission, / Aloneness is man's real condition" (*CP* 238).

For this reason, real art encourages "consciousness of differences," while false art encourages a bland self-approbation. Mephistopheles favors "polysyllabic oratory" because he uses language as a means of currying favor or inciting fanaticism; he "flings at every author's head / Something a favorite author said" (*CP* 212–213). Accordingly, the Devil's rhetoric is "idealistic" rather than analytic.

> All vague idealistic art
> That coddles the uneasy heart
> Is up his alley, and his pigeon
> The woozier species of religion,
> Even a novel, play or song,
> If loud, lugubrious and long . . .
> To win support of any kind
> He has to hold before the mind
> Amorphous shadows it can hate.
>
> (*CP* 214)

The Devil's "woozier species of religion / Even a novel, play or song" has not quite the besmirched grandeur of the Grubstreet industry that Pope satirizes in the *Dunciad*, but Auden's Mephistopheles and Pope's Cibber are more than collegial members of the same professional guild.

> [T]he Chaos dark and deep
> Where nameless Somethings in their causes sleep,
> 'Till genial Jacob, or a warm Third day,
> Call forth each mass, a Poem, or a play:

> How hints, like spawn, scarce quick in embryo lie,
> How new-born nonsense first is taught to cry,
> Maggots half-form'd in rhyme exactly meet,
> And learn to crawl upon poetic feet.
> Here one poor word an hundred clenches makes,
> And ductile dulness now meanders takes;
> There motley Images her fancy strike,
> Figures ill-pair'd, and Similes unlike.
>   (1.55–65)

We may discern in Auden's "amorphous shadows" the intellectual offspring, as it were, of Pope's "maggots, " although the catachrestic repugnance of the latter, in which literal and figural meanings collide in a shapeless panic, is more blatant. The description in *New Year Letter* of the Devil's preferred style as "loud, lugubrious and long" might put us in mind of the *Dunciad*'s portrayal of Dulness as "laborious, heavy, busy, bold, and blind" (1.15).

Likewise, *New Year Letter*'s vision of "diversity in unity" (*CP* 213) may be said to bear some resemblance to the Popean vision of the cosmos as a system "Where Order in Variety we see" (*Windsor Forest* 15) and as the Great Chain of Being (*Essay on Man* 3.7–26). Auden, however, modernizes the trope by transferring it from the realm of the cosmological to the realm of the historical or temporal, thus of human being in explicit contrast to divine being. In drawing this distinction, he follows Augustine, who differentiates God and man on the basis of being outside or inside of time: "Your years neither go nor come, but our years pass and others come after them" ("anni tui nec eunt nec veniunt: isti autem nostri eunt et veniunt, ut omnes veniant").[49] This history gives *New Year Letter* the overall contours of its argument, its turnings from aesthetics to ethics to religion, which playfully echo the essential drama staged, according to Auden, in the philosophy of Kierkegaard. The poet's synopsis of this drama, written for a selection of the philosopher's works published in 1952, could be read equally as a statement of *New Year Letter*'s view of human nature as a summary of Kierkegaardian existentialism.

> Every man, says Kierkegaard, lives either aesthetically, ethically, or religiously. As he is concerned, for the most part, with describing the way in which these categories apply in Christian or post-Christian society, one can perhaps make his meaning clearer by approaching these categories historically, i.e., by considering the Aesthetic and the Ethical at stages when each was a religion, and then comparing them with the Christian faith in order to see the difference, first between the two rival and incompatible Natural Religions and, secondly, between them and a Revealed Religion in which neither is destroyed or ignored, but the Aesthetic is dethroned and the Ethical fulfilled.[50]

Auden in his explication of Kierkegaard seems to give particular priority to *Either/Or* and *Stages on Life's Way* and in so doing perhaps undue importance to the notion of the "stages" or spheres of existence, although he complicates such an emphasis by adding that in the religious sphere "neither [art nor ethics] is destroyed or ignored." Kierkegaard should not be understood to propose any hard and fast distinction between these stages or any sort of quasi-Hegelian dialectical structure to human consciousness. Yet the point that the Kierkegaardian "categories" ought to be treated historically contains a basic insight about Kierkegaard's picture of ethical existence. The necessity of religious faith must be experienced as a natural element of everyday life. This is the absurdity of the human predicament. "The eternal truth has come into being in time: this is the paradox. . . . [I]f the individual does not existentially and in existence lay hold of the truth, he will never lay hold of it."[51] In the *Journals* this is laid out as a gap between human history and Christian eternity that must be overcome in the individual's quotidian actions: "there cannot be any direct transition from an historical fact to the foundation on it of an eternal happiness. . . . *To be related to spirit means to undergo a test*; to believe, to wish to believe, is to change one's life into a trial; daily test is the trial of faith."[52]

The determination to ground the religious in the secular, to build the City of God out of the city of the human, as it were, and to grasp the eternal "existentially and in existence" is recapitulated in the final two verse paragraphs of *New Year Letter*. The poem apostrophizes God in a wildly Orphic invocation before turning to Auden's friend Elizabeth Mayer, the *New Year Letter*'s human addressee, in more intimate, vernacular tones.

> O Unicorn among the cedars . . .
> O Dove of Science and of light . . .
> O sudden Wind that blows unbidden,
> Parting the quiet reeds, O Voice
> Within the labyrinth of choice . . .
> Instruct us in the civil art
> Of making from the muddled heart
> A desert and a city where
> The thoughts that have to labour there
> May find locality and peace
> And pent-up feelings their release,
> Send strength sufficient for our day,
> And point our knowledge on its way,
> *O da quod jubes, Domine.*
>
> Dear friend Elizabeth, dear friend
> These days have brought me, may the end

> I bring to the grave's dead-line be
> More worthy of your sympathy
> Than the beginning; . . .
> We fall down in the dance, we make
> The old ridiculous mistake,
> But always there are such as you
> Forgiving, helping what we do.
> O every day in sleep and labour
> Our life and death are with our neighbour,
> And love illuminates again
> The city and the lion's den,
> The world's great rage, the travel of young men.
> (CP 241–243)

The language of the penultimate strophe, with its insistent use of the vocative *O*, catches much of the lyricism of Rilke's *Duineser Elegien*, one of the texts Auden lists as a "modern source" of *New Year Letter* in his notes. Indeed, the line "O sudden Wind that blows unbidden" in addition to being an allusion, as Hecht notes, to the biblical wind that "bloweth where it listeth" (John 3:8), may be inspired by Rilke's invocation of love, the "Neptune of the blood," in the Third Elegy: "O der dunkele Wind seiner Brust aus gewundener Muschel." Hecht feels that "the prayer for the 'release' of 'pent-up feelings' seems very likely a prayer for erotic fulfillment."[53] This commingling of religious and erotic desire would be in keeping with the Rilkean spirit, which is always lapsing from one to the other. Our only hope of divine, unconditional love, in other words, resides in our willingness to embrace the earthly.

The moral is reinforced in the divide between the two paragraphs, which signifies the transition from the sublime to the mundane. At its end, the epistolary fiction of *New Year Letter* retreats from the vision of a redeemed hereafter in order to linger on the view of a purgatorial here and now. The poet reminds us that inevitably "[w]e fall down in the dance, we make / The old ridiculous mistake." But, he adds, we may be redeemed from our errors by the forgiveness of our neighbors. "The world's great rage, the travel of young men" may be a messier and more painful reality than the ideal of "locality and peace," but this reality has the virtue of being wholly ours.

> We can at least serve other ends,
> Can love the *polis* of our friends
> And pray that loyalty may come
> To serve mankind's *imperium*.
> (CP 224)

In the end, *New Year Letter* may be said to be a satire in a highly specific sense; the poem presents us with a modern reality that is absurd ("ridiculous") and debased (full of "rage") but not contemptible. This reality supplies the ground of an ideal of civil coexistence—"the *polis* of our friends"—that is nearer in texture to the social agitation of Roman life captured by Horace when he complains that in Rome "a hundred / other matters assail my head, leaping / abroad from all sides" ("aliena negotia centum / per caput et circa soliunt latus," Satire 2.6.33–34) than to the agony imagined by Juvenal, who sees only "the thousand savage perils / of the city" ("mille pericula saevae / urbis," Satire 3.8–9).[54]

A later poem entitled "The Sabbath," which appears in *Homage to Clio* (1960), severely revises the account of creation given in Genesis in order to throw a harsher light on this modern reality. This tour de force revisits the morning of "the Seventh Day of Creation," when the animals—"herbivore, parasite, predator"—awaken to find "not a trace" of man, "whose birth on the Sixth had made of that day / An unnecessary interim" (*CP* 672). The only signs of human activity that the animals can detect are "holes in the earth, / Beaches covered with tar, / Ruins and metallic rubbish in plenty." This barren mass of detritus leads the beasts to conclude that man has destroyed himself through his "unnecessary" pursuits: "Well, that fellow had never really smelled / Like a creature who could survive." Free of his vulgar and brutal intrusion (and relishing the license to tell one another that man had "No grace, address or faculty like those / Born on the First Five"), the animals resume their instinctive modes of behavior only to be interrupted by an unforeseen and lethal new turn of events.

> Back, then, at last on a natural economy,
>   Now His Impudence was gone,
> Looking exactly like what it was,
>   The Seventh Day went on,
>
> Beautiful, happy, perfectly pointless. . . .
>   A rifle's ringing crack
> Split their Arcadia wide open, cut
>   Their Sabbath nonsense short.
>
> For whom did they think they had been created?
>   That fellow was back,
> More bloody-minded than they remembered,
>   More godlike than they thought.
>
> (*CP* 673)

That man's introduction back into the order of things represents a revelatory or revolutionary moment in the history of creation is dramatized cunningly here at the conclusion of the poem by means of a number of subtle formal effects: the rapid compression of the "rifle's ringing crack" in a trimeter line, the reverberation of the shot within the line through the insistent repetition of the phoneme [r], and, most strikingly, the sudden deviation in the last two stanzas from the rhyme scheme (xbyb) that informs the preceding five. The moment is revolutionary because it solemnizes man's usurpation of God's place—because it arrives not as one more moment in a continuous series but as a point of departure, a new and ominous beginning. The egomaniacal question posed by man (to himself) at the start of the final stanza ("For whom did they think they had been created?") implies that this usurpation is a *fait accompli*, that there now exists no higher authority to whom the animals can appeal. This question may be read as a perverse reversal or inversion of the questions posed *to* man by the poem in the third epistle of Pope's *Essay on Man*:

> Is it for thee the lark ascends and sings?
> Joy tunes his voice, joy elevates his wings:
> Is it for thee the linnet pours his throat?
> Loves of his own and raptures swell the note:
> The bounding steed you pompously bestride,
> Shares with his lord the pleasure and the pride...
> (3.31–36)

Pope asks these questions on his way to a description of the "State of Nature" as an image of social cooperation, where part and whole exist in equilibrium: "Self-love and Social at her birth began" (3.149). Auden also draws a picture of the state of nature as an image of society, but to very different effect. Behind both of these pictures, of course, looms the portrait of creation drawn in Genesis 1:26: "And God said, Let us make man in our image, after our likeness: and let them have dominion over the fish of the sea, and over the fowl of the air, and over the cattle, and over all the earth, and over every creeping thing that creepeth upon the earth." The variation that Pope runs on this theme is to emphasize the responsibilities that come with "dominion": "One all-extending, all-preserving Soul / Connects each being, greatest with the least; / Made Beast in aid of Man, and Man of Beast" (3.22–24). The variation that Auden runs on this theme is to emphasize the potential for abuse of such "dominion": "For whom did they think they had been created?"

Even more powerfully, however, "The Sabbath" may be said to travesty the story in Mark 2:23–28 regarding the harvesting of corn on the sabbath by the followers of Jesus. On witnessing the actions of his followers, the Pharisees are provoked to ask: "Behold, why do they on the sabbath day that which is not lawful?" Jesus replies by reminding them of the story of David's eating of the bread reserved for priests on his flight from Saul (recounted in 1 Samuel 21:1–10), to which he adds an explicit moral: "And he said unto them, The sabbath was made for man, and not man for the sabbath: Therefore the Son of man is Lord also of the sabbath." Yet Jesus in his reference to the story of David's flight presents the violation of ritual as consorting with a more pressing purpose: "Have ye never read what David did, when he had need, and was an hungered, he, and they that were with him?" This emphasis on "need" signals David's subservience to a higher law, a point underscored in the account in 1 Samuel by the assistance David receives in his need from the priest Ahimelech (compare also the passage that tells us "And the spirit of the Lord came upon David from that day forward," 1 Samuel 16:13). By contrast, in Auden's poem "The Sabbath," natural law or need, aligned with "natural economy," is just what manmade violence attacks, what it has "cut . . . short." In the poem Auden tarnishes a familiar narrative paradigm as if to say to the reader: here is the sordid modern truth in place of the fiction to which you are accustomed (and the presence of the rifle, "tar," and "metallic rubbish" all testify to the modern character of this truth). Neither the archaic parable nor the contemporary reality quite seem like they can be restored to innocence once Auden is finished with them.

The dour terseness of the epithets applied to "that fellow" in the last two lines, a relentlessness heightened by the omission of a conjunction (asyndeton) and by the formulaic sameness of the beginning of both clauses (anaphora), summons up much of the chilling single-mindedness captured by the image of "iron-hearted man-slaying Achilles" that ends "The Shield of Achilles," where the adjectives "iron-hearted" and "man-slaying" convey Achilles' ferocity all the more vividly for their redundancy. Put more broadly, the agreement of the two poems hinges on a shared pessimism concerning human nature and a shared hope with respect to the work of art as a means of uncovering that nature. Like "The Sabbath," "The Shield of Achilles" argues that the work of art may play a revisionary role in bringing a previously unbearable truth to light. As the end of the poem tells us, the "thin-lipped armorer" Hephaestos knows better than Thetis "of the shining breasts" how "to please her son" (*CP* 598).

Unlike its Homeric model, then, Auden's "Shield" cannot be classified as an ekphrasis of a notional *objet d'art* that, because of its divine nature, enhances the earthly world it depicts. Homer gives the reader the impression that the shield reorders the Greek cosmos into a new, idealized configuration and that the beauty of the idealization rubs off in turn onto the poetry. The theory of art that Auden propounds is something else again. Because of its origin in the mind of an artist whose self-trust has been tempered by direct knowledge of the arbitrariness of justice (note the poem's last glance at Hephaestos's lameness as he "hobbled away"), the shield of Auden's poem bears more honest witness to the harshness or monstrosity of historical reality. What helps to drive home the argument is the queasy feeling we have on reading "The Shield of Achilles" that history is falling into an all too familiar pattern before our eyes. The poet concocts here a nightmarish mélange of the Homeric figures for which Thetis hunts in vain, a crucifixion scenario that evokes the end of imperial Rome ("As three pale figures were led forth and bound / To three posts driven upright in the ground"), and the "million boots in line," "statistics," and "barbed wire" of twentieth-century prison camps and ghettoes. Of course, history is doomed to repeat itself, the poem mockingly seems to say.

A similar argument informs Auden's other ekphrastic masterpiece, "Musée des Beaux Arts." What he admires about Brueghel's painting "The Fall of Icarus" is the impassive clarity with which it renders a death that the bystanders in the painting overlook either on account of callousness or shallowness. As the poet writes, "everything turns away / Quite leisurely from the disaster" in "The Fall of Icarus": everything, that is, except the painterly care or attention that refuses to let us, who stand outside the picture, ignore "the splash, the forsaken cry" and the "white legs disappearing into the green / Water." Brueghel's *chef d'oeuvre* places him in the ranks of the other artists whose works are on display in the eponymous museum of the poem, because it proves the ability, shared with his peers, to be truthful on a difficult topic: "About suffering they were never wrong / The Old Masters." The designs of the painter stand directly opposed to the purposes of "the expensive delicate ship" in the painting that "had somewhere to get to and sailed calmly on," leaving the drowning Icarus and the viewer of Brueghel's handiwork equally in its wake. This ship of state, or *navis bonorum omnium*, to use a more Ciceronian turn, bears a conspicuous family resemblance to the flotilla of modern American "ships on the dazzling blue" of Auden's later poem "Fleet Visit," vessels that

> Look as if they were meant
> To be pure abstract design
> By some master of pattern and line,
> Certainly worth every cent
> Of the millions they must have cost.
> (*CP* 550)

As in the case of their ancestor displayed in Brueghel's painting, the expense of these warships quite matter-of-factly gives the lie to their delicacy. The sly vagueness of the measurement attached to "the millions they must have cost" makes evident that the craft in question are anything but "pure abstract design."

Next to such substantial engines of force, it is difficult at first to see of what possible use or importance such humble contrivances as poems might be. Ridiculing our vanity, arousing us to the construction of a new city, Auden's poetry constantly asks us one overriding question that, in the words of the poem "The Epigoni," runs:

> No point pretending
> One didn't foresee the probable ending
> As dog-food, or landless, submerged, a slave:
> Meanwhile, how should a cultured gentleman behave?
> (*CP* 605)

Speak honestly, we can imagine the poet answering. Avoid the earnest note. And remember it is more humane to laugh with one's friends than to suffer in isolation.

5

Imbued with Otherness

Merrill's Mock-Epics of Desire

"Form's what affirms," declares a nameless schoolteacher, a character who represents both the poet's spokesman and straw man in James Merrill's poem "The Thousand and Second Night," one of two brilliant lyric sequences from his 1966 collection *Nights and Days*. The pronouncement approvingly reflects back on the poem itself and enlarges the teacher's observation that three enigmatic prose intermissions in the sequence refer "to mind, body, and soul (or memory)."[1]

The emphasis of the terms on form, on memory, and on the distinction between the physical and metaphysical suggests a flirtation with the terms of Platonic philosophy. The argument on behalf of poetry is generally in keeping with Diotima's praise of literary artists in the *Symposium* for being lovers of "wisdom" (*phronesis*) and "excellence" (*arete*).[2] Perhaps with the *Symposium*'s erotics of knowledge in mind, Merrill sets the scene of his pedagogical commentary in the classroom of an all-male academy, where the instructor addresses his students as "gentlemen" (*CP* 185). Yet, in the final reckoning, the involvement of "The Thousand and Second Night" with Platonic idealism seems less than sincere. After delivering his comment on the poem, the speaker awards himself the tribute "that's well said," and his comic spasm of self-congratulation before his students, and the reader, may cast doubts on his qualifications as a Socratic lover of wisdom.

On an irreverent note, then, the narrator abruptly switches language-games, shifting from the didactic to the persuasive, from exposition to valuation, from the vocabulary of knowledge to that of aesthetics as he praises himself for the beauty of his own rhetorical performance. If form's what affirms, the oddly intransitive formulation begs the question: what precisely gets affirmed? In the absence of a direct object ("form affirms *x*"), the reader is left with a vanishing sense of the poem's logic and a fixed image only of the social site of the classroom itself. The setting seems to owe a debt to W. H. Auden's mythologizings of the British public school system (one thinks of the passages on education in "Letter to Lord Byron" and the lines on schoolchildren in "September 1, 1939"), as the pedagogue's borrowing of "Spender's phrase" in the course of his ruminations signals (*CP* 185). Merrill shares with Plato an apparent persuasion that masculine desire, in particular for other men, properly is expressed through sublimation in culturally productive works. Who enjoys the authority to legislate what constitutes a proper or culturally productive work, however, is a more troublesome question for the American poet than for the Greek philosopher.

The retreat from theoretical reasoning in "The Thousand and Second Night" indeed suggests some discomfort on the author's part with an epistemology that has come to serve as the foundation of the normative Western idea of civilization and thus has been tainted through force of tradition with homophobia, to some degree in spite of itself. From this perspective, the heterosexist circumscription of culturally permissible roles for gay men demonstrates the failure of straight society to abide by its own supposedly rationalist standards and thereby reveals itself as a sign of the uncivilized. By articulating the poet's skepticism toward such ideals, Merrill's writing elaborates an incisive satirical critique of the psychologically confining pressures of social decorum.

The twenty-one-line poem "Graffito," in his 1988 collection *The Inner Room*, sharply illustrates this satiric undertaking. The first stanza rehearses the poet's encounter, during a walk through the outskirts of Rome, with a dilapidated church, "originally a temple to Fortuna," from whose cornice a piece of stone has fallen into the pedestrian pathway. On the fragment a graffiti artist has scrawled the image of a forearm "wearing, lest we misunderstand / Like a tattoo the cross-within-a-circle / Of the majority—Christian Democrat" (*CP* 567). Merrill's description of the picture continues:

> Arms and the man. This arm ends in a hand
> Which grasps a neatly, elegantly drawn
> Cock—erect and spurting tiny stars—
> And balls. One sports . . . a swastika?
> Yes, and its twin, if you please, a hammer-and-sickle!
> The tiny stars, seen close, are stars of David.
> Now what are we supposed to make of that?
>
> Wink from Lorenzo, pout from Mrs. Pratt.
> Hold on, I want to photograph this latest
> Fountain of Rome, whose twinkling gist
> Gusts my way from an age when isms were largely
> Come-ons for the priapic satirist,
> And any young guy with a pencil felt
> He held the fate of nations in his fist.
>
> (*CP* 567)

In place of the paradigmatic Horatian meeting with the parasite seeking advancement (as in Satire 1.9), Merrill stages a confrontation between the sightseeing narrator and the handiwork of a moralistic zealotry that, succumbing to the appeals of what the speaker concisely calls "isms," mistakes propaganda for principle. To the poet's eye, the garbled farrago of political symbols nullifies the artist's attempt at sexual provocation, revealing it as empty macho self-indulgence. Falling for the "come-ons" of ideological doctrine, the "priapic satirist" perverts his own moral and intellectual vocation—what Locke meant by the celebrated phrase "the labour of his body, and the work of his hands"—into an obscene, onanistic public display.[3] By applying a cool, photographic gaze to the scene, the speaker reduces this spectacle to the status of an anachronistic curio ironically voided of its original cult value. Like an instant photo, the picture of maniacal sexual bravado develops before the reader's sight as the poem's technical resources gradually assert themselves. What at first glance seems a haphazard amalgamation of intrastanzaic rhymes and loose consonances ("misunderstand" in the first stanza is aligned with "hand" in the next and "circle" imperfectly paired with "sickle") coalesces at the poem's conclusion into a scheme of proper rhymes linking alternate lines. The very sequence of rhyming end words—"gist," "satirist," "fist"—frames a derisory parable of the egoistic motivations that underlie political extremism and intolerance.

In this way, "Graffito" exemplifies a general trait of Merrill's poetry, namely an ironizing nonadmiration of literal-mindedness and cultural chauvinism, a wariness here opposed to the demagoguery of the graffiti artist. In a genuine sense, then, Merrill reinvigorates the Augustan sensibility, particularly through the cultivation of a quasi-Horatian playfulness. Yet, at the same time, he revises the critical project of satire—its function as moral critique—in a significant manner. Earlier poets advance such a project by means of a work of imaginary identification with a politically marginalized moral exemplar, as when Horace invokes the chastening ethical ideal of his freedman father or Pope of his Catholic parents. The contrast between the narrator's detachment from "isms" and the dogmatism of his artistic predecessor suggests in one particular respect the negative reversal of this procedure of identification or self-formation. Although Merrill, too, presents his satires of personal misunderstanding as an indictment of conformism on behalf of a neglected minority, he does so by emphasizing his alienation from the available cultural and familial models of self-assertion. In "Graffito," the sexual aggression of the satiric forefather invalidates him as a potential object of incorporation, because such aggression is premised on the unironic repression of its own artificiality as a pose. Distancing himself from the butch essentialism of the "young guy with a pencil," the speaker hints at an alternative libidinal position that constructs masculinity in more flexible, open-ended terms and repudiates the imperial ambition of determining "the fate of nations."

The dialectical tension in the poem between these perspectives thus consorts with the implied satiric aim of assailing the norms of heterosexist culture in the name of the polymorphous, transgressive desires that such a culture seeks to repress. Merrill's renewal of the satiric tradition consequently ought to be understood to coincide with what Judith Butler has called "the notion of [a] gender parody . . . [that] does not assume that there is an original which such parodic identities imitate."[4] Butler famously has linked the politically demystifying operations of gender parody to the psychoanalytic exposure of identification as a phantasmatic mechanism: "Indeed, the parody is *of* the very notion of an original; just as the psychoanalytic notion of gender identification is constituted by a fantasy of a fantasy, the transfiguration of an Other who is always already a 'figure' in that double sense, so gender parody reveals that the original identity after which gender fashions itself is an imitation without an origin."[5] On this reckoning, parody consists in politically oppositional constructions of identity that travesty and thus destabilize the allegedly natural law of sexual development. Following Butler's lead, Diana Fuss has argued that the mutability of gender is inscribed in the very concept of identification as Freud proposed it: "In the very attempt to prove that identification and desire are counterdirectional turns, Freud in fact demonstrates their necessary collusion and collapsability, the ever-present potential for the one to metamorphose into, or turn back onto, the other. The instability of sexual identity lies in the capacity of its psychical mechanisms to desire and to identify with each other."[6] Enlarging on both Butler and Fuss's arguments, José Esteban Muñoz has discerned in the work of recent queer, minority artists the expression of "identities-in-difference" that are "predicated on their ability to disidentify with the mass public and instead, through this disidentification, contribute to the function of a counterpublic sphere."[7] Invoking as a paradigm the response of the linguist Michel Pêcheux to Louis Althusser's theory of subject formation, Muñoz describes disidentification as a "mode of dealing with dominant ideology, one that neither opts to assimilate within such a structure nor strictly opposes it; rather, disidentification is a strategy that works on and against dominant ideology."[8]

Whether explicitly or implicitly, each of these theorists posits the disidentification of gay and lesbian subjects as a challenge to heterosexist norms, hence as a gesture of postmodern incredulity toward the legitimating metanarratives of marriage, family, and social organization. (Fuss's argument might be understood to trace such postmodern skepticism back to its modernist roots in the instability of gender identity intrinsic to Freud's formulation.) We may detect something of the same ironic attitude toward the institutions of bourgeois heterosexist society in Merrill's insistence throughout his career on a hermeneutics of paradox, inversion, and surprise—on what he called the "relativity, even the reversability, of truths." He happens on this formulation during an interview with J. D. McClatchy originally published in 1982. Asked whether his "fondness for paradox" was a "cultivated habit of mind," Merrill replies:

> I suppose that early on I began to understand the relativity, even the reversability, of truths. At the same time as I was being given a good education I could feel, not so much from my parents, but from the world they moved in, that kind of easygoing contempt rich people have for art and scholarship—"these things are all right *in their place*, and their place is to ornament a life rather than to nourish or shape it." Or when it came to sex, I had to face it that the worst iniquity my parents (and many of my friends) could imagine was for me a blessed source of pleasure and security—as well as suffering, to be sure.[9]

Merrill goes on to add a moment later that "the secret" of his resistance to ideology "lies primarily in the nature of poetry—and of science too, for that matter—and that the ability to see both ways at once isn't merely an idiosyncrasy but corresponds to how the world needs to be seen: cheerful *and* awful, opaque *and* transparent. The plus and minus signs of a vast, evolving formula."[10] He aligns poetry together with science, then, as experimental language-games that aim at a perpetual complication and renovation of the rules through the recognition of their "reversability." In so doing, he affirms Jean-François Lyotard's criticism of the attempted revival of the Enlightenment metanarrative of universal progress. The French philosopher attacks such efforts on the grounds that once the legitimating norms of communication have been thrown into question, dialogical exchange can only function to promote paralogy, or the proliferation of logical alternatives, rather than consensus.[11] Consistent with Lyotard's call for "an idea and practice of justice that is not linked to that of consensus," Merrill's observation of the "easygoing contempt" of his parents' social class for both his literary occupation and sexual proclivity subtly encodes a sense of his own reversed allegiance to the practices of a culture not legitimated by the dominant political order.[12]

To deride tradition in order to protect a scandalous freedom of affinity is to perform a work of imagination in the mood of satire. The comic assault on society in the name of culture leaves the poet in a precariously self-contradictory position, with nothing but the most ludicrous resources of argumentation at hand, capable of invoking no greater authority for his assertions than the claim of laughter. Merrill's poetic account of his experience as a gay man refuses to offer any scientific or theoretical rationale for his object-choice, grounding his sexual identity in a reflective rather than determinant judgment, to invoke a Kantian vocabulary. Autobiographically rehearsing his life, he presents his erotic history in terms of an ongoing problematic that must be approached at the level of a judgment of taste.

Kant's proposal of the faculty of taste as the central link in the chain of analogies harmonizing the faculties of scientific and moral reason amounts to an admission, on Lyotard's reckoning, that our "regimens or genres [of knowledge] are incommensurable" and inevitably result in a differend, in an ethical conflict that cannot be resolved by recourse to transcendent principles.[13] Merrill's poems confront us with what remains irreducibly subjective and contingent in queer desire. Consequently, they point up the failure of the law, and of the laws of understanding, to rationally adjudicate the full range of human differences. The poems, as it were, uncover the differend between desire and social cooperation. A work such as "The Thousand and Second Night," which even in its title plays on a suspicion of the poem's irreconcilability to our customary utopian historical views, thus may be said to uphold a Lyotardian conception of the postmodern.

Accordingly, it is of no small interest that one of the names Lyotard gives to the explosive perspectivalism of postmodernity, a condition he defines as a readiness "to confuse . . . reality and fiction, history and narrative . . . diegesis and metadiegesis," is "the metamorphic manner [of] *Satire*."[14] He emphasizes in his use of the word its root meaning of an utterance that exemplifies formal "saturation." Yet the sense of satire as a punitive rhetorical performance inciting to mirth is even more pertinent to the conviction, arising after the demise of the metanarrative of the Enlightenment, that "to speak is to fight, in the sense of playing, and speech acts fall within the domain of a general agonistics."[15] In the preceding chapters, I have suggested that the British Augustan appeal to autonomous judgment upholds a liberal ideal of culture similar in specific respects to the Habermasian notion of an open (*öffentlich*) or public sphere. Without invalidating the historical analysis on which this notion is based, however, I think it is possible to align Merrill's revision of the Augustan project with Lyotard's critique of Habermas's proposed philosophical corrective to the eventual decline of the public sphere. As Eva Płonowska Ziarek has pointed out in her recent call for a recovery of the language of ethics within the field of radical feminist cultural criticism, the value of Lyotard's example is "not . . . to dispense with the necessity of articulating the constitutive contradictions between diversity and equivalence, equality and difference, antagonism and consensus, but to stress the limit cases of articulation—the differends, or the antagonisms that lack the means of expression within hegemonic arrangements."[16] Ziarek contends that, in this light, the problematization of judgment under the aegis of the postmodern corresponds not to an attitude of depoliticized indifference but rather to a concern for justice outside the provisions of the law: "What is . . . at stake in the differend is not a postmodern celebration of the fragmentation of meaning but rather the obligation to redress an injustice that lacks the means of expression."[17]

Merrill's insistence on the artifice of writing, on the availability of poetry as a mode of rhetoric or popular diversion, associates itself with the disreputable concerns of art, scholarship, and sexuality that bourgeois society attempts to reduce to matters of mere "ornament" and thus to put "in their place" outside the bounds of approved discourse. The appeal to the subjective response of taste in order to highlight disputes between language-games repudiates positivist solutions without denying its own lack of a priori validity. Any rebuke of the social order that relies on the authority of metaphor or artistic illusion thus comes to seem an inherently absurd enterprise. Only once the law has been recognized as an instrument of barbarism does the satiric denunciation of injustice seem plausible. The recourse to imaginative methods of redress thus predicates criticism of the polis on an admission of the critic's outsider status. Given the situation, what alternative do we have but to laugh? Merrill's satires advance a liberal politics, then, in a specific sense. As I will show, his poems depict his erotic career as an ongoing process of rueful self-recognition, as his repeated acknowledgment of his identity as a gay man through moments of lapsed or failed identification. (A crucial detour from the Horatian model, it might be remarked, given that the poet's father, Charles, was a founding partner in the investment firm of Merrill Lynch.) What these compositions propose as a substitute for such identification is a sense of belonging to an apocryphal cultural tradition, to a satiric inheritance associated in the writer's mind with stigmatized social and sexual difference. Once again, the consolation of poetic language appears simultaneously emancipating and absurd.

This sense of deviation from the norm is evident, for example, in the poem that I cited at the start of this chapter. "The Thousand and Second Night" recounts the story of the poet's touristic wanderings in Turkey and Greece as a parable of his inability to achieve social communion with family and friends. At the conclusion, Merrill imagines an amiable parting between spouses straight out of the *Arabian Nights*: an aging Sultan and a still beautiful Scheherazade, after all her stories have been told. Once the lovers have declared to each other their mutual longing to be free,

> They wept, then tenderly embraced and went
> Their ways. She and her fictions soon were one.
> He slept through moonset, woke in blinding sun,
> Too late to question what the tale had meant.
> (*CP* 185)

When he awakens, the Sultan crosses over from the willing suspension of disbelief into an unwilling susceptibility to doubt. The blind confusion of his awakening recalls the discomfort of the poet, who confesses at the start of the sequence: "I woke today / With an absurd complaint. The whole right half / Of my face refuses to move" (*CP* 176). As his story progresses and he appears increasingly distanced from former loved ones, however, his complaint (Bell's palsy, according to the diagnosis of the commentator Stephen Yenser) will come to seem less and less absurd.[18] He remembers in particular his abandonment by three "good friends" who accused him of indifference and to whom he replied with meaningless promises that "never saved my face" (*CP* 180).

Celebrating carnival sometime later in an unnamed city that Yenser identifies as Rio de Janeiro, he encounters a male dancer costumed as a skeleton.[19] Possessed of a "savage grace," the dancer "picks you out from thousands," as the poet notes to himself. Yet the covetous gaze reminds its object of "the eyes of those three friends." Only at the moment of this ineluctable return of the repressed, by his own report, does Merrill's aloof composure fail him: "The mask begins to melt upon your face" (*CP* 183).

There are three points about this sequence of events that seem meaningful to me. First, the poem depicts the instability of the poet's homoerotic unions as equivalent in symbolic terms to the fragility of the paradigmatic, heterosexual marriage between the Sultan and Scheherazade. Second, it discovers in the undoing of this marriage one consequence of a larger failure of narrative itself, an inability of "the tale" to be clear about what it meant, to signify and hence to edify. Third, it interprets this failure of narrative as the sign of a parodic historical alienation, of a jadedness possible only the night *after* the original thousand and one. Because the founding myth of patriarchal society has disintegrated as a result of the increasingly heteronomous condition of culture, the gay poet and the straight Sultan, who as Scherehazade's auditor is also a figure for the reader, find themselves in the same hermeneutic position. For each, the narrative of desire only becomes legible in retrospect as a historically accidental construction that reveals every interpretive horizon as a deviation from the norm.

The second of the two lyric sequences from *Nights and Days* further complicates the relation between erotic experience and the act of interpretation. In "From the Cupola," the myth of Psyche and Eros supplies the iconographical trappings for what looks like an allegorized portrait of the marriage of the poet's mother and father, their estrangement, and eventual divorce. The story, it appears, is set in a small town designed, according to the jokey description, in "Greek Revival" style and located somewhere on the northeastern coast, from which the heroine looks back with nostalgia at the edenic Florida where Merrill's mother, Hellen Ingram, grew up. (In keeping with the implied situation, Psyche tells us early on: "I live now by the seasons burn and freeze / far from that world where nothing changed or died," *CP* 209.)

The poem unfolds as a series of verse epistles from wife to husband, each one written in a different meter and stanza, and each headed either by the name of a meteorological or a temporal marker ("sunlight," "star," "rain," "today," "midnight," "noon," etc.). The progress of the letters is punctuated by a dramatic monologue, a novelistic exchange of dialogue between characters, and a passage of prose narration written in a historical past tense that stands in marked contrast to the present indicative of the epistolary voice. Much of these interpolations have to do with the relation between Psyche and her two sisters, Gertrude and Alice.

These sisters, of course, are named for a pair of lesbian expatriates who were founding members of the artistic community that gave rise to what has been termed high modernism. Merrill's autobiography *A Different Person* recounts his befriending by Alice Toklas in 1950 during his own residence in Europe and as the result of a connection through his gay partner.[20] The derivations of the sisters' names suggest the context of their resistance to Psyche's homesick idealizing of Hellen Ingram's Jacksonville and to her acceptance of Eros's conditions of marriage. When a letter received from her distant lover touches off a reminiscence of "a city named for palms . . . / Where nothing died," a paradise where "the bougainvillea bloomed fell bloomed again" (perhaps in evocation of the Miltonic flowers that adorn the bower of Adam and Eve, roses "which the Morn repair'd"), Psyche is reminded by Alice: "That was a cruel impossible wonderland" (*CP* 210).

Along similar lines, Gertrude chastises Psyche for her refusal to turn on the lights in their house after dark and thus, according to the myth, to discover the identity of the deity who visits her at night: "'Oh Psyche,' her sister burst out at length. 'Here you are, surrounded by loving kin, in a house crammed with lovely old things, and what do you crave but the unfamiliar, the 'transcendental'? I declare, you're turning into the classic New England old maid'" (*CP* 214–215). Both sisters, in other words, reprimand Psyche for an idealism that finally represents no more than an escapist fantasy, a covert form of regression. Far from making her into a genuine seeker of the "unfamiliar," the doctrine transforms her into "the *classic* New England old maid."

Against the background of these criticisms, we read Psyche's own formulations of her increasingly divided emotions with respect to her aloof and superhuman spouse, a figure who is, in her words, all "darts and wings and appetites." Admitting her anxiety, she poignantly describes a recent visit with her sisters to the local drive-in movie theater, where, through windows awash with rain, she was struck by a sudden vision (memory? metaphor? hallucination?) of her husband as he was in a more youthful incarnation.

> In the next car young Eros and his sweetheart sit
> fire and saltwater still from their embrace
> Grief plays upon his sated face
> Her mask of tears does not exactly fit.
>
> (*CP* 215)

Who "his sweetheart" is in this tableau is left pointedly uncertain, but the scrupulous adherence to third-person narration implies Psyche's exclusion from the sexual transaction that has just occurred. Meanwhile, a spectacularly histrionic dramatization of the liaison between Venus and Mars plays to the uncontrollable mirth of the audience. "The love goddess . . . overflows [the] screen," the poem grandiosely reports, while "the hero's breastplate mirrors her red lips. " When the mouths of the two divinities meet in a climactic kiss, the response from the crowd is less than reverential.

> My sisters turn on me from either side
>   shrieking with glee under the rainlight mask
>   fondle and pinch in mean burlesque
> of things my angel you and I once tried.
> (*CP* 216)

The knowing, conspiratorial linkage of first- and second-person pronouns here displaces the vaguely impersonal coupling of "young Eros and his sweetheart," as well as the marquee-scale juxtaposition of "goddess" and "hero," from the center of spectatorial attention.

In the interim, the very idea of an elemental, natural, hence unself-conscious heterosexual fusion ("fire and saltwater"), already jeopardized by its assimilation to a rhetoric of masking or concealment, has come in for active ridicule. The transition in these stanzas from a voice of third-person alienation to one of embarrassed first-person intimacy we may understand as the mirror-image reversal of a psychological movement that Merrill attributes to his parents in an anecdote from his memoir.

> They are dining at "21" in New York . . . my father has ordered champagne. He wants my mother to know that he means to break with Kinta [a mistress] and turn over a new leaf. . . . Alas, in the car back to their apartment he goes too far. The worst is over, they're going to be closer than ever, he tells her—falling silent before the glowing embers of his unburdened spirit at last. My mother presses his hand. Then with an amazed headshake, he breathes as if to himself:
>   "But God, I sure do love that little girl."
>   "My heart simply turned to ice," said my mother, ending her narrative.
> (*ADP* 100–101)

A critical failure of understanding is dramatized here by the passage from indirect to direct discourse, as if the ties of sympathy were too fragile to endure a division of the impersonal narrative voice into separate speakers. This scene, also claustrophobically set in a car, might be said to sketch in for us the tragedy lurking underneath the "mean burlesque."

Through their caricature of the lovers, Alice and Gertrude prompt Psyche to recognize the artifice necessary to the maintenance of a responsive emotional decorum. On the one hand, to indulge in prudishness or mere mockery, as the twin sisters do, is dehumanizing. On the other, to obey one's desires in a wholly unconstrained manner is not to feel emotion in an ethically responsive manner but to exist as a force of nature or a god, sans pity, sans fear, sans any potential as well for social integration. "You can feel / lust and fulfillment Eros," Psyche tells her lover with regret, "no more than / ocean its salt depths or uranium its hot / disintegrative force" (*CP* 216). The insight into his character finally will result at home the next evening in her rebellion against the provisions of their domestic arrangement when she lights her lamp, effectively divorcing him: "Then soft light lights the room . . . / yes and I am here alone / I and my flesh and blood" (*CP* 218).

It is in fact the poet, who identifies himself in the sequence only by his first name as "James" and thus inferentially as the "flesh and blood" of Hellen Ingram, if not of Psyche, who has the final word. His apostrophe of the heroine in the last three stanzas of the poem puts the story of her disenchantment in a suddenly enlarged perspective.

> This evening it will do to be alone,
> Here, with your girlish figures: parsnip, Eros,
> Shadow, blossom, windowpane. The warehouse.
> The lamp I smell in every other line.
>
> Do you smell mine? From its rubbed brass a moth
> Hurtles in motes and tatters of itself
> —Be careful, tiny sister, drabbest sylph!—
> Against the hot glare, the consuming myth
>
> Drops, and is still. My hands move. An intense,
> Slow-paced, erratic dance goes on below.
> I have received from whom I do not know
> These letters. Show me, light, if they make sense.
>
> (*CP* 219)

The equivocal approval for Psyche's decision voiced in the first stanza ("This evening it will do to be alone") finds an apt objective correlative in the cautionary, mock-heroic figure of the moth. Precisely by lighting her lamp, Psyche has dispelled the "consuming myth" of heterosexism: that matrimony, obedience to the law, is a woman's predestined fate. Unlike her miniature alter ego, she has just avoided self-immolation. The poet's campy, punning apostrophe of his "tiny sister, drabbest sylph" identifies the moth on the one hand as a missed or transmuted version of the self and on the other as a part of an animistic psychological machinery that receives its fullest literary exposition in *The Rape of the Lock*.

The sylphs in Pope's comic *chef d'oeuvre*, of course, play the part of angelic but ultimately ineffectual guardians of the heroine's chastity. At stake in the determination of the sylphs' proper role, in other words, is the tenor of the male poet's sympathy for his female heroine. Alastair Fowler has remarked that Pope's sylphs come to stand for the poet's "conspiratorial fellow feeling for the poignantly mutable beauty—for one who aspires to airy lightness in a world of heavy prudes."[21] Merrill's reappropriation of the trope in one sense amounts to a feigned or simulated show of empathy with a feminized erotic drive that in its single-mindedness can hope to achieve only its own self-annihilation.

Yet given the obvious conflation of "sylph" with "self" here, there is also a deeper sense in which the metaphor acknowledges Merrill's internalization of the maternal role model. The gratuitous indulgence of this identification, the narcissistic interpretation of the Other as a reflection of the ego, obliges the author in the following lines to admit that his presumptuous attempt to evoke a female genius from the "rubbed brass" of the poem may be no better than masturbation. "My hands move. An intense, / Slow-paced, erratic dance goes on below," announces the narrator, referring both to a mechanical act of self-arousal and the manual labor of typing that will result in the completion of his story (*CP* 219). Finally, he vacillates between a sadistic insensibility to the suffering of the female Other and a naive identification with that other, which the poem itself interprets as potentially narcissistic and masturbatory. This very ambivalence in turn presents the male psyche in a farcical light. The satirical upending of the masculine that Merrill implies through his critique of the feminine redeems the mute, erotic dance of the senses in the self-qualifying "erratic dance" of meaning. At the end, we leave behind the gross literalism of the body for the purer figuration of "these letters." Yet the poet's self-mocking depiction of the production of such signs as a wholly mechanical and autoerotic process raises pointed questions regarding how culturally successful this work really is.

"The Thousand and Second Night" and "From the Cupola" together propound an idea of reading as an erotic activity that leaves the reader in a state of social isolation. Both poems give emphasis to the private or radically personal nature of the task of interpretation and thus to the solipsism of the reader: hence the Sultan who awakens only after Scheherazade's disappearance, "too late to question what the tale had meant," and hence the "me, James," who finds in his mother's divorce of his father a mock-paradigm for his own refusal of bourgeois respectability in favor of artistic and sexual experimentation. Both poems picture the heterosexual desire of one spouse for another as the textual (i.e., symbolically encoded) paradigm for the homosexual desire of one man for another. The works imagine the gay subject in an attitude of intellectual engagement with the enigma of an alternate, socially sanctioned pattern of sexual experience: in a posture of balanced reception and resistance.

Merrill's masterpiece, *The Changing Light at Sandover*, hits on an ingenious symbol to bring to light the communal aspect of the critical enterprise: the Ouija board. The séance-like pretense of spiritual possession associated with Ouija of course suggests an image of critical reception as a shared pastime, a game to be played out in tandem with at least one other "medium" or reader. Indeed, the narrator introduces both the poem and his fellow medium to us in one breath when he announces the commencement of "The Book of a Thousand and One Evenings Spent / With David Jackson at the Ouija Board / In Touch with Ephraim Our Familiar Spirit" (*CLS* 4).

By giving this playful subtitle to the poem, Merrill both evokes and assuages the sense of estrangement from history conveyed by the title of the earlier "The Thousand and Second Night." *Sandover*, in other words, does not wholly share the cynicism toward narrative per se that characterizes "The Thousand and Second Night." Thom Gunn's often-quoted commendation of the epic for offering "the most convincing description I know of a gay marriage" nicely captures the more magnanimous outlook of the later work.

> Much of what makes any marriage successful is the ability to take the importance of one's partner for granted, to *depend* on the other's love without being in a state of continual erotic or passional tension. Merrill's indication of these abilities is the firmer for being indirect. The men's life is presented to us in detail which is almost casual: we see them choosing wallpaper, keeping house, traveling, entertaining, and above all sitting at the Ouija board. It is not a minor triumph and it is not an incidental one.[22]

This is not to say, however, that the ideal of gay marriage is unproblematic in the poem nor that the particular marriage between Merrill and David Jackson (or JM and DJ, to use the poem's labels) is depicted as being untroubled. Perhaps we receive our first inklings in the poem of the specific anxieties that underlie the shared private life of the protagonists during a sustained exposition of Merrill's doctrine of metempsychosis, a discussion chiefly occupying sections C through I of the first volume of the epic, *The Book of Ephraim*, but which continues to be expanded and revised throughout the rest of *Sandover*.

On the testimony of Ephraim, the Ouija-board mediums' tutelary spirit, every living human being is the "representative" of a divine "patron" who educates the young soul "in the entr'acte between / One incarnation and another" (*CLS* 10), until the pupil has lived through enough existences to gain "a footing on the lowest of NINE STAGES" in heaven and qualify as a new patron. A patron may not interfere in the life of his or her assigned representative, but inhabitants of the netherworld may petition the divine bureaucracy for changes in the fates of living souls to whom they are bound by a special sympathy.

So no small commotion surrounds the news of Hans Lodeizen's intercession on behalf of JM in *The Book of Ephraim*, section G. Hans is described carefully in the poem's "Dramatis Personae" as "Dutch poet.... Clever, goodnatured, solitary, blond, / All to a disquieting degree," and his relation to the narrator is glossed in a manner so tactful as to border on the cryptic: "Plays a recording of the 'Spring' Sonata / One May night when JM has a fever; / Unspoken things divide them from then on" (*CLS* 12). Merrill discusses the attachment more openly in his memoir:

> Hans was a graduate student at Amherst when we met in 1946....
> True to form, I fell in love.... Between my eighteenth and twenty-fourth birthdays there must have been ten or twelve young men *en fleurs*... whom I was smitten by in succession, or two or three at a time. Of these, Hans was by far the most meaningful. (*ADP* 46)

The reminiscence refrains from any attempt at reconstruction of Hans's motivations (other than by noting the willingness with which he offered Merrill his "mothering" in response to the poet's complaint of an incipient cold on the night of the missed musical seduction), for the sake of delicacy leaving intact the "unspoken things" alluded to in *The Book of Ephraim*.

Despite these "unspoken" tensions, we are told, Hans in the afterlife still bears "SOME POWERFUL MEMORY OR AFFINITY" for Merrill and "HEARS THRU U JM A VERNAL MUSIC" (*CLS* 24). It is this "affinity" that prompts "HL" to intervene with the cosmic authorities in order to advance JM beyond the realm of earthly incarnations directly to the nine stages of celestial patronage. As Ephraim tells the poet, "THIS WILL BE YR LAST LIFE THANKS TO HIM." The privilege, however, exacts a high price, as it is revealed that DJ still has "one or two, at most / Three lives more" (*CLS* 24) to undergo on earth before his own elevation to the nine, meaning that he must be separated from JM, potentially for several lifetimes. The narrator responds to this news with an uncharacteristic vehemence:

> Ephraim, this cannot be borne. We live
> Together. And if you are on the level
> Some consciousness survives—right? Right.
> Now tell me, what conceivable delight

> Lies for either of us in the prospect
> Of an eternity without the other?
> Why not *both* be reborn? Which at least spares one
> Dressing up as the Blessed Damozel
> At Heaven's Bar to intervene—oh hell,
> Stop *me*. You meant no harm. But, well, forgive
> My saying so, that was insensitive.
>
> <div align="right">(<i>CLS</i> 25)</div>

What "cannot be borne" as an emotional or spiritual experience is a life lived in the other's absence, an incarnation that ought not to be "born." For a life to be "born" is for a life to be "borne": the latent pun confers on the very act of propagation a certain burden, underscoring the weighty responsibilities imposed by the event of birth on the participants. The wordplay reminds us that this particular married couple can participate in the reproductive process only in a metaphysical, rather than in a literal, biological sense. Taken together with the farcical image of JM in drag "as the Blessed Damozel" in order to argue DJ's case, the lines suggest the poet's anxiety that even heaven may be unprepared to accommodate such an attachment between two adult men and may require the rigmarole of a pretended heterosexual arrangement in order to sanction the union. The pall cast by the continuing influence of Hans on JM, an influence that threatens to separate JM and DJ in the hereafter, is reinterpreted a moment later in psychologically more naturalistic terms as "nothing, dearest heart / But the dim wish of lives to drift apart" (*CLS* 25).

Explication of the Ouija-board spirits in overtly psychoanalytic terms takes place two sections later when JM visits his "ex-shrink," Tom, to get the psychoanalyst's opinion of the couple's exchanges with the other world. The poet's visit to his analyst occurs after "the miscarriage of plans for Joselito" (*CLS* 29), Han's representative, for whose rebirth DJ believed he had found a suitable mother, the wife of an "ex-roommate." In fact, however, he had misremembered her name and, as a consequence, Joselito is born to the wrong woman. Along similar lines, JM has suggested his niece Betsy (short for Beatrice, appropriately) as a host for Ephraim's "all but bestial" (*CLS* 8) representative, Simpson. Although the reincarnation of Simpson as Betsy's son Wendell goes more smoothly and congenially than Joselito's rebirth, it is revealed that the authorities who govern the spirit world are "FURIOUS" at Ephraim, HL, DJ, and JM for having interfered in the routine distribution of souls. Ephraim subsequently is brought to trial before "Heaven's Bar," as JM has dubbed it, but receives no word of support from the mediums, who reply to his expressions of fear with "flippancies" (*CLS* 29). "Whereupon," we are told, "the cup went dead," leaving JM and DJ without fresh material for transcription.

Tom swiftly renders his opinion that "what you and David do / We call folie à deux" and leads JM to the insight that "somewhere a Father Figure shakes his rod / At sons who have not sired a child" (*CLS* 30). This appraisal of the situation makes clear that the punishment of Ephraim by the divinities, a rebuke to which JM and DJ make no small contribution, represents a disciplining of the ego by the superego for violating the rule of paternal succession. Because the Ouija-board mediums have succeeded in bringing children into the world, thus in circumventing the conventional economy of heterosexual relations, they must be punished by the father, which is to say by themselves.

The two men share a similar identification with the figurative father whom each has disobeyed by persisting in a queer existence. Punishing their own erotic genius, JM and DJ assume the dead father's role of lawgiver and thus atone for their crimes. The scenario is reminiscent of Freud's account in *Totem and Taboo* (1913) of the development of taboo prohibitions in tribal societies. The organization of gangs of young males within a clan, an organization that "may have been based on homosexual feelings and acts," eventually leads to the murder of the aggressive patriarch by his sons, their completion of a guilty identification with the father by devouring him in cannibalistic celebration, and their acceptance of the incest taboo, hence of exogamous heterosexuality, out of remorse.[23]

If there is any father against whose word the poem rebels, however, it is in fact Tom himself. The too-easy explanation for which he settles in this case is undercut slyly by the Ouija board, which relays a message from a higher authority.

> FREUD
> We learned that evening DESPAIRS
> OF HIS DISCIPLES & SAYS NIE
> ZU AUFGEBEN THE KEY
> TO YR OWN NATURES.
> (*CLS* 30)

The slapstick overtones of this bit of ventriloquism, replete with pidgin German, suggests discomfort with a theory that would relegate the homosexual to the position of a regressive, pre-Oedipal step on the way to the fulfillment of a heterosexual evolutionary ideal.

Freud names "regard for the father or fear of him" in the essay "Some Neurotic Mechanisms in Jealousy, Paranoia, and Homosexuality" (1922) as one of four factors contributing to same-sex object-choice (18:231). However, he clearly holds in this essay, as in other works, such as *Group Psychology and the Analysis of the Ego* (1921), that it is strong identification with the mother that disposes the male child to unrepressed homosexuality. Such an identification requires the subject to renounce the mother as an object of libidinal cathexis, but she is retained as an object of remembrance after the fashion of melancholia. While this renunciation seems to raise the possibility of an escape from the Oedipal complex, then, it exposes the mother-identified gay son to an incessant "self-tormenting" that "signifies . . . a satisfaction of trends of sadism and hate which relate to an object, and which have been turned round upon the subject's own self" (14:251). Given this argument, it is tough to see how in the context of Freudian psychoanalysis a homosexual subject could be conceived that would not be pathological by definition.

Contrary to this line of reasoning, *The Book of Ephraim* propounds a theory of the emotions according to which the gay son defines himself in the course of refusing or rejecting identification with a parent, especially the mother.[24] Instead of such an object-identification, the subject arrives at what might be called a language-identification. The notion is advanced most sharply in section Y, where the narrator asks himself why he has persevered over a long span in working out his bizarre narrative: "How sensible had *we* been / To dig up this material of ours" (*CLS* 87)? The question comes in response to a memory of a session with the ghost of W. H. Auden, shortly after his death, during which the older poet, before being censored by the divine powers that preside over the poem's cosmology, tried to request the destruction of some private papers stored in Oxford. JM's pang of self-doubt merely underscores how incapable he has found himself of emulating Auden's scrupulosity, how many of his own secrets already have been aired.

Ruminating on Auden's anxious regard for his personal affairs brings to mind the thought of DJ, freshly arrived home from the "senior / Citizen desert ghetto" where his aging parents live (*CLS* 88). As JM listens to his lover's descriptions of the bickering between "the poor old / Helpless woman and the rich old skinflint," who intermittently make peace to "Bask in the tinted conscience of their kind," he arrives at a tentative rationale for his own need to put his experiences with DJ into words.

> Feared and rejoiced in, chafed against, held cheap,
> A strangeness that was us, and was not, had
> All the same allowed for its description,
> And so brought at least me these spells of odd,
> Self-effacing balance.
>
> (*CLS* 89)

It is the very "strangeness," or *Unheimlichkeit*, of existing in the plural, of being an "us," that teaches the narrator the equanimity to admit the limits of the erotic bond, to know when to regard himself simply as "me." Such a fine sense of "balance" may only be developed through the work of writing or "description." This is because, as the witty closing lines of the section testify, we come to possess our self-knowledge only when, through an exercise of satiric perception, we disclaim it.

> My father in his last illness complained
> Of the effect of medication on
> His real self—today Bluebeard, tomorrow
> Babbitt. Young chameleon, I used to
> Ask how on earth one got sufficiently
> Imbued with otherness. And now I see.
> (*CLS* 89)

The tone here is brilliantly complex. The offhand pun that colors the "illness" of the narrator's father—it is "last" in both senses of being most recent and final—allows us to forget momentarily that JM's only access to Charles Merrill at this point is through the Ouija board, as if the poem were trying to domesticate any trace of Oedipal anxiety by passing over the father's death with an air of nonchalance.

If a touch of disquiet invades our perception of the poet's seeming breeziness on this score, we should note by way of contrast that the cartoon images JM offers us of his father under medication ultimately serve the purposes of commiseration rather than disregard. It must be recalled, of course, that Charles's natural inclinations, amplified by the drugs, run toward heterosexual ebullience (Bluebeard) and bourgeois conformism (Sinclair Lewis's Babbitt) and James shares neither impulse at all. Although the admission of this difference precludes any sense of identification between father and son, however, it nonetheless can be said to sponsor a feeling of compassion. Because what the poet, in a wry mood of self-deflation, at last recognizes of himself in his father is an equal, if in libidinal terms dissimilarly configured, vulnerability or instability of the "real self." In the end, JM sees his own "otherness" as no less absurd and self-contrary than his father's. To achieve this perspective, however, is to hone a kind of poetic judgment, to shape one's self-presentation in the pointed manner of a joke.

A poem collected in Merrill's collection *Braving the Elements* (1972), the book that preceded the first appearance of *The Book of Ephraim* in *Divine Comedies* (1976), develops this wary sense of self as a defense against maternal influence. "Up and Down" employs a loose, iambic pentameter quatrain rhymed abba and divides into two sections of fourteen quatrains each. The first section, "Snow King Lift Chair," recounts the poet's memory of a ride with a lover in a ski lift to the top of a mountain, where the couple had their photograph snapped and "gazed our little fills at boundlessness" before returning (*CP* 340).

The second section, "The Emerald," holds the most interest for us, however. Here Merrill describes a "drive downtown" with his mother a short time after the death of "the gentle General," her second husband (identified in *A Different Person* as General William Plummer). Mother and child stop at the "Mutual Trust" bank, where "palatial bronze gates shut like jaws / On our descent into the innermost vault," within which the security deposit boxes are kept (*CP* 341). Merrill's mother searches through the contents of her own until she finds first a bracelet given to her by Merrill *père* ("Teardrop to fire, my father's kisses hang / In lipless concentration round her wrist," *CP* 342) and then a ring also given her by her first husband, this time on the occasion of the poet's birth. The setting houses an emerald in which the narrator discerns a miniature symbol of both the tomblike vault wherein his mother now appears as a "girl-bride jeweled in [her husband's] grave" and the living room of sustained domestic fidelity: "A den of greenest light, it grows, shrinks, glows, / Hermetic stanza bedded in the prose / Of the last thirty semiprecious years" (*CP* 342).

Merrill's mother presses the ring on him, imploring him to give it as an engagement token to his "bride" when he should decide to marry. The gift prompts a highly equivocal refusal.

> I do not tell her, it would sound theatrical,
> *Indeed this green room's mine, my very life.*
> *We are each other's; there will be no wife;*
> *The little feet that patter here are metrical.*
>
> But onto her worn knuckle slip the ring.
> Wear it for me, I silently entreat,
> Until—until the time comes. Our eyes meet.
> The world beneath the world is brightening.
>   (*CP* 342)

The catachrestic figure on which hinges the poet's admission of his gay sexuality, hence inability to meet the conditions attached to the gift, depicts poetic production not so much as a usurpation of the parental role traditionally belonging to the heterosexual as rather a modest, and in the end perhaps unsatisfying, imitation of parenthood ("The little feet that patter here are metrical"). Ultimately, the poet has to settle for the figural, rather than the literal, pattering of childish feet. Of course, knowingly to opt for such an outcome means to transgress the bounds of social legitimacy or propriety. No wonder, then, that the poet delivers his refusal of paternal responsibility and thus of the social contract in an alexandrine, a hypermetrical line that represents a deliberate violation of the metrical compact with the reader.[25] Such a flouting of the rules at the same time exercises its own peculiarly exemplary authority, because the self-moralizing overdetermination of the alexandrine belongs to a tradition that finds its locus classicus in Spenser's tribute to

Chaucer in *The Fairie Queene* ("I follow here the footing of thy feete, / That with thy meaning so I may the rather meete," 4.2.34).

This tribute in turn elicits numerous similar acknowledgments of influence from subsequent poets, including, crucially, Milton in *Il Penseroso*.[26] Such expressions of humility encode more or less latent claims to genuine artistic license, and in this sense we may regard Merrill's insertion of the twelve-syllable, six-stress line into the pentameter framework of "Up and Down" as a craftsman's flourish, as a show of credentials earned within the guild of professional poets. But Merrill deploys the inflated line in a particularly irreverent way that seems out of sorts either with the Spenserian paradigm or with the imitations of later admirers. The formulation from "The Emerald" clearly depends on the surprise achieved at the end of the line by the obtrusion of the prosodic term "metrical," by the wrenching of a cliché onomatopoeia for the noise of a small child's running ("the *pattering* of little feet") into a figure for the sound of poetic diversion. (We might measure this surprise if we substitute in place of "metrical" an adjective that maintains the initial, putative sense of the cliché and compare the effect, as in: "The little feet that patter here are infantile.")

The hypermetrical line in "Up and Down," in other words, embodies the same sort of purposefully outrageous mixing of metaphors that we are used to encountering in Pope rather than in the rhetorically less anxious models of Spenser and Milton.

> Maggots half-form'd, in rhyme exactly meet,
> And learn to crawl upon poetic feet.

These lines from the *Dunciad* (1.59–60) offer an example of an especially severe catachresis that works as an emblem of the poem's confrontation with twisted or distorted rivals. A perfectly conventional specimen of the heroic couplet, the verse eschews the Spenserian legerdemain of juggling pentameter and hexameter together. Nevertheless, a close mythographic relation connects these Grubstreet "maggots" to the "wounded Snake" described in the celebrated lines of representative versification on the alexandrine in *An Essay on Criticism*: "A needless Alexandrine ends the Song / That like a wounded Snake, drags its slow length along." In both cases, a poetic misstep exemplifies a larger and dehumanizing aesthetic insensibility.

Both texts parody the creation myth that occurs at the beginning of Ovid's *Metamorphoses* and that details the *abiogenesis*, or spontaneous coming-into-being, of natural freaks (*nova monstra*) on the banks of the Nile. This chronicle immediately precedes an explanation of the instituting of the Pythian games to celebrate Apollo's killing of the *serpens* that terrorized humanity in the primitive wilderness (1.416–451). At any rate, both Pope's "snake" and "maggots" stand for a monstrous threat of corruption from beyond the bounds of civilization (perhaps meant to resonate with the Roman distrust of Egypt, the great barbarian rival empire) that infiltrates the polis through the misapplication of language. Both *An Essay on Criticism* and *The Dunciad*, in other words, propose verbal judiciousness as the determining criterion of the civilized or human.

Then what do we say when society or civilization itself does not wish to listen to us? Clearly, the question is one that in some version Merrill wishes to raise, because he explains his response to his mother's present of the emerald ring in terms of what "I do not say to her." Just how much of her son's private life does she know about, we might ask ourselves. His reticence with her on the topic of his sexual orientation, his refusal to be pathetic or "theatrical" in devising a reply to her offering, may indicate his high level of trust in his mother's intelligence, his conviction that nothing *needs* to be said between them on this score because everything of importance is already understood. On the other hand, his silence also may imply his embarrassment in the face of her wistful denial of the all-too-obvious truth, a denial that in the end he cannot wholly indulge.

As readers we perhaps are not privy to the exact nuances of the communication that takes place between them. But then as agents, mother and son perhaps are not fully aware of the joke that underlies their reconciliation through his return of her gift, a joke set up in the poem's retelling of the episode by the proleptic punch line of the alexandrine and shared between poet and reader. For after being told by the poet that his only possible progeny are "metrical," after coming to grasp positively his identity as a gay man, we cannot fail to interpret his replacement of the ring onto his mother's "worn knuckle" as a parodic rejection of the heterosexual marriage contract. The very gesture of asking her to wear the ring for him, which sends up the traditional, ceremonial exchange of rings between bride and groom, would seem to seal his identification with her, thus affirming his commitment to a queer object-choice. It is the mutual, unspoken recognition of their shared freedom from the burden of perpetuating the Merrill family name that enables them to look back with their own reflective clarity at the "brightening" underworld of dead progenitors.

On a deeper level, however, the poet's overt naming of himself in these lines as a gay man who is also a gay writer prevents any but the most qualified expression of sympathy across generations. By avowing his authorship of strictly "metrical" progeny, he admits his fundamental sexual dissimilarity from his mother. The host of literary allusions summed up in the line "The little feet that patter here are metrical" ironizes or undercuts the sense of identification between himself and his mother that is played out in the giving back and forth of the ring. The line signals Merrill's deliberate embrace of the life of a gay poet and rejection of a life of attempted conformity to the social "norm" of heterosexuality. At the end of the poem, then, it is strongly implied that in order to fulfill his contracts with readers present and future, the poet must be willing to break his contracts with the larger society. To do so, however, is to risk an overly literal expression of Oedipal rage, a murdering of parents that has no symbolic value.

In the concluding sections of *The Book of Ephraim*, the poet increasingly seems occupied with the anxious forethought of his mother's death, an event that remains imminent throughout *The Changing Light at Sandover* but never quite materializes. (The poem's last real reference to her, in *Mirabell's Books of Numbers*, book 7, tells how the poet's "heart contracts in terror" when she takes an especially long time to answer his unexpected phone call on a "free evening," *CLS* 232–233.) Musing on Giorgione's enigmatic masterpiece, *La Tempesta*, during a trip to Venice in the light of a scholarly article only recently published by Nancy Thompson de Grummond at the time of *Ephraim*'s composition (*L'Arte* 5, 18–19/20 (1972): 4–53), an essay that interprets the painting as a depiction of the legend of Saint Theodore, helps JM to shed light on a more personally perplexing mystery,

> as scholarship
> Now and then does, a matter hitherto
> Overpainted—the absence from these pages
> Of my own mother.
> (*CLS* 83–84)

The painting as explicated by de Grummond provides a suggestive figure for Merrill's treatment of his mother in the poem on a number of counts, as follows.

First, the Christian myth, which reports both Theodore's rescue of his own mother from a menacing dragon and his destruction of a temple of the pagan Magna Mater after being imprisoned for his faith, helps to dramatize, admittedly on a somewhat grandiose scale, the ambivalence of JM's attitude toward *Sandover*'s central, if oddly elusive, feminine figure. Second, *La Tempesta* constitutes a monument or memorial to the Christian martyr that cannot be viewed as a linear narration of Theodore's life through a sequential arrangement of scenes but only as a conglomeration of symbolic attributes or elements from different moments in his life, and thus illustrates the subjectivity and cognitive instability of the very work of memory, hence of the sense of shared history intrinsic to family relations. (The image consists of a young man standing in the left foreground and leaning on a staff while gazing at a nude woman who sits nursing a baby on the right side of the painting. According to de Grummond, the young man represents Saint Theodore after having slain the dragon, while the woman personifies his mother, meaning that the child she nurses is also Theodore, but at the age of infancy.) Third, because the very process of the painting's composition exemplifies the work of sublimation that structures human perception per se and qualifies any conception of memory as a factually or historically transparent medium. Indeed, the poem begins its ekphrasis of *La Tempesta* by alluding to an earlier stage of composition, revealed by modern photographic analysis, at which a female nude emerges beneath the male figure visible on the painting's surface, and thus by focusing on what the finished product omits: "X rays of *La Tempesta* show this curdling / Nude arisen, faint as ectoplasm, / From flowing water" (*CLS* 83). The emphasis here on the ghostly nature of the "overpainted" nude, on her state of existence as "ectoplasm," argues that the necessary precondition for the formation of the masculine subject in the painting is the death of the feminine.

As Merrill proceeds from this meditation on Giorgione to take up the "matter" of his mother, he makes a show of avoiding the elegiac or somber note and insists rather on her importance as an active presence to his own project of self-invention.

> Because of course she's here
> Throughout, the breath drawn after every line,
> Essential to its making as to mine;
> Here no less in Maya's prodigality
> Than in Joanna's fuming—or is *she*
> The last gasp of my dragon? I think so:
> My mother gave up cigarettes years ago
> (And has been, letters tell, conspicuously
> Alive and kicking in a neighbor's pool
> All autumn, while singsong voices, taped, unreel,
> Dictating underwater calisthenics).
>
> (*CLS* 84)

Framed by parentheses, the closing addendum offers a glimpse of a world of quotidian experience outside the poem's boundaries, a view that may strike the reader with a certain surprise. We are reminded that JM's mother has a life independent of his thoughts of her, that she even may be animated by a chorus of spectral, "singsong voices," which, however canned or dully utilitarian, are her own (as the pool is not) and keep her "alive and kicking." While the image of her exercising her autonomy with a splash is a playful one, it is worth noting that, immediately before the parentheses, an association between his mother and Joanna, the *femme fatale* of the lost novel summarily reconstructed by the poetic narrator in *Ephraim*, crosses JM's mind. The idea is dismissed because Joanna's "fuming" already has been traced back to his chain-smoking stepmother (at the end of section J), whom he apparently invokes here as "my dragon." Yet in itself the thought's occurrence is telling. Still more telling is the identification of the narrator's mother with

Maya Deren, the "doyenne of our / American experimental film" (*CLS* 11) and student of voodoo ritual who blesses DJ and JM early in the poem with a heart-shaped emblem drawn on the floor of their Stonington home (*CLS* 23–25).

Section R relates Maya's death from heart failure in a New York hospital and resurrection as a voice speaking through the Ouija board to the friends she has left behind: "DAVID JIMMY I AM YOUNG AT LAST" (*CLS* 64). She informs the men that Erzulie, the voodoo goddess of love, rules in the afterlife as "THE QUEEN / OF HEAVEN" and is of "ONE QUINTESSENCE" with the eternal feminine in all her divine incarnations (Mary, Kuan Yin). "I AM HER LITTLEST FAUVE," Maya announces with a curious mix of triumph and self-deprecation. "The moment brought back Maya in a whiff / Of blissful grief," comments JM, to whom she revealed in life a "small figure boldly hued" and now again discloses a paradoxical multitude of qualities: "Touches of tart and maiden, muse and wife / Glowing forth once more from an *Etude / De Jeune Femme* no longer dimmed by time" (*CLS* 65).

If on this latest occasion the observer recognizes what was always constant in his friend, he also discovers what is new and changed in himself since her loss. He sees her anew, "no longer dimmed by time," because he views her in admitted rather than denied retrospect, "brought back" to him through a memory "activated" by grief, hence all the keener as an index of historical difference. Apprehending Maya's femininity in her various parts of "tart and maiden, muse and wife," he has glimpsed the greater sum of her individuality, hopefully as a prelude to releasing her from the clutch of anguish by means of anguish.

Acknowledging the difference of the feminine, and thus implicitly of the maternal, JM prepares himself for a coming-to-grips with the radical extraneousness of the world at the end of *The Book of Ephraim*, an antagonistic encounter that also constitutes a reconciliation of sorts. In the poignant concluding lines of the poem, the narrator decides not to burn an old box of Ouija-board transcripts that already have been translated into verse. This display of mercy is rewarded with a last, revelatory image not of election but of compromise, not of the supernal but of the domestic, not of paradise but of purgatory.

> Too much
> Already, here below, has met its match.
> Yet nothing's gone, or nothing we recall.
> And look, the stars have wound in filigree
> The ancient, ageless woman of the world.
> She's seen us. She is not particular—

> Everyone gets her injured, musical
> "Why do you no longer come to me?"
> To which there's no reply. For here we are.
>
> (*CLS* 92)

The question does not eschew the possibility of embarrassing the listener and in its self-regard may be compared to the speech by the poet's companion in the second section of *The Waste Land*, "A Game of Chess":

> 'My nerves are bad to-night. Yes, bad. Stay with me.
> 'Speak to me. Why do you never speak. Speak.
>   'What are you thinking of? What thinking? What?
> 'I never know what you are thinking. Think.'
>
> (111–114)

Whereas Eliot's depressed lover harangues the poet in an accusatory and, for the most part, imperative manner, Merrill's more indulgent "woman" puts to the poet and his lover a single question that she poses "everyone" alike in a tone both "injured" and "musical."

Like Cordelia standing in dismay before Lear (another parent linked with dragons), JM finds himself unable to verbalize an appropriate rejoinder to this demand. And like Cordelia's sharper and more public "nothing," the assertion with which he privately answers to himself represents at once a refusal to play along with the questioner and a corrective to the question that, given certain allowances, might permit the continuation of the game. Gay, childless, a survivor of the deaths of friends, JM does not quite say "here we are" to the "ancient, ageless woman of the world," does not quite tell her in so many words, we are present, separate, not with you but close at hand. Instead he counts on her intelligence, despite the nearly Proustian potential for misunderstanding he risks by such self-restraint.

In the poem "Days of 1971," Merrill in fact formulates the human principle on which his satiric vision of society is premised and dubs it "Proust's Law":

> Proust's Law (are you listening?) is twofold:
> (a) What least thing our self-love longs for most
> Others instinctively withhold;
>
> (b) Only when time has slain desire
> Is his wish granted to a smiling ghost
> Neither harmed nor warmed, now, by the fire.
>
> (*CP* 349)

To desire the "least thing" unguardedly is already to anticipate the mourning of the object: to precipitate its sweeping flight or withdrawal from the desiring subject. Only when nothing remains to be mourned save for "slain desire" itself does the mourner achieve the "smiling" impartiality that enables lover and beloved to inhabit the same social continuum. Such a moment marks not only the death of an isolated sentiment but of a pervasive sensibility; in the interim between clauses (a) and (b) of Proust's Law, we might say, a certain life led by the passions is transmogrified into its own dispassionate "ghost."

According to Merrill, however, the true casualty of this *peripeteia* is not the self as such but merely "self-love." Yet we cannot name such a death as an object of mourning, it should be added, unless we have passed beyond the limits of mourning and emerged into the open terrain of mirth. For to acknowledge what we have lost in the course of time as frustrated "self-love" is to admit not only that we are "smiling" but that we are smiling at our own blind vanity, our egomaniacal reflex of projection onto the world, and so to admit the justice of our fate. In a very real sense, then, Merrill is anything but an adherent to Proustian law. If Proust is the great modernist connoisseur of mourning, Merrill is its most charming postmodern demystifier.

The target of Merrill's poetic hilarity is not any one isolated configuration of the erotic life—neither straight nor gay, neither female-identified nor male-identified. Rather, it is our clumsy tendency, no matter with which categories of being we tend to label ourselves, to mistake the desires of others for confirmations of our own and to attempt to legislate away the discrepancies. In so doing, we deny the terms that give us our eccentricities and aptitudes as unique individuals. Against the overidentification that seeks to repress difference, the resistance to postmodern dispersal by what Merrill calls, near the end of *Sandover*, "THE DULLWITTED, THE MOB, THE IDIOT IN POWER, THE PURELY BLANK OF MIND" (*CLS* 476), sounds the liberal laughter of the satirist. The poet associates the behaviorism of mass society with the threat of apocalypse against which his grand mock-epic persistently and anxiously warns: "THE GREAT THINNING TO COME" that will result from a betrayal of the biological life force (GOD B in the poem's terminology) by "THE JUDAS, THE CAIN, THE GREAT OPPOSING FORCE TO MATTER ITSELF" (*CLS* 476). It is thus on the brutality of the postmodern technocratic state that Gabriel, the Angel of Fire and Death who presides over the poem as JM and DJ's judge and ultimate tutor, bestows "THE NAME OF THE ONE SIN: / PAIN. PAIN GIVEN, PAIN RECEIVED" (*CLS* 455). As the peacock Mirabell, another of the protagonists' supernatural instructors, informs them, humankind now confronts the specter of "NUCLEAR DISASTER" because "THE DREAD MACHINE BECAME MAN'S FRIEND" during the Industrial Revolution, thus putting an entirely new magnitude of destruction at the fingertips of human cruelty (*CLS* 183).

How are we to resist a blankness of mind apparently enforced by the weight of historical circumstance? In the previous chapter, I proposed that Merrill's poetic mentor, Auden, articulated one possible answer when he declared that "the mere making of a work of art is itself a political act [that] . . . reminds the Management of something managers need to be reminded of, namely, that the managed are people with faces, not anonymous members, that *Homo Laborans* is also *Homo Ludens*."[27] Throughout *The Changing Light at Sandover*, Merrill affirms his predecessor's insistence on the ludic function of art by elaborating the conceit of the poem as a Gothic parlor game, what the ghostly *dramatis personae* of "Maria Mitsotáki" and (not accidentally) "W. H. Auden" themselves describe as an entertainment "LIKE A BALL / COSTUMES & DANCING / . . . OR MY DEARS A MASQUE" (*CLS* 207). Recalling Merrill's avowal of discomfort at the "easygoing contempt rich people have for art and scholarship," we might conclude that he, like Auden, perceives the playfulness of culture and the rationality of the market as antithetical ideals. On this reckoning, both poets give satiric voice to the ethical dilemma that Lyotard named as the differend of capitalist postmodernity par excellence:

> If culture (culture of the mind, at least) requires work and thus takes time, and if the economic genre imposes its stakes of gaining time on the greater part of phrase regimens and genres of discourse, then culture, as a consumer of time, ought to be eliminated. Humans will thereby no longer feel even sorrow before the incommensurability between realities and Ideas, since they will lose their capacity to have Ideas. They will become more and more competent at strategies of exchange, but exclusively so. The word *culture* already signifies the putting into circulation of information rather than the work that needs to be done in order to arrive at presenting what is not presentable under the circumstances.[28]

Culture as seen under the sign of the postmodern is not simply another regimen subject to the hegemonic pragmatics of discourse but a system of redistributing and decentralizing "information" that threatens to undo such a pragmatics altogether. As Lyotard puts it a moment later, "the only insurmountable obstacle that the hegemony of the economic genre comes up against is the heterogeneity of phrase regimens and of genres of discourse." This is the condition of the differend, which "summons humans to situate themselves in unknown phrase universes, even if they don't have the feeling that something has to be phrased."[29]

From such a standpoint, poetry's ancient entreaty, *nil admirari,* looks like an invitation not to a nostalgic ritual but rather to a game of chance from which we may hope to win some insight into our individual limitations and mutual needs. The "making of a work of art" reminds us that we are all makers, hence that each of us is an end rather than a means. Neither Auden nor Merrill, in other words, would have viewed the shift of poetry away from the old commonplaces of civic discourse as a lamentable abdication or retreat, an admission of the imagination's inconsequence in the face of terror. Rather, the two poets teach us that even an irreverent defense of our personal eccentricities may offer us a saving hope of freedom and a chastening awareness of our reciprocal obligations. Rediscovering our appetite for play, they seem to imply, we may achieve at last a kind of freedom from our habitual presumptions and self-protections. In our posterior age, surrounded by reminders of loved ones we have lost, oppressed by the monumental weight of our traditions, we can wish for no more liberating form of affirmation.

NOTES

Introduction

1. Angela J. Wheeler, *English Verse Satire from Donne to Dryden: Imitation of Classical Models* (Heidelberg: Carl Winter Universitätsverlag, 1992), 54–63.

2. *The Arte of English Poesie* (1589) (New York: Da Capo Press, 1971), 24.

3. *De Satyrica Graecorum Poesi et Romanorum Satira* (1605).

4. For more on the ritual background of the *lanx satura*, see C. A. Van Rooy, *Studies in Classical Satire and Related Literary Theory* (Leiden: Brill, 1965), 1–13.

5. *Satire: A Critical Reintroduction* (Lexington: University Press of Kentucky, 1994), 186.

6. *The Difference Satire Makes* (Ithaca: Cornell University Press, 2001), 42.

7. Ibid., 258.

8. John Dryden, "Preface to Ovid's Epistles Translated by Several Hands," in *The Works of John Dryden*, 20 vols., ed. Edward Niles Hooker, H. T. Swedenberg, Jr., et al. (Berkeley: University of California Press, 1956–2000), 1: 114.

9. *The Material Word: Literate Culture in the Restoration and Early Eighteenth Century* (Baltimore: Johns Hopkins University Press, 1991), 8–9.

10. *The Augustan Idea in English Literature* (London: Edward Arnold, 1983), 213.

11. *Pen for a Party: Dryden's Tory Propaganda in Its Contexts* (Princeton: Princeton University Press, 1993), 270.

12. *Augustan Idea*, 232–233.

13. *Dryden and the Problem of Freedom: The Republican Aftermath 1649–1680* (New Haven: Yale University Press, 1997), 236.

14. *Satires of Rome: Threatening Poses from Lucilius to Juvenal* (Cambridge: Cambridge University Press, 2001), 117.

15. Ibid., 50–51.

16. In his magisterial biography of Dryden, James Winn has noted that there is historical evidence to suggest that the religious conviction of the poet and his family probably played a part in the failure of his sons, Charles and John, Jr., to obtain university educations as well as in the family's abandonment of its house of nineteen years in Longacre for a new residence in the suburbs sometime after Easter of 1687. Pat Rogers has remarked that the proscriptions against the formal

education of Catholics and their residence within ten miles of London forced the retirement of Pope's father from his business as a linen merchant, the relocation of the poet's family during his childhood, and his clandestine course of studies as a youth. Winn, *John Dryden and His World* (New Haven: Yale University Press, 1987), 415, 436. Rogers, *Essays on Pope* (Cambridge: Cambridge University Press, 1993), 129–131.

17. *Poetry of Opposition and Revolution: Dryden to Wordsworth* (Oxford: Oxford University Press, 1996), 4.

18. "In making the one structural alteration in Hobbes's theoretical system that was required to bring it into conformity with the needs and possibilities of a possessive market society, Locke completed an edifice that rested on Hobbes's sure foundations.... The basic assumptions of possessive individualism—that man is free and human by virtue of his sole proprietorship of his own person, and that human society is essentially a series of market relations—were deeply embedded in the seventeenth-century foundations.... The assumptions of possessive individualism have been retained in modern liberal theory, to an extent not always realized. Yet they have failed as foundations of liberal-democratic theory." *The Political Theory of Possessive Individualism: Hobbes to Locke* (Oxford: Oxford University Press, 1962).

19. This sense of Latin as a birthright available to all Britons dates back at least to Geoffrey of Monmouth's legend of Britain's discovery by Brutus, grandson of Aeneas.

20. As J. G. A. Pocock has pointed out, it is the invention of public credit on which this last fiction hinges: "Since a credit mechanism was an expansive and dynamic social device, the beliefs men had to form and maintain concerning one another were more than simple expectations of another's capacity to pay what he had borrowed, to perform what he had promised; they were boomtime beliefs, obliging men to credit one another with capacity to expand and grow and become what they were not. Far more than the practice of trade and profit, even at their most speculative, the growth of public credit obliged capitalist society to develop as an ideology something society had never possessed before, the image of a secular and historical future." *Virtue, Commerce, and History: Essays on Political Thought and History, Chiefly in the Eighteenth Century* (Cambridge: Cambridge University Press, 1985), 98.

21. *Romantic Imperialism: Universal Empire and the Culture of Modernity* (Cambridge: Cambridge University Press, 1998), 136–137.

22. In this sense, Byron ought to be regarded as knowingly taking a position antithetical to that of his contemporaries. "Poets in the long eighteenth century imagined poetry to be a unique and privileged literary form for the enunciation of a puissant (and plastic) vocabulary of nation, particularly one appropriate to a Britain proving itself (in fits and starts, to be sure) great at home and abroad." Suvir Kaul, *Poems of Nation, Anthems of Empire* (Charlottesville: University of Virginia Press, 2000), 5.

23. "The fundamental function of world-maintaining interpretive systems is the avoidance of chaos, that is, the overcoming of contingency. The legitimation

of orders of authority and basic norms can be understood as a specialization of this 'meaning-giving' function." *Legitimation Crisis*, trans. Thomas McCarthy (Boston: Beacon Press, 1973), 118.

24. José Esteban Muñoz, *Disidentifications: Queers of Color and the Performance of Politics* (Minneapolis: University of Minnesota Press, 1999); see especially 11–19.

25. *Gender Trouble: Feminism and the Subversion of Identity* (New York: Routledge, 1990), 138–139.

26. As an example we might take David Wooton's statement in the introduction to his edition of Locke's political writings: "Locke could not see us coming. The word 'liberalism' did not exist in his vocabulary." *Political Writings of John Locke*, ed. Wooton (New York: Penguin Books, 1993), 11.

27. "Two Concepts of Liberty," in *Four Essays On Liberty* (Oxford: Oxford University Press, 1969), 118–172.

28. *New Studies in Philosophy, Politics, Economics, and the History of Ideas* (London: Routledge and Kegan Paul, 1978), 119.

29. Ibid., 123.

30. Ibid., 124.

31. Locke, *Second Treatise*, in *Political Writings*, 325, 286 (paragraphs 123 and 50).

32. *New Studies*, 132.

33. *Classical Liberalism: The Unvanquished Ideal* (New York: St. Martin's Press, 1995), 11.

34. Ibid., 8.

35. *Classical Liberalism and International Economic Order: Studies in Theory and Intellectual History* (New York: Routledge, 1998), 15.

36. Ibid., 17.

37. *New Studies*, 149.

38. *Political Writings*, 288–289 (paragraph 57).

39. Introduction (1960) to John Locke, *Two Treatises of Government*, ed. Laslett (Cambridge: Cambridge University Press, 1988), 102.

40. Ibid., 105.

41. *The Political Thought of John Locke* (Cambridge: Cambridge University Press, 1969).

42. Locke, *Political Writings*, 332 (paragraph 138). Dunn, 222–241, 245–261.

43. *Political Thought*, 246.

44. *Political Writings*, 395, 396.

45. Ibid., 292 (paragraph 63).

46. Ibid., 288 (paragraph 55).

47. Ibid., 288 (paragraph 56).

48. Ibid., 292 (paragraph 63). On the parallel between filial consent to parental rule and popular consent to civil rule, see ibid., 319 (paragraph 112).

49. Ibid., 318 (paragraph 110).

50. *Political Thought*, 265–266.

51. *New Studies*, 148–149.

52. Ibid., 119–120. See also *The Constitution of Liberty* (Chicago: Henry Regnery, 1960), 160–175, 193–204, 220–233.

53. *Two Faces of Liberalism* (New York: New Press, 2000), 26.

54. Ibid., 26–27.

55. Ibid., 1–33, 105–139.

56. Ibid., 139.

57. Ibid., 25. See also Gray, "Hobbes and the Modern State," in *Post-liberalism: Studies in Political Thought* (New York: Routledge, 1993), 3–17.

58. Horace, Epistle 1.6.1–2 and 1.6.15–16. The English rendering is mine; I've avoided citing Pope's imitation here so as not to have to ponder the complicated relationship of his version to the original.

59. See in this regard Kroll's thought-provoking discussion of the Epicurean background of Dryden's linguistic practices in *The Material Word*, 33–48 and 305–325, and Douglas Lane Patey's instructive *Probability and Literary Form: Philosophic Theory and Literary Practice in the Augustan Age* (Cambridge: Cambridge University Press, 1984).

60. Freudenburg, *Satires of Rome*, 51.

61. Ibid., 51.

62. *The Skeptical Sublime: Aesthetic Ideology in Pope and the Tory Satirists* (Oxford: Oxford University Press, 2001), 135.

63. Ibid., 29.

64. Ibid., 132.

65. Ibid., 27.

66. *Politics, Language, and Time: Essays on Political Thought and History* (Chicago: University of Chicago Press, 1960), 85.

67. *Virtue, Commerce, and History*, 109.

68. Ibid., 115.

69. Ibid., 61.

70. Ibid., 121.

71. Ibid., 71.

72. Ibid., 122.

73. The Miltonic source is *The Readie and Easie Way to Establish a Free Commonwealth* and the citation and commentary are from Patterson's *Early Modern Liberalism* (Cambridge: Cambridge University Press, 1997), 5.

1. Satura Redux

1. Eclogue 4.4. See Jonson, "Part of the King's Entertainment," in *Works*, ed. C. H. Herford and Percy Simpson (Oxford: Oxford University Press, 1941), 7:92.

2. *The Augustan Idea in English Literature* (London: Edward Arnold, 1983), 196.

3. *Pen for a Party: Dryden's Tory Propaganda in Its Contexts* (Princeton: Princeton University Press, 1993), 270.

4. *Lives of the English Poets*, ed. George Birkbeck Hill (Oxford: Clarendon Press, 1905), 1:373.

5. *The Structural Transformation of the Public Sphere*, trans. Thomas Burger (Cambridge, MA: MIT Press, 1991), 4.

6. Ibid., 32, 25–26.

7. Ibid., 32–33, 32.

8. *The Postmodern Condition: A Report on Knowledge*, trans. Geoff Bennington and Brian Massumi (Minneapolis: University of Minnesota Press, 1991), 65–66.

9. For Habermas's account of the surrender of the public sphere to commercial imperatives and the consequences of that surrender, se *Structural Transformation*, 180–250, and *Legitimation Crisis*, trans. Thomas McCarthy (Boston: Beacon Press, 1975).

10. I am thinking here of the work of historians such as J. G. A. Pocock and Linda Colley, who have revised sharply the view prevailing virtually throughout the twentieth century of the ineffectuality and irrelevance of Tory opposition during the period of Whig hegemony. I examine Pocock's arguments as a potential avenue to a revision of the still habitual equation of liberal with commercial culture in the next chapter. For Colley's views, see *In Defiance of Oligarchy: The Tory Party 1714–1760* (Cambridge: Cambridge University Press, 1982).

11. *Literary Patronage in Augustan England, 1650–1800* (Cambridge: Cambridge University Press, 1996), 76.

12. *Dryden and The Problem of Freedom: The Republican Aftermath 1649–1680* (New Haven: Yale University Press, 1997), 4.

13. Ibid., 3.

14. Ibid., 3.

15. Ibid., 236.

16. *Lives*, 1:469.

17. *Leviathan*, ed. Richard Tuck (Cambridge: Cambridge University Press, 1991), 9.

18. Ibid., 284, 285.

19. See chap. 18: "For there is no Covenant with God, but by mediation of some body that representeth God's Person; which none doth but God's Lieutenant, who hath the Soveraignty under God," ibid., 122. And in the same chapter: "And as the Power, so also the Honour of the Soveraign, ought to be greater, than that of any, or all the Subjects. . . . And though they shine some more, some lesse, when they are out of his sight; yet in his presence, they shine no more than the Starres in presence of the Sun," ibid., 128. See as well chap. 40, where Hobbes recounts the history of the transmission of God's covenant with the people of Israel.

20. James Winn notes that Dryden lifts the phrase "mountain belly" from Jonson's description of himself in the lyric "My Picture Left in Scotland" and applies it to Shadwell at line 193 of *MacFlecknoe*. *John Dryden and His World* (New Haven: Yale University Press, 1987), 290. See also Jonson's "An Elegy" (poem 42 in *Underwoods*): "Let me be what I am: as Virgil cold, / As Horace fat, or as Anacreon old."

21. For the derivation of "Barbican," see Strype's *Survey* (book 3, 93), as quoted in *The Works of John Dryden*, 20 vols., ed. Edward Niles Hooker, H. T.

Swedenberg, Jr., et al. (Berkeley: University of California Press, 1956–2000), 2:318n.

22. Susan C. Greenfield, "Aborting the 'Mother Plot': Politics and Generation in *Absalom and Achitophel*," *ELH* 62 (1995): 285.

23. Abraham Cowley, *Poems*, ed. A. R. Waller (Cambridge: Cambridge University Press, 1905), 244.

24. The exact date of composition is unclear, but sections of a manuscript, now in the Bodleian Library and transcribed by John Oldham, are dated 1678 in his hand. Winn places the writing somewhat earlier, in 1676.

25. *Works*, 2:326n.

26. In his preface to *Ovid's Epistles, Translated by Several Hands*, Dryden refers to Jonson's version of Horace more than once. *Works* 1: 109–119.

27. *The Material Word: Literate Culture in the Restoration and Early Eighteenth Century* (Baltimore: Johns Hopkins University press, 1991), 320.

28. Winn gives a detailed account of how Shadwell's unwarranted sniping at Dryden on account of the latter's pensioned position as laureate may have motivated *MacFlecknoe*. *Dryden and His World*, 289–290.

29. *Pen for a Party*, 161.

30. Joseph Spence, *Observations, Anecdotes, and Characters of Books and Men, Collected from Conversation*, vol. 1, ed. James M. Osborn (Oxford: Clarendon Press, 1966), 28.

31. *Works*, 2:40–41.

32. Michel Foucault, *The Order of Things* (New York: Pantheon Books, 1970), 209.

33. *Works*, 2:41.

34. *Order*, 188–189.

35. Ibid., 209.

36. The mythology is common in English literature from the Renaissance to at least the late eighteenth century; it is one of the central sources of the metaphor, for instance, in Pope's *Dunciad*. See Douglas Brooks-Davies, *The Mercurian Monarch* (Manchester: Manchester University Press, 1983).

37. *Works*, 1:53.

38. *Leviathan*, 21.

39. Ibid., 22.

40. "*Absalom and Achitophel* and Dryden's Political Cosmos," in *John Dryden*, ed. Earl Miner (Athens: Ohio University Press, 1972), 158–159.

41. Ibid., 159.

42. The poet also sent two of his three sons to study at Westminster under Busby. On this matter see Winn, *Dryden and His World*, 41, and on the school generally, 36–57.

43. *Works*, 2:5.

44. Edmund Plowden, *Commentaries or Reports* (London, 1816), 212a. Cited in Ernst H. Kantorowicz, *The King's Two Bodies* (Princeton: Princeton University Press, 1957), 7.

45. Ibid., 8.

46. Especially pertinent on this score is the last line of the chapter, which reads in the King James Version: "But the thing that David had done displeased the Lord." For Winn's comment, see *Dryden and His World*, 328.

47. *Eikon Basilike*, ed. Philip A. Knachel (Ithaca: Cornell University Press, 1966), 14.

48. Ibid., 3.

49. With regard to the "sparks" of revolution in Parliament, for instance, the elder Charles ruefully maintains, referring to the Eleven Years' Tyranny, that "by forbearing to convene for some years, I hoped to have extinguished [them]" (3).

50. *Pen for a Party*, 113–114.

51. "Satire and the Constitution of Theocracy in *Absalom and Achitophel*," *Studies in Philology* 91, 3 (1994): 341.

52. From *The Earl of Shaftesbury's Expedient for Setling the Nation*, quoted in *Pen for a Party*, 75.

53. For Weinbrot's views, see his *Augustus Caesar in "Augustan" England* (Princeton: Princeton University Press, 1978). See also David Bywaters, *Dryden in Revolutionary England* (Berkeley: University of California Press, 1991), 133–147, for a fine discussion of Dryden's application of the Tacitean view to William III in the *Discourse of Satire*.

2. Arm'd for Virtue

1. *Patriotism and Poetry in Eighteenth-Century Britain* (Cambridge: Cambridge University Press, 2002), 56.

2. Ibid., 56.

3. Ibid., 58.

4. The catchphrase was invented by Douglas Brookes-Davies in his *Pope's "Dunciad" and the Queen of Night: A Study in Emotional Jacobitism* (Manchester: Manchester University Press, 1985).

5. "1688: Pope and the Rhetoric of Jacobitism," in *Pope: New Contexts*, ed. David Fairer (New York: Harvester Wheatleaf, 1990), 17.

6. Ibid., 19.

7. *The Skeptical Sublime: Aesthetic Ideology in Pope and the Tory Satirists* (Oxford: Oxford University Press, 2001), 16.

8. Ibid., 16–17.

9. Ibid., 17.

10. Ibid., 23.

11. Ibid., 29.

12. Ibid., 14.

13. Ibid., 29.

14. Ibid., 99.

15. *Essays on Pope* (Cambridge: Cambridge University Press, 1993), 129.

16. Ibid., 133.

17. "Pope and Slavery," in *Alexander Pope: World and Word*, ed. Erskine-Hill (Oxford: Oxford University Press, 1998), 45.

18. Samuel Johnson, *Lives of the English Poets*, 3 vols., ed. George Birkbeck Hill (Oxford: Clarendon Press, 1905), 3:233.

19. *An Essay Concerning Human Understanding*, ed. Peter H. Nidditch (Oxford: Clarendon Press, 1979), 508.

20. "Not 'The Only Trifler in the Nation': Pope and the Man of Leisure in *The Dunciad*," in *More Solid Learning: New Perspectives on Alexander Pope's "Dunciad,"* ed. Catherine Ingrassia and Claudia N. Thomas (Lewisburg, PA: Bucknell University Press, 2000), 130, 132.

21. Emile Audra and Aubrey Williams, the editors of the Twickenham Edition of the *Essay*, cite Bouhours's *Les Entretiens d'Ariste et d'Eugène* (1671) as the chief precedent for such a position. See *Pastoral Poetry and An Essay on Criticism* (New Haven: Yale University Press, 1961), 247nn76–79, 248n79, 255nn141–180, 256n144.

22. *The Critique of Judgment*, trans. James Creed Meredith (Oxford: Clarendon Press, 1952), 90.

23. Ibid., 55.

24. *Probability and Literary Form* (Cambridge: Cambridge University Press, 1984), 130.

25. Ibid., 131.

26. Nicolas Boileau-Déspreaux, *Oeuvres Complètes* (Paris: Gallimard, 1966), 351.

27. *Les reflexions sur la poétique de ce temps et sur les ouvrages des poètes anciens et modernes*, ed. E. T. DuBois (Genève: Librairie Droz, 1970), 60. For commentary, see particularly Samuel Holt Monk, "A Grace Beyond the Reach of Art," in *Essential Articles for the Study of Alexander Pope*, ed. Maynard Mack (Hamden: Archon, 1968).

28. *Probability*, 131.

29. Ibid., 133.

30. *Alexander Pope* (Oxford: Blackwell, 1985), 64.

31. *Probability*, 118.

32. *The Structural Transformation of the Public Sphere: An Inquiry into a Category of Bourgeois Society*, trans. Thomas Burger (Cambridge, MA: MIT Press, 1989), 57.

33. Ibid., 63–64.

34. Ibid., 60.

35. From *Essays on the Law of Nature*, no. 8 (1664), in *Political Writings of John Locke*, ed. David Wootton (New York: Penguin Books, 1993), 182.

36. *Pope and Bolingbroke: A Study of Friendship and Influence* (Columbia: University of Missouri Press, 1984), 88–89.

37. *Virtue, Commerce, and History: Essays on Political Thought and History, Chiefly in the Eighteenth Century* (Cambridge: Cambridge University Press, 1985), 109.

38. In addition to the previously quoted *Virtue, Commerce, and History*, see particularly *Politics, Language, and Time: Essays on Political Thought and History* (Chicago: University of Chicago Press, 1971) and *The Machiavellian Moment:*

Florentine Political Thought and the Atlantic Republican Tradition (Princeton: Princeton University Press, 1975).

39. *Politics, Language, and Time*, 86.
40. Ibid., 90.
41. *Virtue, Commerce, and History*, 122.
42. *Politics, Language, and Time*, 87.
43. Ibid., 90.
44. Ibid., xi.
45. Ibid., xi.
46. *Virtue, Commerce, and History*, 245.
47. *Bolingbroke and His Circle: The Politics of Nostalgia in the Age of Walpole* (Ithaca: Cornell University Press, 1968), 160.
48. *Politics, Language, and Time*, 103.
49. Hammond gives a more detailed account of the parallels and differences between Pope and Bolingbroke's political views in his exposition of the poet's knowing use of the term "corruption" in the *Epilogue to the Satires*. See *Pope and Bolingbroke*, 133–137, 146–149.
50. *Essays*, 148.
51. Ibid., 150.
52. *The Augustan Idea in English Literature* (London: Edward Arnold, 1983), 303.
53. Ibid., 303.
54. *Skeptical Sublime*, 135.
55. Ibid., 135.
56. Ibid., 143.
57. Ibid., 32.
58. *Pope and Bolingbroke*, 92.
59. *The Structure of Complex Words* (Cambridge, MA: Harvard University Press, 1989), 84.
60. Ibid., 99–100.
61. *Essays Moral, Political, and Literary*, ed. Eugene F. Miller (Indianapolis: Liberty Classics, 1985), 227.
62. Ibid., 227, 237.
63. Ibid., 239.
64. "On Liberty," in *Three Essays*, with an introduction by Richard Wollheim (Oxford: Oxford University Press, 1975), 45.
65. Ibid., 81.
66. *Politics by Other Means* (New Haven: Yale University Press, 1992), 99.
67. *The Augustan Age: Approaches to Its Literature, Life, and Thought*, ed. Ian Watt (Greenwich, CT: Fawcett, 1968), 18.
68. *Selected Poetry and Prose*, ed. Frank Brady and William Wimsatt (Berkeley: University of California Press, 1977), 156.
69. *Order from Confusion Sprung* (London: George Allen and Unwin, 1985), 256–257.
70. Ibid., 257.

71. Compare Dryden's translation in *Fables Ancient and Modern* of the metamorphosis of Pygmalion's statue into a woman at the sculptor's touch: "Soft, and more soft at every touch it grew; / Like pliant wax, when chafing hands reduce / The former mass to form, and frame for use" (84–86).

72. *Augustan Idea*, 327.

73. *Melodious Guile* (New Haven: Yale University Press, 1988), 149.

74. *Satire and Sentiment 1660–1830* (Cambridge: Cambridge University Press, 1994), 16.

75. *Augustan Idea*, 295.

76. *The Complete Odes and Satires of Horace*, trans. Sidney Alexander (Princeton: Princeton University Press, 1999), 251.

77. Hammond, *Pope and Bolingbroke*, 65–66, and Mack, *Alexander Pope: A Life* (New Haven: Yale University Press, 1985), 570–573.

78. Hammond, *Pope and Bolingbroke*, 64; Mack, *Pope: A Life*, 569.

79. *Essays on Pope*, 96.

80. *Pope and Bolingbroke*, 67.

81. *The Works of Lord Bolingbroke* (Philadelphia: Carey and Hart, 1841), 2:394.

82. H. T. Dickinson, "The Precursors of Political Radicalism in Augustan England," in *Britain in the First Age of Party 1680–1750*, ed. Clyve Jones (London: Hambledon Press, 1987), 73.

83. Ibid., 72.

84. Ibid., 72.

85. *Augustan Idea*, 314.

86. See, for example, Aubrey Williams, *Pope's "Dunciad"* (London: Methuen, 1955), 26–29, and Brookes-Davies, *Pope's "Dunciad" and the Queen of Night*, 1–33, 121–127.

87. Brookes-Davies, *Pope's "Dunciad" and the Queen of Night*, 21.

88. Ibid., 65.

89. *The Correspondence of Alexander Pope*, ed. George Sherburn (Oxford: Oxford University Press, 1956), 4:340.

90. Ibid., 4:347. The note to Caryll probably was written in January 1733, since it contains a sentence in which Pope tells his friend: "This or the next post will bring you under two covers, my Epistle to Lord Bathurst," a poem published that month. Hammond characterizes the period in which the poet made these statements to Caryll and Swift as one of extraordinarily conspicuous political activity on Pope's part: "Pope's poetry written between 1732 and May 1735, when the defeated Bolingbroke left England once again for France, would appear to be responding in no uncertain terms to the latter's suggestion that Pope 'direct [his] satire . . . to political subjects,'" *Pope and Bolingbroke*, 61.

3. Byron, Laughter, and Legitimation

1. *The Complete Odes and Satires of Horace*, trans. Sidney Alexander (Princeton: Princeton University Press, 1999), 16.

2. *The Skeptical Sublime: Aesthetic Ideology in Pope and the Tory Satirists* (New York: Oxford University Press, 2001), 183.

3. For Pocock's full account, see *The Machiavellian Moment: Florentine Political Thought and the Atlantic Republican Revolution* (Princeton: Princeton University Press, 1975), 156–218, 423–505. Of special importance for my purposes is Pocock's reading of Defoe and Addison's defense of Fortuna in its modern incarnation as Credit, which leads to the following summary of the opposing view: "Virtue must involve the cognition of things as they really were; the power of Credit was irredeemably subjective and it would take all the authority of society to prevent her from breaking loose to submerge the world in a flood of fantasy. It seems possible that she is part of Pope's Great Anarch" (457).

4. *Skeptical Sublime*, 14.

5. *The Romantic Ideology* (Chicago: University of Chicago Press, 1983), 130.

6. Ibid., 127, 130.

7. *Lord Byron's Strength: Romantic Writing and Commercial Society* (Baltimore: Johns Hopkins University Press, 1993), xx.

8. Ibid., xx, xxi.

9. Ibid., 229–231.

10. *England in 1819: The Politics of Literary Culture and the Case of Romantic Historicism* (Chicago: University of Chicago Press, 1998), 368, 372.

11. Ibid., 388.

12. In a letter of January 5, 1819, Hobhouse advised Byron against publishing the attack on Castlereagh in the introduction, asserting: "You could not publish it unless you were over here ready to fight him." After admitting that the poem as a whole could not be expurgated without irrevocable damage, he adds: "This consideration, therefore, makes me sum up strenuously advising a total suppression of 'Don Juan.'" Quoted in Leslie A. Marchand, *Byron: A Biography*, vol. 2 (New York: Knopf, 1957), 765. For a lively account of some of the critical responses to the appearance of the first two cantos, see Christensen, *Lord Byron's Strength*, 214–257.

13. Benita Eisler neatly summarizes the essentials of the situation: "When the first two cantos were published in July, 1819, neither author nor publisher was mentioned on the title page. Even then, the dedication was suppressed, appearing in print only after the poet's death." *Byron: Child of Passion, Fool of Fame* (New York: Random House, 1999), 609.

14. Byron's point on this score might be related to Austin's claim that "a performative utterance will . . . be in a peculiar way hollow or void . . . if introduced in a poem." J. L. Austin, *How to Do Things with Words*, ed. J. O. Urmson and Marina Sbisà (Cambridge, MA: Harvard University Press, 1962), 22.

15. *The Structural Transformation of the Public Sphere*, trans. Thomas Burger (Cambridge: MIT Press, 1991), 25–26.

16. Ibid., 188.

17. *Legitimation Crisis*, trans. Thomas McCarthy (Boston: Beacon Press, 1975), 23.

18. On this score, I disagree with Chandler, who writes that the exasperation of Byron's friend Thomas Moore regarding *Don Juan*'s first installment—he writes, "There is . . . a systematic profligacy running through it which would not be borne"—demonstrates that "the poem poses no case against the reigning normative framework it superficially seems to flout." Two responses come to mind. First, the fact that *Don Juan* "poses no case" in a sense that technically consorts with Chandler's interest in the casuistry of Romantic historicism does not mean that the poem's resistance to "the reigning normative framework" is "superficial." To say so is simply to uphold the framework's normative status. Second, Chandler's conclusion as just cited rests entirely on Moore's opinion. Chandler's own reading of the poem instead leads him later in his essay to a somewhat vague position that nonetheless clearly complicates his initial assessment: "*Don Juan* is thus haunted by a historicism with which it can neither dispense nor quite come to terms." Moore's comment is cited by Chandler in *England in 1819*, 350; Chandler's own remarks may be found on pages 351 and 380.

19. *The Machiavellian Moment*, 452–257. See Pocock, *Virtue, Commerce, and History: Essays on Political Thought and History, Chiefly in the Eighteenth Century* (Cambridge: Cambridge University Press, 1985), 98–99.

20. Saree Makdisi, *Romantic Imperialism: Universal Empire and the Culture of Modernity* (Cambridge: Cambridge University Press, 1998), 124.

21. Quoted in *Lord Byron: The Complete Works*, ed. Jerome J. McGann (Oxford: Oxford University Press, 1980–1993), 5:726.

22. *Satire and Sentiment 1660–1830* (Cambridge: Cambridge University Press, 1994), 116.

23. *Lord Byron: Works*, ed. McGann, 5:728.

24. For more on this topic, see Claude Rawson, *Order from Confusion Sprung* (London: George Allen and Unwin, 1985), 204–207.

25. Claude Rawson, *Satire and Sentiment 1660–1830* (Cambridge: Cambridge University Press, 1994), 100–101.

26. Peter J. Manning, *Byron and His Fictions* (Detroit: Wayne State University Press, 1978), 212.

27. *Lord Byron: Selected Letters and Journals*, ed. Leslie A. Marchand (Cambridge, MA: Harvard Belknap, 1982), 34, 31.

28. Ibid., 31.

29. Sara Suleri, *The Rhetoric of British India* (Chicago: University of Chicago Press, 1992), 32.

30. Ibid., 33.

31. "Byron and the Empire in the East," in *Byron: Augustan and Romantic*, ed. Andrew Rutherford (London: Macmillan, 1990), 68.

32. Ibid., 75.

33. "Totemism and Totalitarianism: Pope, Byron, and the Hanoverian Monarchy," *Forum for Modern Language Studies* 30, 4 (1994): 329.

34. Ibid.,332.

35. Ibid., 331.

36. Nicola J. Watson and Mary A. Favret, eds., *At the Limits of Romanticism: Essays in Cultural, Feminist, and Materialist Criticism* (Bloomington: Indiana University Press, 1994), 196.

4. Auden in the Polis of the Absurd

1. David Bromwich, *Skeptical Music: Essays on Modern Poetry* (Chicago: University of Chicago Press, 2001), 134.

2. Auden's estrangement in later life from the poems he composed during the 1930s that treated historical events in overtly political terms is a matter of public record; in the foreword to *Collected Shorter Poems 1927–1957* (New York: Random House, 1967), he condemns such works as "dishonest, or bad-mannered, or boring." The opinion owes its force to a discovery he made shortly after his arrival in New York in early 1939, while helping to raise money for refugees of the Spanish Civil War, that he "could make a fighting demagogic speech and have the audience roaring." The discovery left him feeling "just covered with dirt afterwards." Edward Mendelson, in a probing and judicious account of this crucial period in the poet's life, reminds us that Auden delivered the speech in March 1939, just a month before meeting his long-term lover and companion, Chester Kallman, for the first time. Kallman inspired Auden to a "Vision of Eros" that resulted, according to Mendelson, in a renunciation of the search for political solutions to his own alienation: "Once Auden stopped trying to cure his personal life through politics, his personal life seemed to cure itself." Although I think Mendelson gives an excellent account of the poet's own explanation of his work and motivations, I will be arguing here that the poetry often belies that explanation, offering its own view of the relation between *cultus* and *res publica*. Edward Mendelson, *Later Auden* (New York: Farrar Straus Giroux, 1999), 31–60; Auden's report of the disillusioning experience of "demagogic" speechmaking is quoted on page 37.

3. W. H. Auden, *Collected Poems*, ed. Edward Mendelson (New York: Vintage International, 1991), 248. I will give quotations of Auden's poetry from this volume or from one of two other sources, both of which have been issued under Mendelson's editorship as well: *Selected Poems* (New York: Vintage Books, 1979) and *The English Auden: Poems, Essays and Dramatic Writings 1927–1939* (New York: Random House, 1977). Hereafter all page citations will be given in the text; the three sources will be abbreviated, respectively, *CP, SP,* and *EA.*

4. *The Dyer's Hand* (New York: Random House, 1962), 88.

5. Richard Davenport-Hines, *Auden* (New York: Pantheon Books, 1995), 325.

6. *The Human Condition* (Chicago: University of Chicago Press, 1958), 322.

7. Ibid., 56.

8. *Poets in Their Time* (Oxford: Clarendon Press, 1991), 227.

9. Ibid., 227–228.

10. See, for example, the anatomization of the culture industry in Adorno's crucial work with Max Horkheimer, *Dialectic of Enlightenment* (1947), trans. John Cumming (New York: Continuum, 1994), 120–167.

11. *Later Auden*, 370.

12. *Prisms*, trans. Samuel and Sherry Weber (Cambridge, MA: MIT Press, 1967), 34.

13. G. W. F. Hegel, *Introduction to the Philosophy of History*, trans. Leo Rauch (Indianapolis: Hackett, 1988), 24.

14. On this score, it is helpful to recall a comment Auden made in a newspaper interview in 1965: "A poet enchants for the purpose of disenchanting people with their illusions about themselves and the world." *Daily Telegraph*, November 29, 1965, as quoted in Davenport-Hines, *Auden*, 323.

15. *Shakespeare's Language* (New York: Farrar Straus Giroux, 2000), 270.

16. It is always dangerous to read any sort of biographical self-referentiality into Auden's writing, as he was famously vocal in his abhorrence of the confessional note. In a rather mean comic spirit, he once publicly heckled Anne Sexton as she read her self-exposing poems, remarking "Who the hell cares about Anne Sexton's grandmother?" However, Auden's playful identification with trickster figures such as Autolycus and Hephaestos and the chronological insistence of the title "Forty Years On" may prompt a curious reader to wonder whether the poet is not encoding an oblique glance back at his own youth. If so, the moment specified by the title is a significant one in Auden's biography: 1928, which precedes the year of the poem's composition by exactly four decades, was the year in which *Poems*, his first collection, was privately printed and in which he made his first trip to Berlin, a city that he called "the buggers' daydream" and made his home for several months. For Auden's remark on Sexton, see Davenport-Hines, *Auden*, 328; for his characterization of Berlin, see Humphrey Carpenter, *W. H. Auden: A Biography* (New York: Houghton Mifflin, 1981), 90.

17. *Later Auden*, 485.

18. Richard R. Bozorth, *Auden's Games of Knowledge: Poetry and the Meanings of Homosexuality* (New York: Columbia University Press, 2001), 6.

19. *Human Condition*, 147, 151.

20. Boswell asserts that Johnson, in his knowledge of Latin, "was exceeded by no man of his time" and reports that he preferred to use the ancient Roman language when talking to French acquaintances, despite their occasional mystification. James Boswell, *Life of Johnson*, ed. R. W. Chapman, (Oxford: Oxford University Press, 1970), 34, 659–661.

21. Erwin Panofsky, *Meaning in the Visual Arts* (Chicago: University of Chicago Press, 1982), 295–297.

22. Ibid., 296.

23. Boswell may be helpful here again, as he reminds us that Johnson, although a man of extraordinary "personal courage," had "an awful dread of death, or rather, 'of something after death.'" *Life*, 579.

24. *The City of God*, trans. Marcus Dods (New York: Random House, 1950), 477.

25. *The Politics of Modernism: Against the New Conformists*, ed. Tony Pinkney (London: Verso, 1989), 45.

26. *Human Condition*, 81.

27. W. H. Auden, *Forewords and Afterwords* (New York: Vintage International, 1973), 4.

28. *Later Auden*, 441.

29. *Forewords and Afterwords*, 4.

30. Eve Kosofsky Sedgwick, *Epistemology of the Closet* (Berkeley: University of California Press, 1990), 141–157.

31. Ibid., 156.

32. *Disidentifications: Queers of Color and the Performance of Politics* (Minneapolis: University of Minnesota Press, 1999), 121.

33. *Human Condition*, 38.

34. Ibid., 41.

35. Ibid., 43.

36. "To gauge the extent of society's victory in the modern age, its early substitution of behavior for action and its eventual substitution of bureaucracy, the rule of nobody, for personal rulership, it may be well to recall that its initial science of economics, which subtitutes patterns of behavior only in this rather limited field of human activity, was finally followed by the all-comprehensive pretension of the social sciences which, as 'behavioral sciences,' aim to reduce man as a whole, in all his activities, to the level of a conditioned and behaving animal." Ibid., 45.

37. For the most illuminating considerations of this issue, see Mendelson, *Later Auden*, 477; Davenport-Hines, *Auden*, 319.

38. *The Dyer's Hand*, 401, 402.

39. Ibid., 403.

40. *Auden's Games*, 167.

41. For a sense of the influence of Layard's friendship and Lane's ideas on Auden's thinking, see Davenport-Hines, *Auden*, 90–96.

42. *The Hidden Law* (Cambridge, MA: Harvard University Press, 1993), 192.

43. *Auden's Games*, 153.

44. Due to a contract dispute, the British edition shared the title of the central poem.

45. *The Descent of the Dove* (Grand Rapids, MI: Eerdmans, 1939), 192.

46. Carpenter, *Auden: A Biography*, 298.

47. *The Courage to Be* (New Haven: Yale University Press, 1955), 165.

48. *Later Auden*, 75.

49. *Confessions*, trans. R. S. Pine-Coffin (London: Penguin, 1960), 263 (11.13).

50. *Forewords and Afterwords*, 172.

51. *Concluding Unscientific Postscript*, trans. David F. Swenson (Princeton: Princeton University Press, 1941), 187.

52. *The Journals of Søren Kierkegaard: A Selection*, ed. and trans. Alexander Dru (New York: Oxford University Press, 1938), 367–368.

53. *Hidden Law*, 241.

54. *The Complete Odes and Satires of Horace*, trans. Sidney Alexander (Princeton: Princeton University Press, 1999), 294.

5. Imbued with Otherness

1. James Merrill, *Collected Poems* (New York: Knopf, 2001), 185. All further references to the poetry are from either this volume, hereafter abbreviated *CP*, or from *The Changing Light at Sandover* (New York: Knopf, 1992), hereafter abbreviated *CLS*.

2. *The Collected Dialogues of Plato*, ed. Edith Hamilton and Huntington Cairns (Princeton: Princeton University Press, 1963), 560.

3. The phrase is from the fifth chapter, "Of Property," of *The Second Treatise of Government*. See *Political Writings of John Locke*, ed. David Wooton (New York: Penguin Books, 1993), 274. The classic account of Locke's notion of property and its grounding in a Puritan understanding of duty or vocation is John Dunn, *The Political Thought of John Locke* (Cambridge: Cambridge University Press, 1969).

4. *Gender Trouble: Feminism and the Subversion of Identity* (New York: Routledge, 1990), 138.

5. Ibid., 138.

6. *Identification Papers* (New York: Routledge, 1995), 69.

7. *Disidentifications: Queers of Culture and the Performance of Politics* (Minneapolis: University of Minnesota Press), 7.

8. Ibid., 11.

9. "An Interview with J. D. McClatchy," in *Recitative*, ed. McClatchy (San Francisco: North Point Press, 1986), 80.

10. Ibid., 80.

11. *The Postmodern Condition*, trans. Geoff Bennington and Brian Massumi (Minneapolis: University of Minnesota Press, 1991), 60–67.

12. Ibid., 66.

13. *The Differend*, trans. George Van Den Abbeele (Minneapolis: University of Minnesota Press, 1988), 135.

14. "Philosophy and Painting in the Age of Their Experimentation: Contribution to an Idea of Postmodernity," in *The Lyotard Reader*, ed. Andrew Benjamin (Oxford: Blackwell, 1989), 183. 185. Lyotard's insistence on this "metamorphic" function, I think, resonates with Merrill's characterization of his own poetics as a reflection of the "reversability of truths."

15. *The Postmodern Condition*, 10.

16. *An Ethics of Dissensus: Postmodernity, Feminism, and the Politics of Radical Democracy* (Stanford: Stanford University Press, 2001), 86.

17. Ibid., 86.

18. Stephen Yenser, *The Consuming Myth* (Cambridge, MA: Harvard University Press, 1987), 126.

19. Ibid., 130.

20. *A Different Person* (New York: Knopf, 1993), 74–75. Hereafter abbreviated *ADP*.

21. Alastair Fowler, "The Paradoxical Machinery of *The Rape of the Lock*," in *Alexander Pope: Essays for the Tercentenary*, ed. Colin Nicholson (Aberdeen: Aberdeen University Press, 1988), 164–165.

22. Thom Gunn, "A Heroic Enterprise," in *A Reader's Guide to James Merrill's "The Changing Light at Sandover,"* ed. Robert Polito (Ann Arbor: University of Michigan Press, 1994), 157.

23. Sigmund Freud, *The Standard Edition of the Complete Works*, ed. and trans. James Strachey, 24 vols. (London: Hogarth Press, 1953–1974), 13:144. All further citations of Freud are from this edition.

24. A possible channel of communication back to Freud is opened here, however, since Merrill might be taken to elaborate the relation drawn by Freud in "Some Neurotic Mechanisms, Etc." between the "receding into the background" of identification with the mother (18:232) and the emergence of unrepressed homosexuality.

25. Admittedly, this compact is relatively loose in "The Emerald," since the verse is written in accentual pentameter rather than a true iambic, but no other line in the poem contains six stresses.

26. John Hollander, *Melodious Guile* (New Haven: Yale University Press, 1988), 164–179.

27. W. H. Auden, *The Dyer's Hand* (New York: Random House, 1962), 88.

28. *The Differend*, 181.

29. Ibid., 181.

INDEX

Addison, Joseph, 21, 205n3
Adorno, Theodor, 125, 131, 207n10
Aeschylus, 139
Alaric, 129, 131
Alighieri, Dante. *See* Dante Alighieri
Althusser, Louis, 170
Andrault, Alexandre-Louis, comte de Langeron, 102, 103
Anne, Queen, 72
Arbuthnot, John, 58, 78, 82–83
Arendt, Hannah, 124, 137, 142, 145, 147
Aristotle, 60, 63, 82, 142
Auden, Wystan Hugh, 4, 9–10, 11, 22, 109–110, 123–166, 167, 183, 193, 194, 207n2, 208n14, 208n16, 209n41
   Dyer's Hand, 207n4, 209nn38–39, 211n27
   "Don Juan," 147
   "Epigoni," 166
   "Epitaph on a Tyrant," 9, 151
   "Et in Arcadia Ego," 133–134, 137–140
   "Fleet Visit," 109
   "Forty Years On," 132–137, 140
   "For the Time Being," 154
   "Friday's Child," 151
   "Greeks and Us," 143, 144
   "Homage to Clio," 132
   "In Memory of Sigmund Freud," 151
   "In Memory of W. B. Yeats," 123–124, 149
   "In Sickness and in Health," 146
   Letter to Lord Byron, 147–154, 168
   Letters from Iceland (with Louis MacNeice), 147, 148
   "Musée des Beaux Arts," 125, 165–166
   New Year's Letter, 140, 146, 155–162
   "Poet and the City," 123–124, 141, 193
   "Prologue at Sixty," 140, 141
   "Sabbath," 162–164
   "Secondary Epic," 127–132
   "September 1, 1939," 10, 125, 146, 155, 157–158, 168
   "Shield of Achilles," 9, 109–110, 151, 164–165
   "Sir, no man's enemy . . . ," 140
   Thanksgiving for a Habitat, 141, 143
      "Encomium Balnei," 141
      "Grub First, Then Ethics," 141, 143, 144, 145
Augustan metaphor, 4–7, 8, 9, 23–24, 35, 40, 48, 62, 70–71, 74, 75, 85, 86, 89, 92, 101, 114, 127–132, 169

Augustine, Saint, 140, 141, 159
Augustulus, Romulus, 132
Augustus, *princeps*, 5, 23, 26, 27, 40, 48, 73, 74, 75, 90, 127–129
Austen, Jane, 149
Austin, J. L., 205n14

Baudelaire, Charles, 153
Bethel, Hugh, 64–66
Bogel, Fredric, 3–4
Böhm, Franz, 12
Boileau-Déspreaux, Nicolas, 55, 56
Bolingbroke, viscount. *See* St. John, Henry, viscount Bolingbroke
Bonaparte, Napoleon. *See* Napoleon Bonaparte
Bonhoeffer, Dietrich, 151
Boswell, James, 208n20, 208n23
Bouhours, Dominique, 202n21
Bozorth, Richard R., 137, 148, 152
Brecht, Bertolt, 141
Bromwich, David, 69
Brookes-Davies, Douglas, 84, 201n4
Brown, Laura, 57
Browne, Thomas, 80
Brueghel, Pieter, the Elder, 125, 165
Busby, Richard, 41, 200n42
Butler, Judith, 10, 170
Butler, Marilyn, 116, 117
Byron, George Gordon, Lord, 4, 8–9, 11, 22, 86–122, 128, 129, 146–148, 152–154, 196n22, 205n12, 206n18
  Beppo, 86, 92, 96–99
  Childe Harold's Pilgrimage 4, 87–93, 98, 128
  English Bards and Scotch Reviewers, 86
  Don Juan, 8, 9, 86, 87, 92, 93, 94, 99–122, 129, 206n18
  Giaour, 116–117
  "On This Day I Complete My Thirty-Sixth Year," 86
Bywaters, David, 201n53

Caroline of Brandenburg-Anspach, Queen, 80
Caroline of Brunswick, Queen, 120–121
Carpenter, Humphrey, 208n16
Caryll, John, 85, 204n90
Casaubon, Isaac, 3
Castelnau, Gabriel, marquis de, 102–104, 108
Castiglione, Baldassare, 135
Castlereagh, Robert Stewart, viscount, second marquess of Londonderry, 92, 94, 205n12
Catherine the Great, 102
Cato, the Elder, 126
Chandler, James, 93–94, 206n18
Charles I, 23, 36, 44, 120, 201n49
Charles II, 4, 5, 20, 23, 24, 25, 29, 32, 40, 42–45, 48, 72
Charron, Pierre, 8
Chaucer, Geoffrey, 186
Chillingworth, William, 25
Christensen, Jerome, 93
Cibber, Colley, 105, 114, 158
Cicero, 83, 165
Coleridge, Ernest Hartley, 106
Colley, Linda, 199n10
Conway, David, 12
Cowley, Abraham, 29–30, 31
Cromwell, Oliver, 40

Damas, comte de. *See* Roger, Joseph-Élisabeth, comte de Damas
Dante Alighieri, 110, 136–137
Davenport-Hines, Richard, 207n5, 208n14, 208n16, 209n37
Defoe, Daniel, 21, 205n3
Dennis, John, 114
Deren, Maya, 190
Dickinson, H. T., 81
disidentification theory of gay subject-formation, 169–171, 173, 183, 187–188
Disney, Walt, 150

Dolben, John, 42
Downie, J. A., 49–50
Dryden, Charles and John, Jr. (sons of poet), 195n16
Dryden, John, 4, 6–7, 8, 11, 19, 20, 22, 23–48, 51, 52, 80, 89, 95, 107, 112–113, 195n16, 198n59, 199n20, 200n26, 200n28, 201n53, 204n71
  Absalom and Achitophel, 5, 25–26, 29, 32, 41–48, 107
  "Annus Mirabilis," 39
  "Discourse of Satire," 201n53
  MacFlecknoe, 26–34, 38
  Medall, The, 34–40
  Preface to Ovid's Epistles, Translated by Several Hands, 195n8
Duchamp, Marcel, 143
Dunn, John, 14, 16, 210n3

Eisler, Benita, 205n13
Eliot, T. S., 191
Elyot, Thomas, 135
Empson, William, 68
Erskine-Hill, Howard, 4–5, 6, 23, 52, 65–66, 73–74, 82
Etherege, George, 31, 33
Eucken, Walter, 12
Everett, Barbara, 125

Ferguson, Adam, 63
Filmer, Robert, 29
Fletcher, John, 30, 32
Fortuna (Fortune), 90, 98, 168, 205n3
Foucault, Michel, 35–36, 38
Fowler, Alastair, 178
Frederick Lewis, Prince of Wales, 49, 67
Freud, Sigmund, 170, 182–183, 211n24
Freudenburg, Kirk, 6
Fuss, Diana, 170

Gassendi, Pierre, 8

Gay, John, 58, 80, 91, 105
gay poetics. *See* satire: of heterosexist repression
George II, 71, 73, 74, 75, 80, 138
George III, 116
George IV, 116, 120
Gide, André, 150, 152
Giorgione, Giorgio Barbarella, 188, 189
Godwin, William, 64
Goethe, Johann Wolfgang von, 156
Granville, George, baron Lansdowne, 72
Gray, John, 17–18
Greenfield, Susan C., 29
Griffin, Dustin, 3, 25, 49, 52–53
Grotius, Hugo, 21
Guercino, Giovanni Francesco, 138
Guicciardini, Francesco, 20
Gunn, Thom, 179

Habermas, Jürgen, 9, 24–25, 58–59, 95, 172, 196–197
Haley, David B., 5, 25
Hammond, Brean, 60–61, 67, 77, 80–81, 203n49, 204n90
Harrington, James, 21
  Harringtonian theory of property, 61, 64
Harth, Philip, 5, 24, 34, 45
Hayek, F. A., 11–13, 16–18, 21, 62
Hecht, Anthony, 151, 161
Hegel, G. W. F., 8, 152
Herford, C. H., 198n1
Herrick, Robert, 23
Hobbes, Thomas, 18, 21, 27, 39, 60, 135, 196n18, 199n19
Hobhouse, John Cam, 63, 64, 205n12
Hollander, John, 74
Homer, 79
  Iliad, 89, 110
  Odyssey, 114–115
Hooker, Edward Niles, 195n8, 199n21

Horace, 5, 9, 19, 23, 31–33, 49, 64–66, 70, 71, 74, 75, 77, 78, 82, 83, 87–89, 114, 162, 169, 200n26
  as son of *libertus* (freedman), 5, 82, 169
  See also Pope, Alexander: *Imitations of Horace*
Horkheimer, Max, 125, 207n10
Howard, Robert, 39
Hume, David, 8, 12, 17, 68–69
Hyde, Catherine, duchess of Queensbury, 80
Hyde, Henry, viscount Cornbury, 67

Ingram, Hellen, 174, 175, 177
Isherwood, Christopher, 148, 154

Jackson, David, 10, 179
James I, 23
Johnson, Samuel, 7, 24, 26, 53, 70–71, 138–140, 208n20
Jonson, Ben, 23, 30–32, 74, 122, 200n26
Joseph, Charles, Prince de Ligne, 102, 103
Juvenal, 162
  Juvenalian indignation, 78, 95

Kallman, Chester, 207n2
Kant, Immanuel, 54–56, 172
Kantorowicz, Ernst, 43
Kaul, Suvir, 196n22
Kelsall, Malcolm, 120
Kermode, Frank, 132
Kéroualle, Louise de, duchess of Portsmouth, 43, 45
Kierkegaard, Søren, 159, 160
Knight, Frank H., 12
Kramnick, Isaac, 63
Kroll, Richard, 4, 32, 50, 198n59
Krook, Anne K., 46

Lane, Homer, 150, 209n41

Langeron, comte de. *See* Andrault, Alexandre-Louis, comte de Langeron
Laslett, Peter, 13–14
Laud, William, 25
Laverne, Tranchant de, 106
Lawrence, D. H., 150
Layard, John, 150, 209n41
Lenin, Vladimir Ilyich, 63, 64
Lewis, Sinclair, 184
liberalism (as such), 7, 11–22, 51, 52, 58–59, 69–70, 116–117
  classical, 7, 11–13, 17, 53
  cultural, 7–8, 9, 11, 18–22, 25, 53, 95, 173
libertas, Horatian and Lucilian ideal of, 6, 9, 19, 53
Licensing Act (1662), 24
Ligne, Prince de. *See* Joseph, Charles, Prince de Ligne
Locke, John, 7, 11, 12, 13–17, 20, 21, 29, 53, 62, 169, 196n18, 197n26, 210n3
  Essay Concerning Human Understanding, 53
  "Letter Concerning Toleration," 15
  Two Treatises of Government, 13
  The First Treatise of Government, 29
  The Second Treatise of Government, 7, 11, 13–16
Lodeizen, Hans, 180
Longinus, 89
Lord, George, 40–41
Lowther, William, earl of Lonsdale, 112
Lucilius, 9, 75
Lyotard, Jean-François, 24–25, 171, 172, 193, 210n14

Macaulay, Thomas Babington, 17, 62
Machiavelli, Niccolo, 20, 90
Mack, Maynard, 77
MacNeice, Louis, 147, 148

Macpherson, C. B., 7
Makdisi, Saree, 8, 101
Manning, Peter, 114–115
Marchand, Leslie, 205n12
Marvell, Andrew, 23, 40, 122
Marx, Karl, 21, 22, 62, 63, 64, 129
Mayer, Elizabeth, 160
McClatchy, J. D., 170
McGann, Jerome, 92, 93, 106
McGinley, Phyllis, 143
Mendelson, Edward, 129, 137, 144, 158, 207nn2–3
Merrill, Charles (poet's father), 173, 184
Merrill, Hellen Ingram (poet's mother). *See* Ingram, Hellen
Merrill, James, 4, 10–11, 22, 167–194, 210n14, 211n24
   Changing Light at Sandover, 10, 179–191, 192–193
   Different Person, 175, 176, 180
   "Days of 1971," 191–192
   "From the Cupola," 10, 174–178
   "Graffito," 168–169
   "Thousand and Second Night," 10, 167–168, 172, 173–174, 178, 179
   "Up and Down," 10, 184–188
Metternich, Klemens Lothar Wenzel von, 92
Mill, John Stuart, 64, 69
Millar, John, 63
Milton, John, 22, 30, 110–111, 186, 198n73
   Paradise Lost, 30, 110–111, 175
Mises, Ludwig von, 12, 62
Monk, Samuel Holt, 202n27
Monmouth, Geoffrey of, 196n19
Monmouth, James Scott, first duke of, 42, 45, 47
Montaigne, Michel de, 155
Moore, Thomas, 206n18
Mordaunt, Charles, earl of Peterborough, 77–78

Muñoz, José Esteban, 144, 170
Murray, John, 94

Napoleon Bonoparte, 92, 111, 115
Newcomen, Thomas, 152
Newton, Esther, 144
nil admirari, principle of, 7, 19, 66, 67, 88, 194
Noggle, James, 19–20, 50–51, 66, 89, 92

Odovacer, 132
Ouija, 10, 179, 181, 182, 184, 190
Ovid, 34, 35, 84, 186

Panofsky, Erwin, 138
Pasha, Ali, 115, 117
Pasha, Muchtar, 117
Patey, Douglas Lane, 50, 55, 56–58, 198n59
Patterson, Annabel, 22
Paul, Saint, 100, 146
Pêcheux, Michel, 170
Pindaric ode, 141, 144
Plato, 82, 142, 143, 168
   Symposium, 167
Plowden, Edmund, 200n44
Pocock, J. G. A., 20–22, 61–64, 90, 98, 196n20, 199n10, 205n3
Pope, Alexander, 4, 6–7, 8, 11, 19, 20, 21, 22, 47, 49–85, 89–92, 95, 97–98, 104, 107, 112–114, 120, 122, 128, 131, 148, 158–159, 163, 169, 178, 186, 203n49, 205n3
   Dunciad, 51, 52, 74, 83–85, 89, 90–91, 128, 130–131, 158–159, 186, 187, 200n36
   Epistle to Dr. Arbuthnot, 78–83, 112
   Essay on Criticism, 52, 54–61, 67–68, 74, 186, 187
   Essay on Man, 51, 107, 159, 163
   Iliad, translation of, 59
   Imitations of Horace, 53, 66

Pope, Alexander (*continued*)
    Epistle 1.6, 19, 66
    Epistle 2.1 (To Augustus), 50, 52, 71–75
    Satire 2.1, 49–50, 59, 64, 75–78
    Satire 2.2, 64–66
    Moral Essays
        To Bathurst, 204n9
        To Burlington, 50, 122
    Rape of the Lock, 97–98, 178
    Windsor Forest, 49, 50, 52, 72, 159
Potemkin, Grigori Aleksandrovich, 105, 106
Prior, Matthew, 149
Proust, Marcel, 192
Pufendorf, Samuel von, 21
Puttenham, George, 3

Queensbury, duchess of. *See* Hyde, Catherine, duchess of Queensbury

Rapin, René, 55, 56
Rawson, Claude, 71, 75, 107
Reynolds, Joshua, 138
Richelieu, Armand-Emmanuel du Plessis, duc de, 102, 107–108, 118
Rilke, Rainer Maria, 161
Roger, Joseph-Élisabeth, comte de Damas, 102, 103
Rogers, Pat, 51–52, 64–65, 79, 195n16
Romulus, 127
Röpke, Wilhelm, 12
Rousseau, Jean-Jacques, 9, 117

Sade, Donatien-Alphone-François, marquis de, 36
Sally, Razeen, 12
satire, 3, 8–11, 51–52, 83, 86, 94–95, 127, 135, 172, 184
    as liberalizing practice, 6–7, 95
    of heterosexist repression, 10–11, 143–146, 148, 169–173, 177–179

Savoury, Thomas, 152
Sedgwick, Eve Kosofsky, 144
Sexton, Anne, 208n16
Shadwell, Thomas, 5, 27–29, 31–33, 199n20, 200n28
Shaftesbury, Anthony Ashley Cooper, first earl of, 5, 34–39, 41, 44, 45, 47
Shakespeare, William, 74, 132, 133, 135, 136
    The Winter's Tale, 132–136
Shapin, Steven, 50
Shapiro, Barbara J., 50
Sheffield, John, third earl of Musgrave, 41
Sidney, Philip, 23, 74
Smith, Adam, 7, 12, 17, 135
Southey, Robert, 94, 113
Spence, Joseph, 35
Spender, Stephen, 148
Spenser, Edmund, 84, 85, 102, 185, 186
St. John, Henry, viscount Bolingbroke, 21, 58, 60–61, 63, 64, 77, 78, 81, 203n49, 204n90
Suetonius, 26
Suleri, Sara, 116
Suvorov, Aleksandr Vasilevich, 102, 105, 106, 107
Swift, Jonathan, 51, 58, 64, 71, 85, 91, 104, 105, 109, 204n90

Tillich, Paul, 155
Toklas, Alice, 175
Tonson, Jacob, 85
Tory Party, 24, 25, 34, 49–51, 63
Tümler, Jan, 12

Van Rooy, C. A., 195n4
Viner, Jacob, 12
Virgil, 23, 48, 70, 75, 90, 127, 128, 129, 130, 132
    Aeneid, 26, 90, 127, 131
    Fourth Eclogue, 23, 48

Waller, Edmund, 40

Walpole, Robert, 21, 49, 61, 77–81
Warburton, Thomas, 83
Watson, Nicola J., 122
Watt, Ian, 70
Watt, James, 152
Weinbrot, Howard, 48
Wheeler, Angela J., 195n1
Whig Party, 7, 11, 17, 20, 24, 34, 35, 26–27, 39, 40, 49–50, 53, 63, 64, 77, 120
William III, 201n53

Williams, Charles, 155
Williams, Raymond, 141
Winn, James, 43, 195–196n16, 199n20, 200n28
Wordsworth, William, 111, 113

Yenser, Stephen, 174
Young, Edward, 105

Ziarek, Ewa Płonowska, 172
Zionkowski, Linda, 54